Person and Society
in American Thought

american
university
studies

Series V
Philosophy

Vol. 200

PETER LANG
New York • Washington, D.C./Baltimore • Bern
Frankfurt am Main • Berlin • Brussels • Vienna • Oxford

Cornelius Francis Murphy, Jr.

Person and Society in American Thought

A Study in Christian Humanism

PETER LANG
New York • Washington, D.C./Baltimore • Bern
Frankfurt am Main • Berlin • Brussels • Vienna • Oxford

Library of Congress Cataloging-in-Publication Data

Murphy, Cornelius F.
Person and society in American thought: a study in Christian
humanism / Cornelius Francis Murphy, Jr.
p. cm. — (American university studies. V, Philosophy; v. 200)
Includes bibliographical references and index.
1. Theological anthropology—Christianity. 2. Theology, Doctrinal—History.
3. Christianity and religious humanism. I. Title.
BT701.3.M87   230.0973—dc22   2006022444
ISBN 978-0-8204-8172-2
ISSN 0739-6392

Bibliographic information published by **Die Deutsche Bibliothek**.
Die Deutsche Bibliothek lists this publication in the "Deutsche
Nationalbibliografie"; detailed bibliographic data is available
on the Internet at http://dnb.ddb.de/.

The paper in this book meets the guidelines for permanence and durability
of the Committee on Production Guidelines for Book Longevity
of the Council of Library Resources.

Printed in Germany

To the spirit of New England
Devout and Free
That brought forth my ancestors
And nurtured me.

Contents

Acknowledgements

Many institutions and individuals were helpful to me in the development of this work. I want to acknowledge the assistance given by the Carnegie Libraries of Pittsburgh, the Redwood Library of Newport, Rhode Island, and the Public Library of Middletown in that state. Earlier drafts of various chapters were read by Foster Provost and Wallace Watson of Duquesne University, and Timo Airaksinen, chair of the Philosophy Department of the University of Helsinki, Finland. While thanking them all for their comments, I am, of course solely responsible for the final product.

Jenifer Johnson provided indispensable assistance in the technical development of the manuscript on my personal computer. I am very grateful for her help. I extend my deepest gratitude to my grandniece, Melissa A. Crawford, who graciously edited the manuscript and prepared it for publication. Without her, this book would not have come to be.

Foreword

The American colonies were established by men and women who were trying to escape from the political and religious oppression of the Old World. In the new environment they hoped to experience a unique freedom and take advantage of the abundance of the natural world surrounding their settlements. Those who settled the Massachusetts Bay Colony were motivated by a novel religious inspiration. They wanted to establish a purified form of Christianity which would shed all the worldly attachments that, in their eyes, had compromised the fundamental purposes of the Protestant Reformation.

The New England Puritans tried to codify their religious convictions into a theocratic form of government. They hoped to integrate church and politics in a way that would make their community a "City on a Hill," meaning a beacon of light that would illuminate the outer darkness. Although the experiment failed, their teachings about the relation between God and man would continue to exert an influence upon the shaping of the individual and collective identities of the American people. This is a study of that influence and of the efforts of prominent thinkers to find alternatives to the Puritan cosmology. In the Eighteenth century, the Calvinism espoused by American Puritans was restated by their greatest theologian, Jonathan Edwards. Edwards emphatically defended the central doctrines of Divine Sovereignty, Predestination, and Original Corruption. He directed his reflective and pastoral energies against all forms of thought that placed freedom above Grace, time above Eternity, and the love of man over the love of God.

Edwards threw down the gauntlet. However, within the emerging New England society there were brave souls who were willing to accept the challenge. The theologians, philosophers, and poets who dared to oppose Edwards were acting out of their developing sense of human dignity as well as their own spiritual convictions. They were also continuing a battle between humanism and Christianity which was an essential aspect of the European history from which everyone coming to these shores was trying to escape.

The Renaissance had presented a grave challenge to the authority that medieval Catholicism had long exercised over European culture. By celebrating the ideal of individual fulfillment, the expansion of human powers, and the importance of temporal happiness, the humanists threatened the basic principles and purposes of Christian life. Following the Reformation, the same adventurous spirit appeared in the form of the German Enlightenment.

The struggle to establish new boundaries between human initiative and Divine causality disturbed all Christian churches. The supremacy of theology was toppled and the independence of philosophy and science affirmed. Ultimate questions were being raised that, among other things, called into question the teachings of Luther and Calvin. These issues would remain unresolved when Protestantism was transplanted to the shores of North America.

In the beginning of Chapter I, I describe how the Calvinist orthodoxy was challenged in America by thinkers ranging from William Ellery Channing to Ralph Waldo Emerson. These diverse attacks had the common aim of shifting attention from the severity of the established faith to a new sense of spiritual possibilities. Those who resisted the Puritan hegemony recognized that the will was weak, but they refused to believe that it was essentially corrupt. Conceding the Sovereignty of God, they also wanted to assert the self-sufficiency of man. They could not accept a doctrine of Grace that replaced, rather than perfected, human nature. And while leaving some room for Divine Mercy, they would not allow such benevolence to compromise the value of independent moral effort.

As New England experienced its own renaissance, the moral rigor inherited from the Puritans was gradually softened by the spontaneities of unfettered thought. The American humanists refused to be intimidated by the teachings of Divine Vengeance, and they tried to overcome the excessive humility of their religious ancestors. The prospects of eternal rewards and punishments came to be of less importance than the assertion of their own individual identities.

Channing's Unitarianism marked the transition on the plane of organized religion. Here one could honor God without losing a positive sense of self-respect. With the Transcendentalists, introspection and intuition came into prominence, and with them, a search for new sources of inspiration. They had become disaffected with the rituals and practices of the established churches, and they began to seek some spiritual solace from the resources of the natural world. But this absorption in Nature increased their isolation from the broader community.

At the conclusion of the first chapter, I explain how, in spite of the increasing optimism, a pervasive awareness of the reality of human sinfulness remained. Although Channing rejected the Calvinist teaching on human depravity, he also recognized the ambiguities of moral intention. The sense of personal evil was also dramatically expressed by the best imaginative writers of the period, such as Hawthorne and Melville. Hawthorne believed that there could be no authentic moral growth unless individuals realized that they were drawn to evil as well as to good. Melville explored the dire consequences that follow when one's will is set loose from all objective moral constraint.

As Melville's thought matured, he gained deeper insights into the complexity of motivation and found it impossible to identify a stable personality as the source of action. As the social implications of American Democracy came into prominence, it would become even more difficult to retain a sense of personal integrity.

In the second chapter, I trace the ways in which the flowering of transcendental self-reliance would have to be reconciled with the egalitarian implications of rising immigration and urban development. The post-Puritan understanding of human nature could no longer afford to concentrate exclusively upon the meaning of selfhood. It had to encompass the value of both the person and society.

The difficulty of doing both of these things is revealed in the works of Walt Whitman. Whitman celebrated the democratic ethos in his poems and essays. He believed that the American Republic was becoming the absolute standard of civilization and that the power of its people would match the natural forces of the universe. Yet, in spite of his enthusiasm for collective growth, he was unwilling to renounce liberty in order to promote equality. Whitman's sense of personal freedom made him uneasy about the value of comradeship. His brooding imagination was preoccupied with a deeper need for ultimate satisfaction. Whitman wanted to move within an orbit of himself that, in its independence, would not submit to any higher spiritual or temporal authority.

Whitman welcomed material progress. Henry Adams, whose grandfather and great-grandfather had both served as President of the United States, was less sanguine about the future. Industrial expansion meant an increase in power that allowed a few to control the destiny of many. Even worse, the growth of the economy required methods of manipulation that posed a dire threat to personal integrity. For Adams, the essential problem was the disintegration of Christian culture. Medieval Catholicism represented an all-embracing unity that formed a bridge between time and eternity. Now there was nothing but modern chaos.

The democratic humanism promoted by Walt Whitman was devoid of any theological anchorage. Others would try to reconcile the realities of modern life with the assurances of traditional belief. An amateur theologian, the Senior Henry James, tried to reinterpret the Christian religion in a way that would reunite the Divine and the human. To his mind, Democracy was not just a political phenomenon. It had a sacred character because it revealed the presence of God on Earth. James believed that the reconciliation of God and man was at hand, but it would require the submission of the individual to the good of the common life.

Edward Bellamy reached conclusions similar to those of Henry James through the exploration of self-consciousness. Individuality becomes object to an eternal subjectivity that constitutes the universal soul. Such a contact with the infinite becomes the ground of a prospective self-identity in which the individual reconciles the private with the public aspects of his personality. For Bellamy, social solidarity would be grounded in the efficient administration of the common life.

These attempts to reconcile the tensions between the individual and the group through some measure of impersonal unification were challenged by Henry James' son, William. At the beginning of the third chapter, I indicate how, in his elaboration of a practical existentialism, William James came to embrace the ideal of human singularity. He opposed all philosophies that tried to subordinate the individual to any larger whole. While his pragmatism was attentive to the immediate and practical, ultimate concerns were also an essential aspect of his thought.

James insisted upon the importance of religion to the complete fulfillment of the human person. This orientation toward finalities was closely related to his understanding of the powers of the human will. Henry Adams thought that the spreading power of industrial technology weakened the will more effectively than any inherited sense of original guilt. For him, the only possible solution was an adjustment to necessity balanced by the inward preservation of personal independence. To William James, this approach was cowardly. James defended the power of the individual will to be an agency of social change. His arguments included appeals to higher powers as well as the refinement of psychological insight.

Like Emerson before him, James could not integrate his deep attachment to the value of the individual life with a genuine affirmation of sociability. His humanism enhanced personal life, but it was not sufficiently communal in nature. Changing circumstances in our national life called for a new balance to be struck between the destiny of the one and the fate of many, and the task was beyond James' powers of reflection.

As an industrial community, America was becoming deeply interdependent and more highly organized. Sociological modes of understanding were ascendant and these privileged the objective modes of human existence. The challenge was to work out a positive conception of the relation between the individual and the community. James' friend and colleague, the philosopher Josiah Royce, would assume that responsibility.

Royce tried to reconnect the individual will with common destiny by exploring the dialectic between self and social consciousness. He also tried to transcend the relativism implicit in Jamesian pragmatism. To make the good something more than the expedient, Royce elaborated a substantial ethic whose central virtue was that of loyalty to community.

Royce also thought that James' approach to religion was too self centered. Religion in general, and Christianity in particular, had a communal quality that Royce believed confirmed the gradual socialization of human consciousness being explicated in his time, by the resources of philosophical idealism. From his childhood, Royce had been drawn to the idea that time could intersect with eternity. To advance that closeness, he sought to reconcile the subjective and objective modes of meaningful understanding. He affirmed both the reality of community and the metaphysical possibilities of the individual . Royce thought that the individual becomes what he is meant to be by his honest recognition of the reality of other human beings, who are different from himself, but with whom he can have constructive interactions.

As he considered the relevance of Christian principles to the purposes of life in common, Royce had to confront the problem of personal evil. Like the Puritans, he rejected naive beliefs in original innocence. At the beginning of the fourth chapter, I explain how Royce hoped to make the traditional doctrine of Atonement applicable to the circumstances of modern man.

In Royce's ideal philosophy, Society should become a Beloved Community. But its unity and peace were constantly threatened by individual selfishness. Spiritual reparation was necessary to social salvation. However, forgiveness for the wrongs that shatter human solidarity would not come through the graces merited by the suffering and death of Jesus Christ. It would come instead by way of the redemptive powers of individuals who were able to convert their communal loyalties into a willing suffering for the sins of others.

Royce was significantly influenced by William James' commitment to the centrality of the separate life. To establish an appropriate harmony between the singular and the collective, Royce subjected all encounters with others to the primacy of personal meaning. Unfortunately, this fragile balance could not withstand the encroaching realities. As democratic and economic imperatives gained greater force, egalitarian philosophies would take precedence over all modes of transcendental individualism. The social whole was starting to become more important than the personal existence of any of its members.

The United States was becoming a mass society. As the twentieth century progressed, life was lived increasingly in coordination and interdependence rather than isolation. And the life in common was coming under the control of equalizing economic and political power. Sameness reigned. As technological governance expanded, thought and feeling became subordinated to the demands of an unending prosperity.

These technological developments put Christianity on the defensive. Religious sentiment was being separated from ecclesiastical allegiance, and the established churches withdrew from the dynamics of profane experience. Spiritual significance was being discovered through ways of being human that were enacted entirely within the horizons of this world. As I document these changes, I also explain how the decisive move towards the supremacy of the social was promoted by one of our most distinguished philosophers, John Dewey.

Dewey's earlier studies had convinced him that the pursuit of life required the establishment of organic relationships within an environment of constant change. Dewey wanted to understand as deeply as possible everything that we experience as a people. His instrumental understanding of practical intelligence gave pragmatism a social face. As means became ends, the expedient would be determined by collaborative procedures rather than by individual decision. In the transition to the social, Emersonian individualism would give way to a new understanding of what it means to be a human being. The ideal of personal self-reliance would be replaced by the possibilities of material and cultural enrichment that could only come through participation in a common cause. According to Dewey, what one is to be will be determined by what one does within the various venues of social cooperation that marked the progress of democratic society.

Throughout this study, I have looked upon the American experience as a continuation of the conflict between Christianity and humanism that had begun earlier in Europe. The circumstances here were of course unique; yet the principal themes of the antagonism would reappear, albeit in novel forms. The major controversies began in New England, for it was there that the Reformation was being most forcefully renewed. As a result, there arose an irresolvable tension between an extreme form of Calvinism and the rising expectations of individual and social fulfillment.

The Christianity to which the Puritans bore allegiance gave primary emphasis to the Sovereignty and Justice of God. His majestic, absolute, and arbitrary power was set over against the insignificance and depravity of man. The good news of Salvation was proclaimed but it was qualified by a doctrine of Predestination that restricted its scope. Furthermore, in the order of action, individual freedom was not valued. Whatever good that was accomplished was attributed to Divine Grace rather than to human effort. This was the somber and restrictive background against which those who hoped to affirm the dignity of human nature would have to struggle.

One response was the attempt to establish a more intimate and positive relationship between God and Man. For the Unitarians, the distinction between the Divine and the human would become more a matter of degree than of kind. The Transcendentalists celebrated the holiness of the individual soul, while the senior Henry James thought the divine was in-dwelling in Democracy. William James defended a form of pantheism that could satisfy his deeper need to find meaning in the otherwise impersonal universe. Others who wished to separate themselves from the inherited theology elaborated myths of original innocence that they hoped would overcome the doctrines of innate corruption. The general movement was towards an immanence of ultimate meaning in the social as well as the personal dimensions of existence.

As democratic values began to dominate the culture, some were convinced that The Spirit was at work within the general community. With the acceleration of economic activity and the expansion of national power, the sense of the sacred was withdrawn from the established churches. The expectations of spiritual renewal that were inspired by Protestant Christianity were giving way to the pre-eminence of a humanism that attributed a divine sanction to both collective and individual success.

The humanistic aspirations encouraged by The Enlightenment were also being disappointed. Science and technology brought great advantages to the quality and duration of life, but the hyper-organization of society that they inspired had led to a decline in human freedom. The political order honored a liberty that social experience seemed to deny. As the forces of consolidation intensified, the individual was left without any meaningful sense of personal self-possession.

The confusion over what it means to be a separate human being is not just the result of the technological development of society. It is also rooted in our theological and philosophical history. The Puritans were so preoccupied with the majesty of God that they could not attribute any stable qualities to individual existence. The only valuable identity was that conferred by Grace. As time went on, a feeling that the self was detestable was retained by many who had abandoned their religious faith. Ironically, even those who thought that the individual was irreplaceable could not ground their belief upon any substantial principles. The best that could be said was that the self was a part of the selfhood of the human race.

In Chapter V, I describe the gradual decline of both the Christian and humanist ideals. I see the loss of a sense of substantial self-identity as the central problem. While recognizing that the difficulties are ultimately traceable to a loss of belief in the existence of an immortal soul, I contend that the issues are philosophical as well as theological in nature. Both those who oppose and those who support the value of an independent human existence assume that the self has no ontological status. This failure of being underlies our inability to give adequate recognition to the inviolable qualities of personal existence. The lack of an adequate metaphysics also renders us incapable of reconciling the individual and communal aspects of our experience. We lack the capacity to distinguish situations in which one can legitimately be considered as a part of a larger whole from those in which one has the inherent right to define what one shall be.

In an effort to gain a better understanding of human nature, I draw upon some relevant aspects of the Christian philosophical tradition as these have been developed within Roman Catholicism. In its comprehension of the human, Catholic philosophy maintains a distinction between the individual and the person. It does so without treating the two dimensions as completely separate realities. The principal idea is that every human being is an individual because of the material and biological aspects of his or her existence, and a person by reason of the spiritual qualities. The tradition holds that both aspects must to be taken into account if the quality of being human is to be fully understood.

Classical Catholicism also affirms the existence of a common human nature that dwells within each person and whose order can be discovered by the use of reason. While an exhaustive treatment of the subject is beyond the scope of this study, I treat it in a manner that should stimulate further dialogue. The idea that there is a natural law guiding our created destiny has been a source of great contention between Protestant and Catholic understandings of the human condition. While all Christian persuasions rely upon Gospel values, Catholicism has not restricted the range of its ethics to the direct commands of God as these are found in the Bible. Nor, pace humanism, does it ground its ethics in the self-legislating powers of the individual. Catholicism relies upon an intermediate normative order whose basic precepts are accessible to any reasonable person who desires to know and to do the good.

The idea that there exists an overarching and objective order of values is offensive to some who place supreme importance upon human autonomy. The Catholic view is that the recognition of this higher order is essential to the formation of an authentic personality. In trying to reconcile these conflicting views, I point out that while Catholicism refuses to accept the modern idea that values originate within the self, it does respect the freedom of the individual to either accept or reject the principles that exist independently of the human mind. How one uses one's liberty will determine what kind of person he or she shall become.

To be a person, one must have a substantial existence that is not derived from one's immersion in any group. At the same time, the genuine development of personality has an indispensable social component. To be fully human, one must be generously disposed towards all of life's possibilities. The reason for such inclusiveness lies in the fact that the deepest qualities of being human - the desire to know and to love -are by their nature communicable. As I continue these reflections, I try to identify some of the distinctive features of a well lived life that is both personal and sociable in the fullest sense of these terms. Taking into account our pragmatic inclinations, I concentrate upon the relation between being and doing. Following Karol Wojtyla (Pope John Paul II), I affirm that action makes the person. In every public as well as private situation, a deed is personal if it is done for reasons that are interior to the one so engaged.

In our modern hyper-organized society, the balance between social involvement and inherent self-possession is very difficult to sustain. This is obvious in the dynamics of family life, but it extends, in subtle ways, to every form of human association. Generally, considerable deference to the community is inevitable; but in matters of moral importance, independent judgment cannot be abandoned. A sound humanism recognizes that the imperatives of cooperation never cancel one's obligations to oneself.

In suggesting how one may strike a proper balance between personal and communal existence, I give considerable attention to the phenomenon of opposition. Metaphysically considered, this entitlement has a meaning that runs much deeper than what is legally recognized as the right to dissent. Even when socially engaged, one who is convinced of his or her uniqueness must be willing to object to what others may consider to be desirable for the good of the group. Allegiance can be expressed in disagreement.

The right to resist the views of others does not relieve the individual of his positive responsibilities to promote the good of community. I deplore the fact that there are many who consider themselves to be moral beings, yet refuse to actively cooperate with others to resolve common problems. This is a scandal that offends both Christian and humanistic ideals. To be an authentic person, in any communal context, one must be ready to take initiatives that exceed all enforceable obligations. A genuine person does not abandon community even while insisting that he, and not the social group, is the subject of action.

However expansively one comprehends human possibilities, the question remains whether they can be realized without Divine Assistance. We must ask again, as we did at the beginning of our history, whether Grace and freedom can be reconciled. In the initial chapter we saw how the Puritan mind favored Grace in a manner that admitted of no compromise with liberty. Now the pendulum has swung to the opposite extreme. We privilege freedom in a way that rejects all forms of spiritual subordination. Yet the reality of personal as well as social evil is an undeniable feature of life, and it is obviously not correctable by human effort alone. It remains to be seen if a balance can be struck between the desire for personal independence and the need for supernatural help .

The reader will recall that the position Edwards and his followers took depended upon antecedent assumptions of primal depravity so thorough that they destroyed the natural capacity of the will to pursue the good. According to Catholicism, we are wounded, but not completely corrupted by Original Sin. This more nuanced understanding of the consequences of the Fall can facilitate the shaping of an accord between Divine and human initiative. There then remains the question of where the spiritual resources that can heal sinfulness and enhance freedom are to be found.

In this 'Post-Christian' age, it is assumed that one can become a complete person without an explicit adherence to any established religion. It is of course true that a Democracy draws upon the good-will of citizens who do not share the same philosophical system or religious faith. But that premise and the related doctrine of separation of Church and State are matters of public policy. Valid within their own political frame of reference, they do not address the utterly personal issues of faith and worship. These cannot be avoided by anyone seriously concerned about his or her personal identity and ultimate destiny. Each must alone decide whether there is any spiritual authority that is empowered to heal the deep divisions between good and evil, love and hate, hope and despair, that compete for the affections of the singular human heart.

The futility of trying to discover the basic meaning of life within the self alone, by absorption in the wholeness of Nature, or through the evolution of Democratic society, should be evident to anyone who carefully reads this book. These failures of final meaning inevitably bring us back to the significance of Christian Revelation. Throughout our history as a nation, the quest for self-understanding has always had some relationship to the doctrines and practices of Christianity, primarily in its Protestant post- Reformation forms. But the rise of a modern humanism has transformed the problem of identity into a competition between Christianity and Atheism for the allegiance of the individual soul. For one who is attracted to the Christian way of life, the question then becomes that of determining where he or she might find the fullest institutional expression of the Salvation won by the Suffering, Death, and Resurrection of Jesus Christ.

The relation between the human and the Divine was also of great concern to our most original thinkers, and their reflections may help us to identify some of the deeper needs that must be met by any ecclesiastical manifestation of

Christianity appropriate to this new century. Such a church must be one that preserves the uniqueness of the individual person, even as it celebrates the communal dimensions of fellowship and worship It also must honor the good of society while remaining independent of all temporal power or opinion. Comprehensive in its understanding of the range of human existence, it must be willing to recognize the degree to which it has not been faithful to the fullness of life. An authentic Christian Church must enable the believer to fulfill all his obligations toward temporal life, even as he moves in hope towards the world that is to come.

The fullness of Revelation will only be found in a Church that defends all the essential truths of faith and morals. Such a spiritual authority will maintain the distinction between the Creator and his creation, but do so in a manner that does not diminish our human dignity. While avoiding doctrines of complete depravity, it will recognize the constant struggle between good and evil that occurs daily within each individual soul. A sacramental system that can not only cure our sinfulness but also raise us to the status of children of God will be essential to its mission. And while it preserves the dogmas of Final Judgment, this Church will proclaim that Mercy, rather than vengeance, is the dominant characteristic of the Triune God.

I end these reflections with a respectful appeal that the inclusive and ecumenical claims made by the Roman Catholic Church be examined again, without prejudice. The Church has come to a deeper understanding of its nature through the Second Vatican Council. The Council acknowledged that the Spirit of Christ is operative in other Christian churches but insisted that the Catholic Church alone possesses the full means of Salvation. To some, this is rank Triumphalism; to others, it is offensive to human dignity. But those who give truth the highest priority may find that the claims of Catholicism are worth thoughtful reconsideration. They may find that the basic aspirations towards freedom and fulfillment that have so occupied the American mind are affirmed by the teachings and sacraments of Roman Catholicism. The Church that awaits such further inquiry may truly be found to reconcile the independence and unity of humankind, while also providing an intimacy with God which surpasses the aspirations of our greatest thinkers.

CHAPTER ONE

Freedom, Grace, and Nature

Renaissance and Reformation

In medieval Christendom the human person was understood to possess a value which surpassed in dignity all the rest of the created world. The uniqueness of the person lay in his free will; a freedom which depended upon, and was elevated by, the Grace which flowed from Christ's redemptive sacrifice. The culture as a whole was permeated by a common faith. There was a shared way of life which, while beginning on earth, would only be consummated in eternity. [1].

Within the various communities of Christian Europe each individual had a specific status and function which was fixed by the prevailing social structure, while the rituals and teachings of the Church guided him towards his final destiny. It was an age of unreflective simplicity. Most lived out their lives by looking forward, in hope and fear, toward the life that was to come. The Renaissance shook the foundations of this hierarchical civilization. By the middle of the Fourteenth century, a developing feeling for the abundance and variety of life started to shatter the earlier restraint and tranquillity. As the feudal system began to disintegrate, profound changes occurred in the area of culture as well as in political organization. A spirit of adventure was abroad and it was inspiring a new sense of human possibilities.[2].

The revival of the classics of ancient literature led the humanists of the Renaissance to search for new ideals of human perfection. Ultimate beatitude was becoming less attractive than the mundane expression of individual uniqueness. As a sense of expansion began to include the realm of self-understanding, a feeling for inner complexity began to replace the unsophisticated outlook which had been a distinctive feature of medieval civilization. The spirit of the Renaissance gradually began to shape a new European culture. By the time of the German Enlightenment, the inward powers of the mind were being expanded to a point which began to blur the distinction between the divine and the human. For those who were philosophically inclined, the great abyss between the Creator and his creation was becoming a source of frustration rather than worshipful gratitude. Science was beginning to penetrate more deeply into the mysteries of the physical world, and it was thought that the spiritual mysteries of existence would yield to a comparable mode of inquiry. Western man was finding the source of meaning and inspiration within himself rather than through a dependence upon a supernatural order whose origins were beyond.

In this changing culture a rational understanding of human well-being was being explicated without reference to divine causality. In the philosophy of Leibniz, for example, principles of justice were thought of as eternal, unchanging verities which encompassed both God and man. The human being was being drawn into a fellowship with the divine. Transcendence was viewed as nothing more than a projection of what is best in human experience. In the overall chain of being, the positive qualities of creation were to be realized by self-determining individuals. Most importantly, their potentials should not be inhibited by any external spiritual or political force. [3].

As European society withdrew itself from the authority of the Church, the Protestant Reformation tried to revive the sources of Christian life. In the teachings of Luther and Calvin, the distance between the Creator and His creation was restated with great vehemence. In the reaction against the spirit of the Renaissance, a pessimistic understanding of human possibilities began to grip the ordinary imagination. Traditional themes of predestination and election were magnified and the sovereignty of God was set majestically over against the littleness and perversity of man.

In the Calvinist conception, man was a sinner subject to the terrible power of an angry God. The individual was destined to undergo the torments of eternal damnation unless he humbled himself and accepted the Christian conversion. Even more radically than in the medieval culture, the economy of salvation was one more of grace than of freedom. But at the same time, a humanistic self-consciousness was asserting itself which rejected all forms of blind obedience to any form of higher authority. The individual was beginning to understand himself as a person; as one who, by the use of his own powers, must bring himself to his fulfillment. [4].

As tension grew between the orthodox Protestant dogma of arbitrary divine election and the insubmissive understanding of self-determination, the central issue became that of freedom of the will. The quarrel was not new. Since the beginnings of Christian culture, the power of the human being to do the good on his own initiative had been problematic. The position of Saint Augustine is illustrative.

Augustine defended the freedom of the will against the Manicheans. They had held that evil was an immutable part of nature and, consequently , that moral wrong could not have its source in individual choice. For Augustine, this philosophy was incompatible with the dogma of the Creation. No part of the created world, whether material or spiritual, could be of itself evil. The will, therefore, had the power to do good by being righteous. Being free, however, it was also capable of choosing evil. Sin arose out of the will, independent of any external cause. Neither good, nor evil, could be attributed to anything beyond the one who wills it. [5].

Augustine defended the will against the Manicheans in order to prove that God, as Creator, could not be the cause of moral evil. However, to combat the Pelagians, he felt that it was necessary to emphasize the limitations of the powers of the will. The new challenge was to prove that God was the author of all good.

Pelagius, a British monk, believed that once human reason had illuminated the nature of the good life, there were no significant obstacles to living it. He distrusted appeals to grace because it made men look for divine assistance in circumstances in which they should depend upon the qualities of their own character. If sin was a matter of choice, the will must be the ultimate determinant of human conduct.

To Augustine, the error of the Pelagians was that they left no room for the grace of God. The individual either sins, or lives rightly, but unless freed by grace, he cannot overcome his servitude to evil and enjoy the freedom of the adopted sons of God. Grace must precede the actions of the will; if it did not have this antecedent authority, grace would have to be bestowed for righteous behavior. Such an inversion would contradict the gratuitous nature of the divine assistance which had been merited by the suffering, death, and resurrection of Christ. [6].

After Augustine, it was established Christian teaching that the grace of God is the exterior principle of human acts. The rigor of Augustine's position was to some degree softened in these later reflections. Aquinas, for example, held that after the Fall of Adam the human being is unable to fulfill his nature completely without the aid of grace, but he was careful to observe that the individual person is not entirely corrupted by sin. He could do some good by his own power, even though he could not do all the good which is the created substance of human nature without supernatural help. [7].

Any hope for further development in the distinction between grace and freedom was shattered by the Reformation. For Luther, the will can do nothing by its own power. All comes to pass by God's Providence. For Calvin, man sins willingly, but he does so necessarily because of his passions. Being depraved, he can only move in the direction of evil. When moved by grace, he does the good;

but nothing of the good can be attributed to his own powers. All that is of value comes from the freedom of God. [8].

The struggle between grace and freedom also raised questions about the nature of the good. In Catholic theology an attempt had been made to strike a balance between voluntarism, which attributes all moral meaning to divine intention, and rationalism, which assigns an active role to human understanding of the natural law. Suarez had taught that reason reveals what is good or evil to human nature and that God, as the Author of that nature, commands that actions should be done, or avoided, as reason dictates. With the Protestant ascendancy, the powers of the intellect were disvalued and the moral good was found exclusively in God's commands. Human nature was virtually equated with sinfulness. The only inclinations of importance were those of the heart towards evil or righteousness. [9].

The dialectical struggle between divine sovereignty and human depravity within Protestant theology was carried across the oceans to the Puritan settlement in New England. In the seventeenth century an attempt was made in the Massachusetts Bay Colony to establish a theocracy. It was governed by an Elect whose religious and secular responsibility was to keep the sinful multitudes in the fear of God. Freedom was the prerogative of righteousness. To the Puritan mind, God's unconditional demands had to be realized by the application of his moral law to the community. That law was enforced in order to develop a new "City on a Hill". [10].

Over time, the rigors of the Calvinist dogma began to lose their grip over the general population. By the beginning of the eighteenth century, common experience was contradicting the assumptions of pervasive inner corruption. Some preachers dared to suggest a reconciliation of divine and human purposes. The inhabitants of New England began to feel that it was within their power to create for themselves a greater measure of earthly happiness than the traditional Puritan pessimism would allow. As the theology was losing its social sanction, it stood in need of a powerful restatement of Divine Sovereignty and a vigorous defense of the priority of grace over freedom.

A reconsideration of the basic themes had already begun in Europe. Among the rationalists of the Enlightenment, grace was being thought of as being just a vindication of the rectitude of the conventionally upright. Within Calvinism, a Dutch theologian, Jacobus Arminius, challenged the ideas of election and predestination. He tried to distance himself from the Pelagian heresy of self-sufficiency by acknowledging the effectiveness of God's grace. Arminius recognized that divine assistance illuminates the mind, brings right order to the affections, and directs the inclinations of the will towards the good. However, Arminius also claimed that grace was not irresistible. He insisted that the efficacy of supernatural help required the co-operation of the human will. [11].

In 1619, at the Synod of Dort, the teachings of Arminius were condemned because they deviated from the Calvinist dogma concerning the enslavement of the will to evil. Thereafter, Arminianism became a word of reproach within Protestant countries. But it became influential in North America where self-determination and personal responsibility were of central importance.

The dangers which Arminianism posed to orthodoxy there would be met by the last, and greatest, of the Puritan theologians, Jonathan Edwards. In responding to the Arminian challenge, Edwards drew upon the insights of moral psychology as well as the fundamentals of religious dogma. In his famous treatise on the subject, Edwards argued that the stress which his adversaries placed upon the autonomy of the will overlooks the fact that choice is grounded upon preferences. Liberty may be the power of choosing as one pleases, but the direction of choice is determined by underlying motives. We are free to follow the will, but we are not free to form the act of volition. The will is determined by something prior to itself. Freedom is the attribute of a person, but Edwards insisted that a person's destiny is governed by the love, or hate, which already exists in his heart. [12].

The Arminians stressed the essential indifference of the will in order to protect its autonomy from being compromised by considerations of vice or virtue. They felt that the greater was the neutrality, the greater would be the liberty. Edwards found this intolerable because it offends the basic principles of causation. For him, the idea that everything that exists has a cause applies to ethical as well as material reality. Moreover, moral determination is nearly as absolute as physical necessity. A strong disposition virtually determines the quality of action. In Edward's moral theology, actions are not themselves the cause of their own existence. They are the fruit of the dispositions of the heart. Where the heart is corrupt, wickedness becomes habitual. He argued that the individual cannot on his own love the real good, nor can he direct his actions towards the infinitely holy being of God. According to Edwards, it was irrelevant that some of the unregenerate actually perform a few good actions. The more fundamental reality was the preponderance toward evil which lay at the core of human nature.

This essential corruption was derived from Adam's original sin. Seminal disobedience would lead all of his progeny to damnation unless they were saved by God's gracious election. Whether or not that saving love enters the individual soul is a free and arbitrary divine decision. It is unrelated to a person's choices or personal character. [13].

Edwards insisted that no one can be confident of divine favor. Where grace has not been given, all suffer the consequences of Adams' disobedience. In choosing evil , Adam acted as a representative of the whole human race and his children, in their turn, will be prey to all the perversions of self-love. In his teaching and preaching, Edwards insisted that all who are beyond the realm of grace will be mastered by a carnal law which gives pride of place to inferior goods through innumerable acts of defiance of God's holy will.

In the Edwardian theology, the logic of corruption leads to damnation. Where grace is given, all that has been received is returned to God by a holy and devout life. But where grace is withheld and sin prevails, divine justice will be satisfied by a punishment of eternal duration.

Strangely, to Edwards, such an outcome is perfectly compatible with his more general idea that Beauty is the distinctive quality of divinity. The vindictive justice of God expresses the beauty of the divine character. God can always bring infinite good out of evil; in the case of sinners, the absolute good was the infinite punishment of infinite evil. [14].

Edwards' pessimism, like that of the Catholic Jansenists, came from a profound intuition into the depths of corruption and deceit which lie within the human heart. Yet these insights, however valid in themselves, were out of touch with the spirit of freedom which was gradually asserting itself within the New England experience. Ideals of personal liberty were evolving which could not be reconciled with the Edwardian notion that all was evil until it was changed by grace. Americans tended to think that they had shaken off the moral gloom, as well as the political corruption of the Old World. Many would reject any religious doctrine which viewed them as wretched and despicable in the eyes of God. Freedom of choice was the key to their moral natures. As they became more confident of their own powers of action, they would abandon all explicit obedience to the Puritan theology. Yet they would be unable to completely avoid its influence.

Benjamin Franklin was representative of the transition. He asserted the Puritan moralism but separated it from its theological ends. His catalogue of virtues advised; they did not dictate. Franklin was a man of the world as well as a native of New England, and the distinctions which he drew between vice and virtue were meant as guides to a sober, if not necessarily godly, life. [15].

Within the Calvinist tradition as established by the Puritans, some theologians tried to moderate the severity of its doctrines by making them more realistic. They wanted to bring the orthodox teachings closer to the lives of those who were trying, as best they could, to lead a good and upright life. Others tried to strike a better balance between the ethical and the spiritual factors of the religion. They looked upon the moral laws which God had imposed upon humanity as being as excellent as his grace. The disturbing understanding of the divine nature was recast in terms of a majestic benevolence which might attract the attention of those among the educated who placed a high value upon rationality.[16].

In the end, however, the tensions between the dogmatic teaching which emphasized an extreme dependence upon divine favor at the expense of the desire for individual independence would become intolerable. The infinite distance which Puritan teaching placed between the Creator and His creation would lead the New England mind to search for new ways of comprehending the dignity of the human person. This would involve changes not only in religious doctrine, but also in the ways that the individual would relate to the natural world by which he was surrounded.

A New England Revival

In the New England of Jonathan Edwards, the intellectual life of the community was under the authority of the established church. By the end of the eighteenth century a process of separation had begun; a rebellion which bore some resemblance to Roger William's' defection from the Massachusetts Bay theocracy more than a century earlier. In both instances, the right of the individual to form his own conscience, and decide for himself upon the nature of his spiritual commitments, was of central importance.

The inspirations for the new movement were German Idealism and French Romanticism. Both stressed a subjectivity that found religious expression in the teachings of Unitarianism. Calvinist Puritanism had found an able defender of the faith in Jonathan Edwards; Unitarianism would have its own distinguished advocate in the preaching and writings of William Ellery Channing. Channing would move away from the doctrines of total corruption towards a doctrine of personal righteousness. In the process, he would articulate a new relation between God and man.

Channing held that it is a grave error for a theology to fix attention upon the sovereignty of God while demeaning, or neglecting, the majesty of the human. According to Channing, this was the fatal mistake of the Puritans. They had not only demanded that the faithful be fearfully aware of their sinfulness and the wrath of God; believers were also expected to purge themselves of their particular discrete identities. A sense of self was incompatible with the plenitude of grace. Channing believed that the flaw in the New England Calvinism was that it leads the individual to be unjust to himself. [17].

Channing was convinced that one does not honor God by losing self-respect. For him, the reform of New England Protestantism would have to strike a better balance between the finite and the infinite dimensions of religion. For Unitarianism, it was not enough to recognize that God's power was limitless and irresistible . One must also acknowledge that man is free.

To affirm the possibilities of human liberty within a religious context would involve the implicit retrieval of the Arminian teachings concerning the freedom of the will. Within New England society it was generally recognized that our actions determine our character. At the same time, the population recognized the individual's dependence upon God. Channing insisted that it is not God's will alone that must be done. The ethical power of human action implies an inner nobility which Edwards and his followers simply failed to realize.

Channing also believed that the Puritan Calvinists failed to understand the deeper meaning of the creation of man. All Christians recognize that we are made in God's image, but the understanding of that honor varies with social and political conditions. In the age of monarchies, subordination was stressed and the deeper meaning of our created dignity was obscured. According to Channing, the value would be clearer in a democracy, where there is less deference to superior authority. To this Unitarian mind, we do not honor the privilege of divine likeness by groveling before the Deity as one would abase oneself before an oriental potentate. Instead, we must actively bring out in ourselves, and in others, the elevated image in which we are made. [18].

Edwards had insisted that since all good comes from God, the soul filled with grace returns all these blessings with worshipful acts of devout and pious gratitude. Channing reverses the process. In the Unitarian subjectivity, we rise to the divine by activating the good of our own nature. In Channing's theology, we can only love a God whose supreme excellence is reflected in our own souls. The spirit is within. It is the origin, and determining cause, of all that we may hope to be. To rise to the divine, we must devote to noble ends those inner qualities of reason and moral freedom which distinguish us from the rest of creation.

Channing also had a humanistic argument against Predestination and Election. In the Calvinist theology , all of humanity is by nature corrupt, utterly incapable of spiritual good, and necessarily inclined to evil. Relief from that terrible condition comes from the grace won by Christ's Redemption. Yet those who are saved are but a minority of all the human beings born into this world as the children of Adam. With the exception of the Elect, the human race is left, in this life, to the corruption in which it was born and, at death, is predetermined to suffer an eternal damnation. This dark logic was offensive to the humane sensibility which was being awakened by the New England Renaissance.

Rousseau denounced the dogma of Original Sin as a libel against human nature. Channing preferred to argue that the teaching of predestination could not be reconciled with the goodness of God. The divine goodness was made known by Revelation, but according to Channing it was also manifest by the powers of human intuition. To the Calvinists, the divine sovereignty was unlimited and arbitrary. Channing, like Leibniz before him, believed that God's goodness and justice, while infinite, are not essentially different from the same qualities found in man.

Edwards' insistence that God's justice is vindictive could not be reconciled with the ordinary understanding of the indispensable aspects of righteousness. Channing argued that we cannot attribute any meaning to justice other than what we learn from reflecting upon our natures as moral beings. Since cruelty is a deficiency of man, it cannot be a positive aspect of God's power and beauty. If God were an arbitrary ruler, as the Calvinists contend, He would share man's vices as well as his virtues. [19].

With the advent of Unitarianism, personal faith began to displace normative theology. Rejecting Trinitarian dogma, the religious individual would advance beyond the immaturities of ecclesiastical allegiance and develop expressions of belief, and liturgical practices, which corresponded more closely with his own inner values. The new spiritual ambition was to bring into ourselves all the divinity that flesh is able to assimilate. There will be nothing, -- not even a mediator—between God the Father and His human children. Furthermore, religious renewal was to have a public dimension. Isolated piety could no longer serve as a spiritual ideal. Reason and the bible would join forces to promote an inclusive moral perfection which was as attentive to the values of social and political progress as it was of individual fulfillment.

Unitarianism would issue a call for us to be as perfect as our Heavenly Father is perfect. But perfection would not consist in our imitation of His constant mercy, but by our doing everything in the best possible way and from the highest motives. In the reforms initiated by Channing, Christianity is restated in a manner which will make it appealing to noble hearts that believe in the power of moral reason. [20].

The idealistic theism that inspired the Unitarian revolt against Puritanical Calvinism would have an influence upon important political struggles in favor of freedom of speech and against the monstrous evil of slavery. But in its turn away from theocentric, in favor of an anthropocentric, understanding of creation, the new religious doctrines would soon give way to a transcendental individualism. The holiness of the individual would be sought within a cosmic union which would ratify all his primary intuitions of truth, beauty, and goodness. This transformation would be most fully realized in the life and work of New England's great philosopher -poet, Ralph Waldo Emerson.

Emerson began his adult life as a Unitarian minister, but he abandoned the office, and the religion, while he was still a relatively young man. The motivations were partly doctrinal. His mind could not accept some of the central teachings, such as the Atonement and the Lord's Supper. But the separation was also caused by a deeper contradiction between the Christian life and the needs of his personality.

What Emerson thought of as the good could not be reconciled with the official definitions of goodness. After leaving his clerical position, he continued searching for whatever would help him find himself. He needed some outlet which would accommodate his poetic sensibility and his unquenchable desire for a comprehensive understanding of the human condition. These yearnings could not be satisfied by the orthodox regularities of any established church.

To Emerson's mind, the bounded allegiances of ecclesiastical life prevented the individual from receiving all that his Maker could teach him. He conceded that membership in a church provides some enlightenment , but he wanted something more inclusive. Emerson had a personality which required a deeper understanding of the meaning of life. His search led him to seek for some all embracing light which casts its power over the whole of the universe. How near is God to man! Even more radically than Channing, Emerson would close the gap between the Creator and His creation.

Channing had tried to overcome the alienation of the human from the divine by attributing to the Godhead the moral excellences that can be found in human experience. Emerson wanted to concentrate his attention upon the precious value of the religious sentiment. He would give it a deeper meaning than it had received from Unitarianism. For Emerson, the passion for holiness empowers the individual to find the purposes of life within himself and in a natural manner which made him an intimate of divinity.[21].

Emerson also had a different attitude toward the value of the human will. Channing had tried to counter the Edwardian notion of innate depravity by affirming the capacity of the will to do the good on its own initiative. Emerson detected a weakness in this voluntaristic confidence; a flaw which was unrelated to the divergence between divine grace and human freedom. Emerson was more concerned with the relation between activity and the formation of personality. Emerson understood the importance of action. When public duty called, he responded, especially when fundamental principles of human dignity were at stake. But, in a more general sense, he was disenchanted with the allure of the strenuous life. Doing binds us to the wheels of chance, with all its fears and uncertainties. More importantly, for Emerson, the will did not establish his personal identity. The will had little to do with making him what he was. [22].

There was a further difficulty. Choice raise problems of conscience and, in a culture shadowed by Puritanism, these agonizing deliberations can lead to crippling emotions of guilt and remorse. But, according to Emerson, when mind is removed from the moral battle, it qualifies the condemnation. The sadness of sin is changed by thought. Calm reflection will show that what seems to be a corrupt subjective state is nothing more than an objective diminution of the good. [23].

Unitarianism had tried to restore the human dignity so long humiliated by Calvinism by encouraging the active moral life. Emerson would rather be liberated by the intellect. The role of the mind in the quest for holiness had long been discounted in the Christian tradition, but Emerson was determined to restore its value. He realized that an intellectual revival would not find any welcome within the established churches. In a moralistic environment, God's grace and the contemplative life could not easily coexist.

Something in Emerson' self-understanding also precluded this reconciliation of mind and faith. Although he had disengaged himself from orthodox belief and practice, Emerson retained a mystical sensibility. He wanted to steer a middle course between dogmatism and atheism. He could only do so by relying upon the divinity which he could discover within himself. Emerson shared with Channing a belief that the essential Christian truths were amenable to personal intuition. Beyond that, Emerson believed that the entire world beyond the self had a spiritual significance which could be revealed to the poetic soul. Being, the First Cause, the higher life, would all descend into the receptive and solitary individual.

The villages and farms of Emerson's experience were not, he said, the world I think. In self -consciousness he was building up an absolute self which would determine all things for itself. This deeper subjectivity would reach beneath all the discord of social existence and lay hold of the harmony of the ideal. Ultimate reality would become knowable by the individual through introspection.

Emerson was wise enough to realize that his metaphysical ego could not stand completely on its own. It would need some external support. While self-reliant, Emerson understood that he would never be completely autonomous. In spite of his aspirations for full personal independence, he still had to depend upon something outside of himself. He realized that, in the order of the human faculties, Reason was superior both to logic and to the uncertainties of empirical understanding. This conception of the higher mind, which reflected the influence of Kant, was inspiring, but it was also vague and eclectic. The Emersonian intellect was a medley of the rational and the irrational; the emotional and the poetic. It embraced all that could be known both within self-consciousness and through the medium of the unconscious. [24].

For the Sage of Concord, the important point was to let go of the will. Only by moving to a contemplative state could one find what was immortal in man. To the one who would become reflective, the wholeness and integrity of humanity would be revealed on this higher level. The revelation would come through the marriage of mind with Nature. In Emerson's humanism, man becomes holy when he establishes a pious union with the fullness of the living universe. The objective is Nature which, beneath all its visual beauty, subsists for itself. As the deep force within which all things find their common origin, Nature elevates individual being. It also compensates for all the disappointments of contingent existence. For Emerson, the encounter with Nature was more wondrous than any of the Christian experiences. To his eyes, the miracles of the Churches are no match for "the blowing clover and the falling rain."

Nature also surpasses social experience. As it enhances individual life it testifies to all those qualities of being which are so often absent from the common lives of men. The multitude may be full of malice and deceit, but Nature brings truth and love to the individual in way that is creative. It not only inhabits, but it also makes, everything within which it dwells. With the aid that he receives from Nature, the individual is empowered to become Providence to himself. He brings goodness to his good and evil to his sin. Nature, being unbounded, is always encouraging. The world in which we are embedded not only builds up the self, it also assures its growth. Once in tune with Nature, the individual gradually comes to understand that beyond what he thinks is best, there lies a better. Whispering to the receptive heart, Nature tells it that it is not yet all that it can be. [25].

Nature is the root of personal growth. In silent communication, it announces to self -consciousness vast and universal possibilities. Once enlightened, the self becomes the medium through which heaven descends to earth, and he responds to what is above with love. Jonathan Edwards had directed the religious sentiment toward a love of God in, and above, all things. But the response was tainted with the fear of Divine Judgment. Emerson thought that the spiritual harmonies within Nature were more attractive than the ominous decrees of a Vindictive Justice. Emerson no longer dreads. As his mind contemplates Nature he is drawn out of himself in ecstasy. [26].

In spite of all these flights to the sublime, Emerson tried to maintain some continuity between his romantic naturalism and the Puritan tradition into which he had been born. Like the Calvinists, Emerson understood that humankind is not self-sufficient. He also knew that anyone puffed up with self-complacency is really weak and blind. Emerson shared with his clerical ancestors a profound belief in the value of self-discipline and a conviction that the soul is master of both will and intellect. But for Emerson, the ultimate principle of existence is not an inherent personal attribute. The deepest principle is the Eternal One; the deep power, or Over-Soul, within which all exist. In Emerson's philosophy, a universal being replaces the vengeful God who can eternally condemn the unique individual soul. Emerson believed that worshiping the transcendental would not prevent him from being, like the Puritan believer, a child of light. But he will recover his innocence by contemplating natural beauty rather than by faithfully receiving divine grace. [27].

As Emerson opened his mind to the truth of the universe he thought that a similar enlightenment would come to all. However, most of those who listened to his lectures were unwilling to follow his program of emotional and intellectual liberation. They needed a happiness that was within the range of their capacities and could be determined by their own wills. People generally preferred to follow the direct moral precepts which had immediate relevance to their lives, rather than reflectively pursue the intricacies of abstract goodness.

They also had reason to be suspicious of the call to contemplation. Emersonian mysticism promised the possession of everything in general; they feared that it would require the surrender of everything in particular. One of the ironies of Emerson's philosophy is that it takes away much of what it was meant to affirm. The central human reality was meant by Emerson to be the self-reliant individual, inspired by the powers of his intelligence. But reason is not individualized. It is not his own. Like Dante –also a philosopher as well as a poet – Emerson tended to believe that the world is endlessly moved by a superior mind. In such a cosmic conception, individuals do not think. They are thought into from above. [28].

Emerson praised the divinity that he thought resided within each individual. But the overall tendency of his thought was in the direction of pantheism. He hoped to surmount the radical distinction between the Creator and creation by bringing God and the Universe together as a single whole. The ambition was in keeping with the spirit of democracy. As the fusion of divinity and humanity applied to all, it affirms the spiritual dignity of every individual regardless of his wealth or power. The idea is admirable, but it is also inhuman in its consequences. For it cannot be reconciled with the distinctive existence of every human person. [29]

Emerson defended the sacredness and unrepeatable character .of every existing human being. But the singularity was subject to a universal spirit. He thought that serving that spirit was the vocation for which he had been called into being. Because he is nothing, he serves the all. Like the sages of India, with whose teachings he was familiar, Emerson understood spirituality as a quest for the impersonal essence of the universe. The power being sought was not that of a remote deity, but of an immediate presence that pervades all living things. The Absolute, higher than all the gods, becomes identical with the individual's own deep Self. To attain such a blissful state of being one simply acts as if the ego does not exist. Self—forgetfulness becomes the condition of individual meaning. [30].

Ancient spiritualities had taught that an enlightened one must live for others and help them in their suffering. Emerson shared that belief, although he tended to reserve it for great occasions. The difficulty was that he never fully reconciled his aspirations for unconditional truth with the concrete demands of human interdependence. He would not allow social ties to invade his solitude. And, while he taught that Genius represents all, he also believed that society was a conspiracy against the individual. Like the rest of reality, the communal aspects of existence could not have an actuality that was distinct from his soul. [31].

The attempts of Emerson and the transcendentalists to work out a meaningful humanism were deeply dependent upon the inspiration which the natural world could provide to the individual soul. But as the nation began to develop, the attitude toward the external world underwent a profound change. Since the seventeenth century the forces of European science had begun to grasp the immense possibilities for material well-being which could be drawn from the resources of the earth. Geometric demonstration and inductive reasoning were breaking the resistance of nature to the human will. Nature was becoming a subject of exploitation rather than an object of worship. As these changes became the basis of American industrialization, the corresponding technologies began to create an alternative, self-sufficient universe to what had been a stable cosmic order. The individual trying to develop an autonomous existence would no longer be in touch with a timeless and enhancing presence that permeates the whole of existence. Indeed, he would begin to experience the natural world as something more menacing than benevolent.

As for the Puritan theology, the more it was rejected, the greater would be its lingering influence. Emerson's cancellation of sin by thought would not bear the weight of experience. Men of deeper insight would see the futility of trying to avoid the reality of evil, and they would also give new meaning to the Calvinist doctrines of Predestination and Depravity.

To the imagination of our emerging writers, the sense of sin was coupled with a fear of its inevitability. The world that they experienced would be caught in the grip of evil. As they addressed these issues, they would attempt to craft a conception of personal identity which could in some way be distinguished from any larger social or cosmic whole.

The Lingering Sense of Sin

Theodore Parker was one of the greatest of all the Unitarian ministers. While he thought like a philosopher, he lived among men. Compassionate, he carried the sorrows of men in his heart; righteous, he had the wrongs of the world on his conscience. His personality combined the idealistic theism of Channing with a transcendental individualism which considered its inner being to be divine.

Parker's Sermon on The Transient and The Permanent in Christianity, which he delivered in 1841, established a new phase of Unitarianism. Parker abandoned the supernaturalism which Channing had preserved through his reliance upon Scripture, and in doing so put in its place an evolutionary theism. In this more natural dispensation, God gradually reveals Himself to human faculties and speaks to the depths of the individual conscience. [32].

Reform was meat and drink to Parker. He directed his corrective energies against the hypocrisies which he saw in the institutional expressions of religion. Channing had moved New England Protestantism away from the doctrines of Predestination and Election, and changed what had been the dread of punishment into a more positive religious emotion. But Unitarianism soon became a religion of respectability. Its austere ethic was often used to justify exploitation. According to Parker, regeneration would come through the abandonment of orthodox doctrines and replacing them with a passionate love of God. He hoped for the realization of an absolutely natural religion which could represent the highest aspirations of humanity.

In Parker's schema, the Devil, as well as the Trinity, disappeared in the majesty of an infinite and flawless God. Christ's mediation was no longer necessary. Divinity would dwell within the whole of creation, in its material as well as its spiritual aspects. In this solidarity of Creator and creature, all would be moved forward, with untainted motivation, to a progressively better future and a perfect final end.

The Unitarian reaction against Puritanism had overcome the exaggerated contrasts between God and humanity by accentuating the positive aspects of our personalities and then projecting them on to the Divinity. Released from the curse of innate depravity, the individual would be free to honor his obligations to the moral law. In Parker's ideal, all aspects of religious doctrine and practice were to be subservient to the aspirations of the transcendentally religious individual. The soul would be free to devote all its energies to the advancement of man as well as the love of God. [33].

Parker's reforming spirit reached out to the public world as well as the realm of personal religious practice. He sensed that there was a new feeling for human unity in the air and he wanted to advance the cause. New England society would again become a place where God's justice was enacted into human laws. In pursuing these transformations, Parker was fearless as well as devout. His grandfather's Minute Men had faced the British in 1775 and Parker was prepared to bring the same combative spirit to his social ministry. He named names and passed judgment on many in high places. But his belligerency not only enraged his enemies; it also gave offense to some who shared his values.

The militant radicals of Nineteenth century New England vehemently opposed slavery and other political and economic injustices. These reformers, quite rightly, saw the evil in the world around them. But they were less inclined to recognize the evil in themselves. This moral blindness deeply disturbed Channing, who believed that the dignity of being human included the ability to recognize one's bondage to sin. He disagreed with the reformers who thought that no evil existed other than that which they opposed. [34].

Channing was a responsible pastor. While a friend of Emerson, Channing did not believe that the reconciliation of Creator and creature would come through the worship of the immensity of nature. Channing also resisted the developing cult of subjectivity which he saw as being full of self-deception and a dire threat to the basic doctrines of Christianity. Channing had effectively renounced the Calvinist theory of complete corruption, but he respected his adversaries' insights into the ambiguities of moral intention.

To Channing's mind, the great reform movements of the Nineteenth century were marred by a tendency to oversimplify the divisions between the good and the dammed. While the objectives were highly desirable, those who pursued social justice often acted with mixed motives. Channing believed that the struggle against objective evil was frequently driven by an externalization of sin which was, in effect, an acquittal of the self. Those who were fighting to improve society were too often overlooking their own moral failures. This absent -mindedness was making Christian teaching on the importance of inner reform irrelevant to the future of the nation.

As a theologian, Channing could only note with sadness the loss of a sense of sin among his fellow citizens. But a writer of fiction, such as Nathaniel Hawthorne, could observe and describe its deeper psychological meaning. Hawthorne was a nominal Unitarian, but he did not share the views of those like Theodore Parker who believed in the moral perfectibility of humanity. Nor did he share the genial philosophy of his friend and neighbor, Ralph Waldo Emerson.

Hawthorne distrusted the Emersonian conception of the Oversoul and related notions of divine indwelling. The Salem novelist was also of the opinion that sin was a positive evil and that its existence is not just the occasion for reform. With his deep insight into human nature, he saw that one can never be sure that moral evil will not infect the desire for personal or social improvement. Most importantly, wrongdoing always has dire consequences not just for the individual who fails but for all affected by his or her actions.

Hawthorne was deeply influenced by the whole Puritan tradition .Through his ancestors, the gloom had become part of his family inheritance. Like the New England Calvinists, he was preoccupied with problems of personal evil. As a writer, however, Hawthorne looked upon questions of guilt and shame as food for the imagination rather than as matters of religious investigation.

While he knew many of the transcendentalists, Hawthorne could not accept their metaphysical optimism. To his mind, they had made the mistake of seeking individual fulfillment in the timeless. Hawthorne was certain that it is only under the pressure of actual experience that one can grasp the actual progress, or decline, of the human soul. The universal had to merge in some way with the particular before one could fully understand the human condition. [35].

Transcendentalist optimism was an inverse image of Puritan pessimism. Hawthorne turned away from such broad and simple abstractions in order to concentrate his attention upon the concreteness of individual moral behavior. He carefully observed the psychological dimensions of guilt and recorded the social as well as the personal consequences of a violation of the moral code. In his stories the sense of sin is pervasive. The guilty one sees that he or she is a sinner, but also realizes that those who would impose sanctions upon the offense have evil dispositions of their own of which they can be sanctimoniously unaware.

Through his fiction, Hawthorne was trying to gauge the full complexity of human life. He was convinced that authentic moral growth can only occur when individuals, as well as societies, realize that they are drawn to evil as well as toward good. To promote that understanding, the magnitude of personal wrongdoing is enlarged and multiplied in his fiction.

In stories of persecution, Hawthorne would sympathize with the victim but did not assume that they were totally innocent. Evil was often mixed with good. In *The Blithedale Romance* Hawthorne showed how sinister influences can be at work even in a utopian community. Selfishness can take control over fraternity and interpersonal rivalries mar the ideals of communal love.

Hawthorne's fiction also describes how evil extends its fatal venom. In *The Scarlet Letter*, Hester Pryne has committed adultery, but the sins of her lover, the Rev. Mr. Dimmesdale, and those of her husband, Roger Chillingworth, are of a far graver nature. Dimmesdale had concealed his fault and violated the reverence which he should have had for Hester's immortal soul, while Chillingworth has maliciously devised a plan to destroy the errant Puritan pastor.

Hawthorne's powerful imagination identifies a vast range of moral derelictions, but his writings give scant attention to deliberation and choice. The events are retrospective; his characters have already done something wrong. Predestination takes on a temporal face. A power beyond the control of the characters is influencing their actions just as everything that is done has inexorable consequences. [36].

Hester Prynne's adultery shows that in the opinion of the community she is already dammed. No human or supernatural intervention can remove the effects of the guilt or terminate the remorseless retribution. There is neither grace nor freedom. The only compensation lies in the way that Hester preserves her individuality in spite of the ordeal. She is determined to live by her own sense of right rather than have her life controlled by the merciless imposition of a moral code. And yet while she rebels in the name of human decency and her desire for personal happiness, she cannot find a higher law to which she can appeal for support. Stronger than her lover, she virtually takes pride in her sinfulness and develops a disposition which approaches moral anarchy. [37].

In his stories, Hawthorne did not concentrate his attention upon the phenomenon of willfulness. But his friend, Herman Melville, would probe more deeply into the abyss of human freedom which opens up when the will is set loose from all objective anchorage. Melville would also rethink the whole relationship between man and nature. Recall that for Emerson, nature was a source of enlightenment. This attitude was enthusiastically embraced by the Transcendentalists. Thoreau believed that all seasons of the year nurture the soul. But to Melville, this faith was incredible. For he had contemplated the sea. [38].

Moby Dick, Melville's great work, is based upon the antithesis of land and sea. The land represents all that can be understood and mastered; the oceans are an obscure realm of instincts, dangers, and terror. Land brings comfort and safety, but those who go to sea seek adventure. It is there that one can grapple with the fundamental issues of personal existence.

Once launched upon his voyage, the sailor, like an Emersonian pantheist, senses a deep identity between his soul and the immensities of the ocean. But in its depths, the water becomes a parable on the mystery of evil and the arbitrariness of the universe. Below the surface, one finds a ferocity which none can comprehend or conquer; a fathomless realm from which Divine Providence seems to have withdrawn.

Like the Deity, Nature is an implacable power. The Puritans had taught that God upholds the universe with his inscrutable and arbitrary will, threatening to bring eternal vengeance down upon all who defy his law. In the imagination of Melville, the malignant aspects of divinity are drawn into the fabric of universal nature. The metaphysical transfer dramatizes how far man is cut off from communion with God.

Predestination is also given a more sinister meaning. To Jonathan Edwards, God knows who will be saved or dammed from all eternity and he allows these foreseen ends to be reflected in temporal behavior. While the Elect invariably do the good, the lost continuously do the evil which flows from their corrupt hearts. Melville looks deeper into the darkness. He sees how necessity now governs the normal course of events. As nature follows inexorable laws, so does the human heart. Lacking an end in view, we all seem to be fleeing from what is behind us. Captain Ahab's conduct in Moby Dick leads to disaster for himself, his ship, and his crew, but his actions follows the logic of a depraved willfulness which is determined to seek, and conquer, a transcendental object. His war against the white whale consumes all his thoughts and desires. The struggle becomes a being in itself. Ahab is a monomaniac, but his actions are directed by a desire to destroy the spirit of evil which he sees as embodied in Moby Dick. The great whale, with its intensified whiteness, represents "all the truth with malice" which pervades the heartless universe.

The attempt to destroy the whale pushes the human will beyond the measure of reason. No longer impotent, the will does not acknowledge any order beyond itself. But this extreme expression of transcendental individualism cannot defeat the evil within or without. Blasphemously passing beyond the limits of human powers, Ahab infringes upon the purposes of God. In doing so, he is defeated by the divine surrogate, the forces of the natural world. [39].

Ahab represents the apotheosis of the Emersonian temperament. But he does not so much deify the individual as he denies divine goodness. He cannot believe that God is kind to those who revere Him. Nor does he think that the Creator of such a terror-filled world can be a lover of souls. Overcome by his morbidness, Ahab feels that he has no option except defiance. He replaces the Edwardian faith in a divine sovereignty with the assertion of an unconditioned individuality. This seems to be the only way that he can preserve his personality in the face of an impersonal universe. His self is saved by Pride.

In Melville's exploration of the post-Reformation self, there is no Redemption. Nihilism and despair take the place of damnation. Other figures of his creation, such as the central character in *Pierre,* learn, most painfully, that uncompromising idealism can also lead to social and personal disaster. As Melville's insights into moral complexity mature, he sees how much unconscious desires prey upon principles and make it more difficult to find valid motives for action. In such circumstances, it is hard to determine whether any of our thoughts or actions arise out of a stable personal identity. [40].

Melville never abandoned the quest for personal identity, but he was unable to identify the elements of a self-sufficient freedom. He explored the possibilities of a self defending its integrity from compulsions within as well as pressures without, but the mood, while not vicious, is irresponsible. And withdrawal is not a real solution.

In his short story *Bartleby the Scrivener,* the central figure withholds his consent from life and can only express his position with a pathetic "I prefer not to". When Melville accepts the realities of social existence the results are equally unsatisfactory. *Billy Budd* is the story of a young beautiful and innocent sailor wrongfully accused, but technically guilty, of striking an officer, one Claggert, and causing his death. Claggert is the incarnation of evil. The captain, Vere, is sympathetic to Billy, but feels obliged to enforce the law and imposes the punishment of death by hanging. Budd, whose last words bless his Captain, dies affirming his own passive grandeur. The tale repeats the theme of the inevitability of evil, but it also teaches a more sinister lesson about necessity. The irresistible has a social face. Organizational values have no respect for persons. The order of society is paramount and the individual, even if unjustly treated, ought to submit. [41].

As Melville neared the end of his life he developed a contented disposition. He became more accepting of the contrasts of good and evil which lie at the heart of existence and he also welcomed the inevitable alternations between birth and death which marks the cycle of the natural year. Overwhelmed by his pessimism, he was unable to heed Channing's warning that no lesson of immortality can be learned from nature. [42].

During this same period, others tried to reconcile a belief in eternal life with the acceptance of natural existence. However, their efforts could not secure the independent value of the individual human being. The life and poetry of Jones Very illustrates the difficulty. Very was a New England minister. He shared Channing's reserve respecting nature, treating it as a secondary source of revelation that should never be allowed to usurp God's primacy as stated in the Bible. Yet Very was deeply torn between these two sources of ultimate meaning. He also probed more deeply than Emerson into the relationship between the divine and the human. Emerson played with Pantheism and the Universal Spirit as he attempted to validate his radical subjectivity; Very, however, would not surrender his emotional connection with Christianity. When Emerson tried to persuade him that truth was relative to his sensibility, Very replied that truth was absolute. [43].

The difficulty for Very was that he wanted to maintain some of the transcendental possibilities of the self while at the same time affirming his religious beliefs. Like the Quakers, he thought that by trusting an inner voice, his soul would acquire an immediate contact with God. Grace was irresistible. Very believed that he had passed through the mystical stages of illumination, purgation, and union. Creating a persona of piety, he transcended the bonds of selfhood and asserted for himself a Christ-like role within the society of the unregenerate.

Many thought that Very was mad. But the imbalance of his personality came from his failure to clearly maintain the distinction between God and man. In this respect, he reflected the spirit of his age, which was determined to overcome the humiliation of the human by the Calvinist tradition.

Very was also setting a pattern which will be repeated throughout our intellectual history. As we continue these reflections we shall have other opportunities to see how, once one convinces oneself of subjective sanctification or absolute righteousness, the self becomes destabilized. Very's tragedy, like that of many of the post- Edwardians, was that while poetically cultivating his religious inclinations he lost all sense of his being a unique and distinct person.

When the search for personal identity takes place within powerful religious or cultural influences it becomes very difficult to attain a balanced sense of individual integrity. During the period of Puritan hegemony, the alternatives were stark. If Grace was accepted, selfhood had to be denied. Nature then became an alternative source of personal enrichment but, as we have seen, its attractions could lead to the extinction of the ego. Only the defiant will seemed to be able to preserve its independent value. Unfortunately, the undisciplined power of volition could, as in the case of Captain Ahab, consume the individual as well as those around him.

As the social dimension came into greater prominence, the desire to maintain a sense of individual independence would become even more difficult to realize. As the national economy grew, power and industry would have little tolerance for transcendental self -reliance. Moreover, the egalitarian spirit was starting to tip the balance against the value of the separate life. The sense of the whole that had inspired Emerson and the Transcendentalists would be given a communal, rather than a personal, meaning. As concern began to shift from the one to the many, those who hoped to live an independent existence would have to struggle to create themselves anew.

CHAPTER TWO

Self and Society

Individualism and Fellowship

Ralph Waldo Emerson's personality drove him to seek his own fulfillment in detachment from the lives of his fellow men. Walt Whitman was constantly drawn to others. In 1855 he published a collection of poems entitled *Leaves of Grass*, which announced a new stage in the evolution of a transcendental individualism. The first poem, "Song of Myself" set the egocentric tone, but the new poet would celebrate, with equal enthusiasm, the whole vibrant reality of the larger community that was taking shape before his eyes.

Whitman doted on himself, "that lot of me and all so luscious", but he did so within the richness of the American experience. The forming nation, with all its splendid diversity and magnificent expansion, excited his imagination. He loved all its forms of government, its science and industry, but above all, its common people. With rising population, urban growth, and westward movement, there was now a human project which corresponded to the possibilities of his soul. His intuitive emotion pondered the deeper meaning of the burgeoning democratic society. [44].

Nothing natural, human, or material escaped his sensitive observations. He was a conduit of everything, and everything was affirmed: from the tiniest blade of grass, through every human type and enterprise, to the majestic flocks of birds floating through the heavens. He saw his task as that of being the bard of a people. He wanted to direct their destiny in a way that would reconcile this final stage of human history with the totality of the universe.

"One's Self I sing, a simple, separate person/ yet utter the word Democratic, the word En-Masse". Whitman believed in the principles of self - reliance, but he also realized that individualism had to be tempered with a sense of democratic fellowship. An enduring commitment to personal freedom had to be reconciled with the reality of the multitude. In the process, comradeship would compete with solitude. [45].

Whitman was, to a superlative degree, a romantic. His frank descriptions of sexuality—which even Thoreau found offensive – reflected the disposition of an erotic personality for whom the longings for happiness were of fundamental importance. Whitman realized, more profoundly than his New England predecessors that at the root of personal existence there is a desire for happiness which is emotionally of greater importance than the search for moral righteousness.

The ideal of happiness gave Whitman a means for overcoming the problem of evil. Like Hawthorne, Whitman was deeply aware of the reality of sin, within himself as well as others. However, he would not allow any moral darkness to defeat his art. He wanted to establish the primal conditions of unfallen man in his collective innocence. Depravity, along with the gloom of the Puritans, would be transcended in the joy of his song. There was nothing in the whole of creation more divine than men and women. Their tendencies towards eternal happiness made theories of the supernatural unnecessary. The Calvinist opposition between God and man would also disappear, because the poet would take no account of a God who contends against His creation.

Whitman would be the poet of wickedness as well as goodness. Even the prostitute could be at ease with him. All were redeemed in the glory of their common existence. Every individual was complete in his or herself, and everyone else as good as they. In the equality of democracy, none are to be degraded for their ignorance or for their sinfulness. [46].

The poet will not judge, but he will admonish. American was welcoming an increasing number of immigrants and to some degree improving their material conditions. Whitman welcomed these developments, but he was also aware of the deficiencies. He intuited that the enlarging Republic had no spiritual elevation to match its growing prosperity. As the body expands, the soul withers. The nation was making great advances in industrial development, but it lacked character and conscience. As for personality, there were none among the many who were worthy of the name. All were being drawn together like uniform iron castings. [47].

The forces of compression needed to be balanced with a liberating spirituality. Whitman shared the belief of the New England Transcendentalists and the Quakers that divinity was within and should be developed according to internal moral and spiritual principles. In the soul's ascent to God, there was no longer any need for ecclesiastical intermediaries. The work of the ministers and priests was over. Guidance for the movement toward holiness would come from poets and from a national literature which would trace for the people the path between reality and their own souls. [48].

Viewed in the lump, man displeases. The people are disheveled and their faults ill-bred, but Whitman saw that they are reliable in emergencies and have untapped reservoirs of decency. Even their strong physical constitutions herald a new phase in the evolution of personality. The great mass of men and women have now beginning to fill the continent has immense potentials which cry out for the enlightenment of religion, but their need is one that no organized church fulfill. Whitman believed that the seeds of veneration can grow only in the quiet of one's isolated self. Out of the solitudes there would arise a vital association of living identities. America would be filled with mature men and women who, while not having exceptional genius or superfluous wealth, would be diligent, virtuous, and cheerful in their relations with others. Only literature can fulfill these elevating responsibilities. According to Whitman, the poet and the weaver of stories have always been religious since they are concerned with the mysteries of existence and the problematic of personal identity. Their work matches the amplitude of the human soul. In the future, literature will be the servant of democracy. [49].

Every great society has been built upon a vital interaction between men and their ultimate beliefs. In medieval Christendom, an intimate connection between divine and human principles gave birth to institutions, laws, customs, and personalities, all of which drew inspiration from their original source. Whitman thought that Democracy would provide a modern equivalent for humanity, both here in the United States and in the world at large. In a future now only dimly foreseen, Democracy will be the absolute source and measure of every moral, social, and political expression which claims the status of civilization. Begotten by this new creation, all will be carried by its ideals and principles to heights which it alone can generate. [50].

Democracy will influence ages to come with an amplitude to match the forces of Nature. As we have seen, an encounter with the beauty and power of nature had already been understood as an essential aspect of the quest for personal fulfillment. Whitman believed that in the emerging collective age, there would arise a people whose powers matched the splendor of the universe. In the doings of democratic men and women, there was something to rival the majesty of day and night.

Unlike Melville, Whitman did not see any terrible antithesis between Nature and the human soul. He is struck by the tranquility of the plants and trees and he hoped to bring to his own life a similar measure of composure. He admires the placid animals who do not whine about their condition, or " lie awake in the dark and weep for their sins". Yet his relationship with the external world was never completely serene. Whitman intuitively understood that both man and nature were part of a great unrest which troubled the whole of creation. He was disturbed by the aloneness of natural phenomena. The waves may comfort each other, but they leave him unsatisfied. He senses that he has a destiny which he cannot comprehend. As he walks in the moonlight along a gray beach, he asks the sea to satisfy his 'unknown want', and, in reply, it whispers to him "…the low and delicious word death". [51].

Confident in himself, Whitman could laugh at the prospect of extinction.

Yet he was preoccupied with the inevitability of his passing. Having seen much dying as he tended the wounded during the Civil War, he could, at one level, accept the inevitable. But Whitman was aware of the threat that death posed to his hopes for immortality. There was **a** permanence to his soul which could correspond to the virtual endlessness of the expanding universe. Death was a part of nature, and Whitman wanted future poets to make great poems about it, but he could not allow death to impair his yearnings for the infinite. As he passed through the ebb and flow of life, Whitman realized that deep within him there was a yet untouched part of himself that would only enter his consciousness if he voyaged forth to find his ultimate satisfaction.

Like Emerson, Whitman rejected the Puritan notion of a vengeful God who takes pleasure in sending the unredeemed to eternal perdition. But Whitman also could not accept the loss of his individuality in the service of a Universal Spirit. He had too strong a sense of his own self to accept its annihilation even in the cause of a higher good. In his poem "Passage to India" (1871) Whitman's irrepressible soul circumnavigates the earth, marking the history of man's striving, redeeming the value of the past, while noting the dissatisfaction which accompanies all human explorations. He then journeys forth, to unknown shores, through the interminable oceans of space and time. The soul of the poet rambles near the range of God. But the self is never abandoned. Whitman cannot think or breathe unless it is out of himself. He assimilates the Christian teaching that his soul is greater than the sun or the stars, but he will not accept the gifts of grace which might assure his soul's salvation. With supreme self-reliance, he moves within an orbit of himself.

Only when the voyage is done, will the poet yield to God. But even then he will not submit to any sovereign power. The ambition is cosmic. As Whitman's poem encompasses everything, so must his soul find complete accord with existence. In these imaginings, God is no longer Edwards' omnipotent Ruler. For the humanitarian poet, a supreme being cannot reveal himself outside of Nature, nor can he be beyond the human spirit. God lives through human immortality. All is now; all is eternal. Whitman's sense of divine affiliation leads him to see himself as someone who, at the end, melts into an Older Brother's arms. [52].

The extravagance of Whitman's fancy raises the modern project of terminating the distinction between Creator and creature to an audacious height that Channing would have considered to be blasphemous. But although while contemplating death the poet irreverently claims to be a son of God, he never forgets that he is also a child of earth. His love of human relatedness-civic as well as sexual- is too heartfelt to turn him away from the possibilities of temporal community. Being together and sharing life's burdens were ever present necessities. And his heart never stops crying out for companionship. [53].

In spite of the attractions of association, Whitman was troubled by the effects which comradeship would have upon the individual life. There was an unresolved tension at the heart of democracy, because there was no overarching principle which could reconcile liberty and equality. Whitman sensed that the tendencies towards aggregation had to be subject to a higher ideal of completeness. If leveling was not to overcome the individual life, democracy had to evolve in a way which would make the pride which each should have in himself or herself alone the ultimate purpose of all coming together. [54].

Whitman always returns to the single solitary soul even as he affirms that the future of democracy lies with the people at large. But although his conception of society was more generous than that of Emerson, Whitman shared his predecessors' egocentric sensibility. Neither could see the world around him in a way that was separable from himself. Believing that he was complete in himself, Whitman could see only himself in others. In spite of his enthusiasm for social solidarity, he was acutely alone. There are no real encounters in his writings. Pluralities become subject to the dream. Whitman's creativity was profound, but it was nourished by an imaginative desocialization which subsumed the existence of other human beings within his own. [55].

Whitman's inability to grasp the reality of others also weakened his hold upon himself. As he tried to attain an absolute selfhood, he thought he could secure his personal identity in the depths of his self-consciousness. As a result, the "I" begins to dissolve in an endless regression of reflections turning back upon themselves. Retreating within its own subjective world, the self becomes more outside of common life than within it.

Such reflexivity would endanger the democratic project, which favors social over individual existence. Over time, this preference for what is common would take its revenge upon the sentiment of egocentricity. What was unique or distinguished would be marginalized or subsumed within some broader social whole, and the desire for an independent existence would gradually become spiritually, as well as socially, unacceptable.

Personal Integrity and General Chaos

Whitman was a poet of material civilization. Workmen, their trades and tools, were all elements of his art. He also honored mechanical developments and a poem he wrote for an exposition was a hymn to the glories of technology. Henry Adams had a less sanguine impression of these public events. Visiting great fairs both here and abroad he was enchanted by the splendor of the inventions, but he came away wondering if the people might soon be helpless before the forces that were being commemorated. For Whitman, industrial expansion was a progressive expression of the "great unrest" in which we all share; Adams worried that the end result might be a collective submission to power. [56].

Adams' misgivings about the direction of this machine -driven society were part of his broader concern over the future of democracy. Beginning with his great -grandfather, John Adams, his family had been deeply involved in the public life of the nation. Following initial successes, however, their participation was marked by a growing disillusionment. Henry's grandfather, John Quincy Adams, had served as the sixth president of the United States, but he was defeated by Andrew Jackson in the 1828 election. John Quincy subsequently served in the Congress, but his loss of the Presidency accelerated the family alienation from politics.

John Quincy Adams' personality had reflected both the Puritan and the Unitarian aspects of the New England experience. He had a moral disposition which combined conscientious rectitude with enthusiasm for human progress. He shared some of Theodore Parker's hopes for the moral reform of public life. Adams had looked upon the political sphere as a secularized form of predestination which had as its object the temporal happiness of the American people. Human perfectibility through the exercise of liberty was the primary objective. Adams revered the Constitution as the expression of the moral law and he thought of the nation's development as the realization of transcendental purposes. [57].

In his public offices, John Quincy Adams sought to direct government towards worldly ends which would merit eternal approval. He was certain that natural rights are conferred by God and that scientific discoveries furthered a divine purpose. He also tried to make the common good prevail over the selfish pursuit of private interests. This abstract moral righteousness was bound to be corrected by harsh reality. Mass politics was ascendant, and the rise of Jacksonian democracy meant that the New England patriarchal authority was finished as a public force. John Quincy saw a deeper import in these changes. The political reverses that he suffered led him to attribute his losses to the abandonment of Divine Providence. These afflictions would not only turn the family away from democratic idealism but also from any belief in the eternal significance of human life. [58].

Henry Adams spent the Civil War years in London, serving as a private secretary to his father, Charles Francis Adams, Sr., the Ambassador of the United States to Great Britain. Upon his return, Henry began a career teaching and writing in the field of history. After his marriage, he and his wife moved to Washington, D.C. where he felt he would be in a better position to study life and politics in the growing nation.

Like his grandfather, Henry was appalled by the coarse venality of the politicians whom he encountered in the nation's capital. The teaching of the Puritan Calvinists on the corruption of the human heart was being confirmed on a large and public scale. Greed, and the unabashed pursuit of power, had replaced the austerity and self-restraint of his ancestors. The country had been founded by virtuous men; now those with baser instincts had become the politically successful. [59].

The discouraging facts of national politics were not only repulsive to Henry Adams' conscience. They also fueled doubts about the objective bearing of moral law upon human events. Adams remained a man of principle but, as he lost faith in transcendental norms, he found himself compulsively holding on to his own values without really comprehending their purpose in the general scheme of things. Like Melville, Adams understood the futility of trying to impose ideals upon recalcitrant materials. He also came to realize that the pursuit of the good was not frustrated just by evil men. The impersonal force of circumstances was also becoming a substantial obstacle to the development of a righteous life. Experience resisted, and outlasted, the feeble attempts of fragile men to subject public affairs to a moral discipline. [60].

Adams had too great a need for personal independence to allow his destiny to be completely determined by powers beyond his control. He would not imitate Bartleby the Scrivener. And Adams was too intelligent to believe that total withdrawal from society was a feasible option. He struggled to find some goal outside himself to which he could be committed without suffering the loss of his unique personal existence. [61].

Henry wrote two novels which imaginatively represent his search for personal meaning. In both, the central characters are women. In *Democracy* (1880) a widow, Mrs. Lee, comes to Washington seeking to make some sense of her life by an acquaintance with the democratic values which circulate in the center of power. She is disappointed in the politicians she meets, especially the amoral Senator Ratcliffe, who uses everyone in his quest for advancement and tries to draw her into a loveless marriage. Mrs. Lee serves as a symbol for Adam's conscience. While his moral life had its roots in Puritanism, Adams had passed well beyond the question of whether the will was free. The willfulness which permeated public life had vindicated Arminius. The problem now was to determine what purposes were to be served by the possession of liberty. The novel does not answer the question. Mrs. Lee 's experiences convinced her that political society does not radiate any values which she could imitate, and she had to be content with cultivating moral attitudes that preserved her self-respect.

The second novel, *Esther*,(1884), which Adams published under a pseudonym, probes more deeply into the plight of the individual who is trying to find the basis of a life of self-sacrifice. Here the heroine is courted by a clergyman, rather than a politician, and the reason for the rejection of the masculine overtures has a deeper meaning. Esther cannot accept the faith, or the church, of her suitor, Rev. Mr. Hazard. Like the politician, the man of the cloth is driven by a compulsive pursuit of power. The precedence given to ecclesiastical values and position prevent the Reverend from loving Esther as she is. Her freedom is also imperiled. Seeing her clerical suitor as the vehicle of a moral tyranny, Esther refuses to expose her identity to such intimidation.

Esther also has a quasi-mystical experience which tells us as much about the author's feelings as it does about her fate. A visit to Niagara Falls gives her an insight into ultimate reality which is not incompatible with her search for personal understanding. The falls embody an immense energy which is expressed in the various components of its voluminous water; a spectacle beyond herself which is both impersonal and true. The Falls is a metaphor for life itself which, in its stream of becoming and passing away, is its own end. Each individual caught up in it has a unique truth that is valuable to the degree that it contributes to the significance of the whole. [62].

The study of history had taught Adams, long before Heidegger, that man is a being in time. There being no escape from temporal existence, the one who is wise will make the appropriate adjustments. All action must be calculated within the limits of possibility. Adams' acceptance of the inevitable had to be reconciled with his insistence upon personal integrity and his unquenchable desire for some ultimate unity. In a poem entitled Buddha and Brahma which he wrote after a visit to the South Seas, Adams tries to deal with cosmic reality in a way that preserves his inner freedom. The poem expresses the idea that everything manifests the one divine spirit, Brahma, and all individual existences depend upon this underlying creative force. But Brahma is not just a primal energy; it is also a repository of purpose. Since Brahma is omnipresent, one might as well stay in the world as leave it. But doing has no value in itself. It is meaningful only if it expresses Buddha and leads to a reunion with this final reality. One's actions are, therefore, not one's own. Through the characters in the poem Adams advises a dualism: one should abandon the active life to necessity while directing the subjective life to the unities which can be discovered within. There, the universe, and all its parts, will quietly find their beginning and end. [63].

Puritanism had taught Adams that one must ultimately connect oneself to some all-embracing unity. Adams had studied medieval Catholicism, and he saw that for the people of that age the Church and its doctrines provided the necessary bridge between time and eternity. Unfortunately, that option was foreclosed to him. The great teachers of the Church, such as Thomas Aquinas, thought that the Divine Order of the Universe would attract the human intellect to contemplate its wondrous design, but the Calvinism of Adam's youth had impressed his mind with the idea that the Justice of God is implacable. To Adams' Protestant mentality the Divinity represents itself in a Law which makes no provision for human weakness. It also makes no allowance for free will. To Aquinas, the natural law, which presents the will with choices between good and evil, enhances human dignity; for Adams, a completely rational law coming from the hand of God would make of him a mechanism. Mankind would not be enhanced by such a form of order because, as Adams saw it, humanity would be nothing more than a conductor of divine force. [64].

Adams' interpretation of the Christian order as a closed system of merciless power helped him as an historian to understand why the men and women of the Twelfth century were attracted to the cult of the Virgin Mary. Her tender mercy softened the rigors of divine justice and her generative power inspired believers to think of themselves as participants in a unified universe. However, with the rise of the modern, that venerable vision failed, and, for Adams, the collapse of Christian unity was the greatest catastrophe of Western history. [65].

The disintegration of Christian culture was foreseeable. Adams felt that the passage from medieval synthesis to modern chaos was a change whose seeds were sown when medieval Christendom was at its height. Those who built the great cathedrals in honor of the Virgin were performing acts of religious devotion, but Adams believed that they were also driven by other motives. Those who were so inspired were also motivated by the ambition of sharing in the infinite power of eternal life. With the rise of science, these desires for mastery were transferred to the exploitation of nature. In both instances, significant human activity was a response to the attraction of outside forces. [66].

The rise of the natural sciences led to a dynamic interchange between the powers of man and those of nature. As these activities found expression in industrial development, the American society was beginning to experience tremendous prosperity. But its citizens were bewildered and afraid. Adams too, was alarmed. He felt that the social transformations had left behind the values of his family and the traditions of his beloved New England. He also believed that this progress also posed a threat to the future of the human family. As the Nineteenth century was drawing to a close, the growth of materialism, the decline of the arts, and the ominous increase in armaments were making a mockery of the ideals which had inspired his forefathers. Democratic idealism and theories of human perfectibility were in full retreat. [67].

The theological explanations of the human condition that had been passed down to Henry Adams by the Puritans and the Unitarians were inadequate to the new situation, but he could not abandon his search for some ultimate understanding. If God existed, mankind would do well to do Him homage. Within that framework, Adams mused, humanity had some hope for authentic improvement. But the possibility of God's existence and His sovereignty depended upon an experience of overall unity and spiritual harmony that had been lost with the breakup of the medieval Christian synthesis. The new reality was multiplicity and fragmentation. The human being could now develop only within the chaos of which he was a part. [68].

In the waning years of his life Adams continued his quest for ultimate meaning although he had abandoned any hope of finding an absolute truth. In his youth he had tortured himself with intense self-scrutiny, but in his maturity he became aware of the destructive effects of excessive introspection. Now his modest goal was just to try to account to himself, in some intelligent way, as to his place in the total scheme of things. Adams did not share Whitman's anxiety over the immortality of the self. As he aged, Adams came to believe that the self requires less explanation than does the world in which it is situated. To direct his attention to what lay beyond him, he made his mind a spool upon which to wind the tread of history to the point where he might comprehend some final explanatory unity. [69].

Being intellectually ambitious, Adams wanted to go beyond the conventional boundaries of historical study so that he could reach a deeper understanding of the passage of time. He wanted to know why there had been a descent from medieval Christendom to the multiplicity of the modern world. In the pursuit, he searched for anything that his mind could grasp that might explain the continuous fragmentation.

Developments within science opened new avenues of comprehension. The mechanical phase of science, with its dependence upon the laws of gravitation, was losing its primacy. Belief in the solidity of matter was also declining. The discovery of radium had revealed new, inexhaustible potentials and inert matter was no longer thought of as the ultimate substance. Matter and motion were interchangeable in a field of forces which was being thought of in terms of energy. The new physics, which came into prominence in Adams' later years, understood reality in terms of super-sensuous forces that were at work in an ever expanding universe. The natural laws governing these forces might be the key to the understanding of the human condition.

Adams thought he saw their full explanatory potential. Many who were well educated grasped the first law of thermodynamics which directed the conservation of energy, but they did not fully understand the complementary principle which holds that all animate forms ultimately decline into a state of entropy. According to the second law of thermodynamics, once matter has released all of its energies it is incapable of further motion. Its terminus is death. Adams thought that if this principle was allowed to have its full effects, it would transform our understanding of human history. History would become a science of accelerating decline in human vitality. And what appeared to be progress would in fact be an illusion. [70].

These insights altered Adams' understanding of the powers of the human person as well as his conception of democratic society. Science would undercut some of the premises of transcendental individualism. Most disturbing of all was the conclusion that the will could no longer be thought of as the distinctive human faculty. Within the medieval world -view, the will was seen as capable of making choices that had eternal consequences. Now, as comprehended by science, the will is an enfeebled faculty which reflects forces which are more powerful than itself.

Jonathan Edwards had believed that the will could do no good because it was corrupt. To Adams, the will was weak because it was being overwhelmed by the unseen natural pressures which drive the universe. There was a deeper debilitation. Adams had previously assumed that reason follows the direction of the will; the new physics was teaching him that both reason and will were subject to relentless determinations. All this frightened Adams. He desperately wanted to understand himself as being something more than a thermodynamic mechanism. There seemed to be no solution. In an earlier age Nature had inspired the Transcendentalists, but it could no longer help because it was now known to be just a field of forces. Adams concluded that some sort of salvation could come from the intellect, provided it took a different view of its capabilities and fitted itself into the overall pattern of a determined existence. [71].

At its height, Western culture had believed that the universe in its totality could be understood by the comprehensive powers of human reason. All reality could be known in terms of various stages of being. Francis Bacon, reversing the relation between the mind and the world, taught that the intellect, like the will, was actually shaped by external forces. The hidden powers of nature were conditioning the range of reason. For Adams, the ascendancy of science meant that progress in mental life demands the response of intelligence to the forces of energy. The descending chaos of motion provoked the mind to respond with its inductive logic, but Adams believed that the greatest advances were now being made by those who were able to engage in the speculations of pure mathematics. Quantitative thought acts as a hyper-space which draws to itself all the various phases of material energy. And energy is multiplicity seeking unity. The ideal of coherence attracts the mind as forcefully as the law of gravity attracts the particles of matter. Adams was not sure that the disposition towards unity had a secure foundation, but it was a useful postulate. It delivers the mind from material bondage and confirms the value of our inward self - consciousness.

The developing scientific understanding had applications to the study of human association that reinforced Adams' pessimistic attitude toward democratic society. Advances in psychology and physiology were demonstrating that man did not possess unlimited or unforeseen possibilities. In its alliance with industry, science was proving that humankind was under the control of forces that required an invariable and unavoidable manner of development. This pre-determination was social as well as individual.[72].

Henry Adams had always wondered about the direction of American society. Walt Whitman could make imaginative affirmations about the future, but Adams would only raise questions about how technology might gain control over the direction of our national life. The communal applications of science seemed obvious to Adams. He could no longer think of social history as the gradual unfolding of man's moral and spiritual powers; there was now just a gravitational field within which the forces of man and nature seemed to constantly modify each other. The scientific hypothesis that society seeks to prevent the dispersion of energy by concentrating the human composite into a dense mass seemed plausible to Adams. As in the material universe, there is in political life an equilibrium that is provisional. Compression is followed by an explosive reaction which, in turn, attracts a new balance of energies. From this perspective social law becomes a 'leveling of intensities' that is designed to give priority to the group over the individual. [73].

Adams was of the opinion that progressive theories of social development are no match for the laws of degradation. Humanity was becoming attracted to various forms of organized existence that were bringing material abundance, but the social co-ordinations which this progress demanded were not voluntary. Adams saw that if order was not imposed by the state, it would be enforced by corporate power. The people en masse celebrated in Whitman's poetry had become a crowd. There was an aggregation that lacked authentic bonds of cohesion. Since the weakness of the will was increasing, there was little growth of distinctive character. And there was a corresponding decline in personal initiative. In Adams dark vision, as society seemed to expand, it was, in reality, narrowing. The process left the individual with only the rights and functions that society confers. Surprisingly, some with equally serious minds would welcome these developments. They would give collective tendencies a religious significance as well as a humanistic value [74]

The Religion of Social Solidarity

In Adams' pessimistic appraisal, the nation seemed to be headed in the direction of a drab collective existence. He thought that America was frozen in time-bound ideas and lacked the elevating influence of vital and mature energies. But Adams also realized that modern man was acquiring new attitudes toward questions of ultimate concern. Having abandoned the Christian forms of worship, human beings now had to placate the unseen forces of the universe that were beginning to take control of their destiny. The dynamo was replacing the Virgin as an object of veneration. [75].

The change of allegiance was, to Adams' sensibility, a perverse form of self-reverence. He expressed this insight in one of his poems: "We made our world and saw that it was good/ Ourselves we worship and have no Son…" A shocking inversion was in the air. The French sociologist Auguste Comte, whose thought was familiar to Adams, had generalized this creature deification by calling for the adoration of the 'Grand Etre' of collectivized humanity. But the American mind was not prepared to adopt atheism as an explicit social program. In trying to satisfy its desires for the infinite, reflective Americans were still trying to heal the breach between God and man which had been imposed upon them by New England Puritanism.

Adams attributed to the principles of physics a foundational meaning that had once been found in transcendental sources. Others would try to reconcile the divine and the human. Henry James, the father of William, the psychologist, and Henry, the novelist, was such an innovator. The elder James was a mystical democrat. Like Whitman, James wanted to attribute a spiritual significance to our common experience. Working within the Christian tradition, he reinterpreted the Incarnation in a way that he hoped would bring a new understanding of the relation between the Creator and His human creatures. [76].

James thought of the Divine Substance as taking upon Himself the very being of his primary creation. The fusion was both humanistically and theologically novel. The uniqueness of James' conception was that the unity between God and man was to be achieved in a communal, rather than in an individualistic manner. James' central idea was that the dignity which is common to all humanity reveals the presence of God on earth. He thought that there is an immanence of divinity within the natural community of mankind. [77].

The emergence of society as the paramount human reality is not just a matter of natural evolution, political development, or even the advance of general self-consciousness. It simply marks the overcoming of that alienation from God which had for so long darkened the history of Christianity, especially in the United States. Once they are reconciled in collective existence, God and man will become naturally, as well as spiritually, one. For Whitman, the enhancement of the individual life was the ultimate purpose of all human association. Henry James disagreed. He not only favored society, he also looked upon individualism as a primary form of evil. To his mind, the separate self was the "one damnable thing on earth." [78].

The evil which lurks within the singular human heart had troubled the American mind since the beginning of the new nation. As we have seen, from the time of Jonathan Edwards, leading thinkers and writers have struggled to understand the inner forces which draw the individual away from the good. Henry James echoed these sentiments. He was acutely aware of the many iniquities which flow from inordinate self-love. He also saw that confident assumptions of self -reliance ignore the fundamental tendencies toward pride and avarice which have a corrupting influence upon the human soul. But, more importantly, Self-love was anti-social. The absolute independence which the individual craves detaches the consciousness of 'Me' from the deeper obligations of common existence. Individualism was unacceptable to the senior James because, to his way of thinking, it illicitly tries to identify the values of the whole of creation with the egotistical demands of the private self. [79].

The Senior Henry James' social philosophy was driven by metaphysical as well as religious principles. To his mind, the phenomenal self has no substance. It merely reflects, in a negative manner, the existence of finite man. To move beyond this base contingency one must first have one's heart cleansed by the ministries of conscience and religion. Then, if the path of purification is honestly endured, the isolated individual will gradually form integral relationships with his neighbors. As he becomes socialized, he will begin to approach the divine. James argued that the authentic destiny of the individual is to experience the broadest possible fraternity with his fellow human beings. Togetherness elevates all. As the otherwise pitiful individual draws closer to the abundant common dignity, he will raise himself to a higher and transpersonal way of being. Cultivating social solidarity, the individual will enter into a positive relation with the larger whole to which he religiously, as well as naturally, belongs. As the good of common life becomes a concrete reality, he will overcome the illusions that have led him to think that the independent personality is the ultimate fact of human existence. [80].

James' theory of a religiously inspired social humanism was conceived as a matter of abstract emotional thought. The writer Edward Bellamy attempted to give the new collective ideal an imaginative form in his futuristic novel entitled *Looking Backward* 2000-1887 which was published in 1888. In this fanciful romance, Bellamy sketched the elements of a non-Marxist utopia which would miraculously emerge by the end of the twentieth century. The common life would acquire an ideal form of social and economic equality. Like Henry James, Bellamy thought that unrestricted individualism could not serve as a humanistic ideal. But Bellamy was a reformer as well as a philosopher.

Bellamy's cast of mind was more like that of Theodore Parker. As did Parker, Bellamy was willing to lift the veil of respectability and express his outrage at social injustice. The satisfied classes of post -civil war America looked upon industrial expansion as an unqualified good, but Bellamy, peering beneath the comfortable surface, saw the deeper realities of competitive greed, great disparities of wealth, and the contempt which the rich showed for the poor.

Democratic self-rule had been politically expressed in the creation of constitutional government and Bellamy believed that the people as a whole could make a comparable statement of collective will with respect to the economy. The primitive stage of industrial development then regnant, with its intense and divisive competition, would eventually prove to be unsatisfactory to all, regardless of their status. The ruthlessness of the 'Gilded Age' would then be transformed into a higher state of peaceful cooperation. The physical change would be in the scale of organization. The private monopolies that were preying upon the general interest would become one "Great Trust" in which all the resources of production and distribution had been nationalized. More significantly, the citizens would be mobilized to support the unified system as both workers and consumers.

At the core of this social and economic reconstruction would be the formation of the people into an industrial army. Growing up during the Civil War, Bellamy had been impressed by the discipline and concentration of purpose which is manifest in a well -trained soldiery. Watching a military parade, he could see men turn away from themselves as individuals and join in a common effort to reach unselfish and impersonal ends. Bellamy wondered whether the same attitudes could be formed among the people in order to achieve the material well-being of all. [81].

Such was the inspiration for *Looking Backward.* Set in Boston in the year 1887, the novel is the story of a wealthy young man, one Julian West, who falls into a sleep so deep that he awakes -still young- more than a hundred years later. The urban scene which greets his eyes is one of spacious order and cleanliness. Its architectural arrangement includes a generous number of magnificent public buildings. His host, a Dr. Leete, and Leete's daughter, Edith, explain the new system to their bewildered guest in some detail. They persuade West that the people are experiencing a new freedom in the collective equality that has eliminated the injustices of nineteenth century industrialism. The basic reformation had not been a revolution but a change of heart. The previous chaos, fueled by individualism, had led to great strife between the capitalists and the workers, and the social disintegration had reached a point where the interests of all were in jeopardy. While developments in efficiency had brought tighter forms of social organization, all were unhappy with the existing state of affairs. A progressive movement had then led the people into a new social union which overcame the destructive forces of greed and envy. [82].

As may be imagined, Bellamy's novel provoked a great deal of criticism, especially among those who read it not as a work of the imagination but as a specific proposal for drastic social action. As an explanation of how a coercive system could assure that goods and services be more rationally produced and distributed, the romance anticipates the degradations that actually occurred in various forms of twentieth century communism. But *Looking Backward* is only one expression of Bellamy's attitude toward the problematic of self and society. His other writings and journals, many of which were not published in his lifetime, give a better account of how deeply this New England reformer thought about the fundamental tensions between the individual and the community that permeates all aspects of modern life. [83].

Edward Bellamy was born in 1850 in Western Massachusetts. His early life was generally happy, but it was overshadowed by the negative elements of the Puritan tradition. A paternal great -grandfather, Dr. Joseph Bellamy, was a distinguished Calvinist preacher and a friend of Jonathan Edwards. Edward Bellamy's father was a Baptist minister and, for a while, the son found spiritual consolation in that religious community. But the sense of impending judgment and unrelieved guilt continued to haunt him. In his notebooks and short stories Bellamy began to imagine ways that the individual could be liberated from the moral and spiritual gloom that impeded a full and happy life. [84].

Bellamy discovered that the sense of a hopeless moral burden which Americans had inherited from their Christian founders was in reality a universal human condition. This primal torment had been recognized in great literature throughout the world and was found in cultures so otherwise different as the Hebrews and the Greeks. The common perception was not that the will is debilitated by the natural forces which move the universe; rather, it is impaired by some fundamental rupture of the relationship between creatures and their Creator. And in this universal nemesis every individual suffers a sense of moral corruption which can destroy his personal integrity and his self respect. The phenomenon has an indelible quality. The religious conversion recommended to remove the guilt may lead one to believe he is forgiven; unfortunately, the stain remains in the memory. Psychologically, one needs also to forget. Through writing various stories, Bellamy began to analyze the problem and suggest ways that the inordinate sense of moral failure might be mitigated. The Unitarians had eliminated primal depravity and replaced it with the idea of innate moral goodness. Emerson tried to resolve the problem of sin by treating it as nothing more than the diminishment of objective being. Bellamy's approach would be more subtle than that of his predecessors. [85].

In order to reduce the tragic sense of guilt, Bellamy divided the individual life into several stages of personality. He hoped to thereby reduce the power of memory to harass the self with its past mistakes. For example, when a character in one of Bellamy's stories admits a prior fraud, those who were the victims of her crime can only see the nobility of her present confession. Her earlier self, which actually did the deed repented of, is past forgiving.

Bellamy would resolve the puzzle of how many selves make up a singular human being by thinking of the individual as being composed of a series of changing personalities whose appearance and demise is recorded by memory. These transformations over time are to be distinguished from personal identity, which is the sense which one has of one's present state, in relation to one's capacities and immediately preceding personalities. [86].Personal identity is not just an awareness of the present moment. It is also not a sameness which has continued over the course of a lifetime. Between present and past selves there is not identity, but only gradual differentiation. [87].

Bellamy used his theory of successive identities to correct the persistent sense of guilt. He argued that the old should not do penance for the sins of their youth because the person that they now feel compelled to punish is not the one who was actually guilty of the fault. But what of the future? If the individual can be liberated from his past imperfections, to what ends should he now direct his will? For Henry Adams, whatever will—power the individual can muster should be applied to the adjustment of his life to his present circumstances. Bellamy's recommendation may, in the end, lead to the same result. But it will be a more noble accomplishment because it will be grounded in the depths of self-consciousness.

Bellamy's ideas are of humanistic interest because he saw the quest for individual self-respect as something more than a search for a release from remorse. The search for a serene identity was also an attempt to reach an essential core of being that would be immune from changes in personality. The self needs something which can provide it with a continuous stability. That something must be impersonal. Egocentric concerns bind the self to what is immediate and transitory; only the future will direct the self to values which endure.

Whitman's ambition was to express his entire personality in his poetry. But over time he saw that he did not really understand who he was. Bellamy thought that the individual was divided by a duality of consciousness. The self is aware that part of him is personal, petty, and egocentric; he has another side which is generous and impersonal. According to Bellamy, neither exists in total exclusion of the other. But the more magnanimous part should determine the future course of our lives. [88].

Like Emerson, Bellamy believed that our encounters with the beauties of the natural world give us the hope of finding some universal being within the depths of ourselves. Bellamy's mysticism was, however, closer to that of the senior James than it was to that of the Sage of Concord. For Bellamy, the quest for the infinite should draw us into closer contact with others. During Bellamy's lifetime industrial civilization was replacing Nature as the source of impersonal good, and a social gospel was taking the place of Emerson's cosmic sensibility. There was also a growing dissatisfaction with the original ideal of the self-reliant individual. The intuitionism of Emerson was considered to be too fragmentary and inconstant to constitute an adequate understanding of the individual in a world that was increasingly becoming more social by nature. [89].

Those who sought to reconcile religion and philosophy began to think of the particular human being as being essentially incomplete unless associated with others. Some were drawn to Hegel, who overcame the problem by positing an Absolute mind which becomes conscious of itself in history. The task of the individual -who cannot achieve a fullness of being by himself- is to become a concrete realization of the Universal. Edward Bellamy's essay "The Religion of Solidarity" is an attempt to resolve the tension between the individual and the group in a form of Hegelianism. The introspective turn towards self-consciousness is how Bellamy assumes we come into contact with infinity. The inward movement also becomes the ground of prospective self-identity. At the bottom of the well of our lives, our individuality becomes objective to that eternal subjectivity that is the universal soul. Paradoxically, the experience both draws us out of ourselves and brings us into deeper contact with ourselves. Having passed beyond the ephemeral, we have reached the greater part of our being. Now the purpose of our lives is to constantly recognize what had previously been a passing intuition.

Bellamy realized that the self that has discovered the being within is not immediately transformed. The process of reconciling the particular with the universal is an unceasing, arduous task. Individuality is slowly purified as the desire for infinity that is awakened by an encounter with natural beauty becomes culturally developed. And although the metamorphosis occurs in an externalized context, all self-love is not disparaged in favor of altruism. Bellamy recognizes that the personal, although imperfect, has a right to be. But it must not exaggerate its autonomy. Nor should it allow its finitude to overcome the nobler aspirations toward what is sublime and universal. For Bellamy the important point is that the individual must give primacy to the impersonal life which is within us because it is one with all. [90].

The inclusive ideal is proclaimed in an appropriate ethic. In calling us to sacrifice our lesser to our greater selves, the ethic of solidarity draws us towards an unselfish union with others. The moral goal —which Bellamy postulates as the common essence of human souls —can be found in the varied forms of human association: from a heterosexual love that has disciplined the passions, to every interpersonal, political, and economic relationship which is not characterized by antagonism. [91].

Bellamy's tentative reflections on the future of self—identity raise Henry James' praise of community to a higher philosophical level. [92]. But while these two thinkers affirm the value of association, they both lack the awareness, so evident in Henry Adams' thought, of the basic tension between the attraction of the impersonal and the more elemental desire for personal integrity. Moreover, while the theme of solidarity has a similarity with Whitman's democratic ideals, it cannot be reconciled with the Poet's ambition to place the aggregating tendencies of modern life at the service of the singular man or woman who hopes to lead a complete, but separate, existence. This unsatisfactory situation would lead another member of the James family to tip the balance back in favor of the individual; favoring the singular life as it is experienced under the concrete circumstances of actual living. However, as the nation expanded, the tendencies toward collectivism would intensify. The One and the Many had to be both accommodated and this meant that self-consciousness had to be reconciled with some broader awareness. The quest to understand the spiritual qualities of human nature would also be renewed. As the influence of the established churches declined, efforts would be made to give traditional Christian dogmas a humanistic meaning. The desire to reduce the distance between the eternal and the temporal would again assert itself and the perennial questions of sin and grace would be reinterpreted in order to give them a modern relevance.

CHAPTER THREE

Pragmatism and Idealism

The Affirmation of Practical Life

The increasing industrialization of the United States promoted a general prosperity but at the same time it failed to satisfy deeper desires for personal happiness. There was a growing sense of ennui, doubt, and depression among many of the middle -class, who felt that their lives were increasing restricted in ways that left little room for personal choice. The expansion of material affluence was leading to moral inaction. As Walt Whitman had observed, there were few real personalities to be found within the burgeoning society. The lethargy that lay beneath the social surface would be challenged by the nation's most important public philosopher, William James. William was one of the sons of the theologian Henry James. Under the tutelage of his father, William's' early life was a preparation for the challenges that he and his country faced as one century drew to a close and another began its uncertain future. As William began to grapple with these issues, he brought to the task dispositions of character which had begun to form in his youth. [93].

As is the case with most relationships between father and son, William James would both reflect, and reject, the paternal influence. The Senior James had been deeply offended by his Protestant upbringing, and he would pass his distaste on to his children. In his youth, Henry James had looked for sources of joy in his religious experiences, but he found only severity and dread. He bitterly remembered the somber Sundays in which the demands of Sabbath worship were set over against all child -like desires for pleasurable experience. In the home of the elder James, spontaneity was frowned upon and aesthetic enjoyment excluded. The domestic ethos limited the spiritual life to whatever was conventionally virtuous and the family was content to live righteously in isolation from the larger world beyond its doorstep.

These experiences of Henry James' early years set him at odds with what he believed to be his essential nature. There was a painful conflict between duty and desire. As a father, he was determined to release his children from that debilitating heritage. He assured them of their innate goodness and he allowed them to release their deeper impulses so that they could cultivate an enjoyment of the wider cultural world. The destiny of the family of Henry James would not be predetermined by the commands of an angry God. [94].

The wealth that the senior James inherited enabled him to provide his family with the expansive experiences which come from frequent travel. During a sojourn in Newport, William became interested in drawing and painting and he took art classes with the approval of his father. William had considerable talent, but he decided against a career in art, probably because of fear of failure. The decision was one of many anxious deliberations William would experience as he impulsively shifted from one occupation to another as he searched for a satisfying occupation. Along the way, he suffered an acute depression. William's experience paralleled some of the psychological torments that his father had endured in his own young manhood.

While in England, the senior James had a crisis of personal identity which he came to realize was related to his excessive striving for moral righteousness. As he became aware of the pride which fueled such a struggle, he came to the conclusion that the strain could not be overcome unless he relinquished his illusions of self -sufficiency. By deepening his dependence upon divine power he could begin to share the fellowship that God had designed for all of humanity. In William's predicament, the lack of self-confidence was provoked by a deeper anxiety. William was seized by the fear that he did not have the power to determine his own destiny.

In the agony of his insecurity, William called out in prayer for divine assistance, but the crisis would be effectively overcome only through his assimilation of humanistic ideals. Studying the work of the French psychologist Renouvier, William came to believe in the freedom of the will. The key to his conviction was a reflection upon the inward power we have to sustain a thought under conditions in which we know we are not obliged to do so. This insight brought such relief to James that he claimed as his first act of free will his belief in it. He was beginning to affirm his own individual reality. Other influences were helping to build up the confidence of the maturing man. From Wordsworth and the Romantics James acquired a deeper understanding of his willing nature. As the power of the will was expressed in deliberate acts it would also influence the development of emotional dispositions. Through a blending of thought and feeling the range of individual experience could expand in a way that would make the self more effective in its dealings with the external world. [95].

William's recovery pleased his father but it was leading the son's mind in a direction that could not be reconciled with the paternal vision of human happiness. The elder James would sacrifice selfhood in favor of substantial social union. This was unacceptable to William, who was developing in his own reflective life a pluralistic conception of man and his universe. For him, the fundamental reality was the distinctive and irreplaceable individual. William's anthropology was that of a multiplicity that was characterized by the essential difference which exists between each and every human being. William wanted to defend the right of each individual to be precisely whoever he is. The conception had a theocentric component. The spiritual work of God was not to be realized in the life of a group as his father had thought. According to the son, Divinity would be manifest in the souls of men who were fundamentally different from one another. [96].

As his career developed, William would find opportunities to give public expression to his existential convictions. He moved from natural science and medicine into the emerging field of the mental sciences. His first major work, The *Principles of Psychology* gave expression to the subjectivist turn of his mind. In this study he tried to persuade his readers that they should not objectify themselves in their experiences but rather make those encounters live within them. For James, immediate self-consciousness was the primary datum and nothing had decisive reality beyond the self. Unlike the followers of Kant, James saw no need to postulate a unifying self lying beyond or behind the realities of self -consciousness. From moment to moment, he held, the experiencing self is sufficiently aware of its own continuities. As for 'past selves', they would not be renounced as Bellamy had recommended. Rather they would be integrated into a Present which alone constitutes self - understanding. [97].

In the Jamesian psychology, reason was not given a place superior to sensibility. If a Cosmic Intellect existed, in James' view it would manifest itself in the passing moments of the lives of diverse and finite individuals. The important task for the individual was to draw together all the various factors of thought, feeling, and sensation which, when combined, make us realistically aware of ourselves and of the world which we inhabit. Appropriate discrimination among the elements which exist within the stream of consciousness is made by interest. In James' understanding of conscious life, our interests stimulate attentiveness to something passing before us and give what is otherwise indefinite a proper place in our mental life. But if these interests vary from individual to individual, how broadly could the field of interests legitimately be conceived?

According to James, the scope of human interests should be as natural and as universal as possible. He opposed the social Darwinism that would restrict the interests that influence thought to those which are intelligible as modes of survival. At the same time, James' character and training tended to make him give a conservative interpretation of the ranges of human wants that could rightfully affect behavior. In James' view, the main objective was to preserve a sound balance between habit and novelty. Our general interests rest upon what we already know, and they find objective validation in the regularities of social custom. Nevertheless, in matters of grave importance to the individual, James would defer to personal choice. This position would place him at odds with some who were otherwise sympathetic to his general outlook. [98].

After being appointed to the faculty at Harvard, James became acquainted with a number of individuals who, like himself, were troubled by the way that science was becoming the dominate force in American culture. Scientific method was now the preferred means of bringing about the order that was needed for the smooth growth of the industrial economy. The practical was in the saddle, and it was changing our understanding of the nature and purposes of higher education. Emerson had been adverse to organized study because he was more interested in the insights that could be found in the depths of the individual soul. Unfortunately, this epistemological disposition was unwelcome in the emerging modern society. Expertise became more important with the rise of distinct professions, and this required extensive and concentrated study. The change was reflected in the life of Oliver Wendell Holmes Jr., whose father had been a leading literary figure. The younger Holmes –who would eventually become a famous Justice of the Supreme Court – decided that by confining his mind to the study of the common law he would discover the general knowledge that he needed to make his way in the world.

The new science of sociology was also influencing the scope of knowledge. To the sociologist, the human mind was not an independent faculty; it was simply a reflection of the common thought which appears in the development of culture. The scientific community was convinced that social laws were as fixed as the laws of gravity William James felt a need to challenge that point of view. [99].

The conflict between science and humanism was hotly debated at the meetings of the "Metaphysical Club", an informal gathering that included James and Holmes among its members. Another participant was a brilliant mathematician and philosopher named Charles Saunders Peirce. Both James and Peirce would take strong positions against scientific determinism. But they would disagree over the degree of liberty that can be allowed to individual judgment within a highly organized and efficient modern society. [100].

Peirce had great respect for scientific inquiry, but he wanted to show that the presumptions of invariable order upon which it was based could not be sustained. Peirce understood the importance of spontaneity to the progress of life. He set out to demonstrate that the universe was both intelligible and indeterminate. Peirce insisted that while inductive reasoning has great explanatory power, it is qualified by the contingencies of experience. He also claimed that abstract theories of mechanical necessity are inexact. In addition, the novelties of diversification being uncovered by the life sciences was incompatible with assumptions of perfect repetition. The complexities proved to Peirce's satisfaction that there was something within nature that allowed for chance. Peirce's philosophy of science also affirmed the powers of the human mind to understand the nature of reality. In placing the mind, in its independence, at the foundation of existence, he was recovering for humanity what Henry Adams thought had been lost to the hegemony of science. [101].

William James was not concerned with the debate over the intellectual powers. He was more interested in demonstrating that the human will is not as weak as Adams had assumed. James believed that the will could be an agency of change and an effective counter force to the rising powers of technical reason. James brought his subjective sensibility to the conflict over determinism. The essential point was that whatever happens in the universe is not as important as what we feel or think about it. For him, true liberty was something more than understood necessity. Yet he would not try to develop any elaborate proofs for his thesis. James took upon himself the more modest responsibility of convincing his audiences that they should assume the existence of the power of effective choice and, in their practical lives, act upon that assumption.

James based his argument upon the phenomenon of regret. He pointed to the common experience in which we feel that something which has occurred should not have happened and the collateral belief that something better might have taken place. On this hypothesis, the directions that we wish life to take are rooted in states of responsive self -consciousness. The awareness that culminates in regret implies the existence of possibilities that challenge the inevitability of accomplished facts. To encompass the possibilities requires a theory of reality that can match the ambitions of the will. This would in turn require a reconstruction of empiricism. [102].

Classical empiricism, as refined by Hume, had an atomistic conception of factual reality which was upheld by principles of psychological association. To the Rationalists, this model of reality had to be supplemented by a priori principles of reason. They thought that something had to exist beyond experience that could give coherence to raw data and the habits of organization by which the data is sustained. Because James was anxious to expand the field of action, he did not want the spontaneities of freedom to be subject to any form of transcendental reason. To avoid recourse to abstraction, James would rehabilitate the independent value of empirical reality through a better understanding of its abundant variety. He thought that a persuasive theory of experience had to account for the relations between things as well as the multiplicity of distinct phenomena.

James argued that unless we understand the world of diverse connections we cannot fully comprehend any domain of fact. What is conjoined is as important as what is separated. One must take account of the links, the continuities, and the pluralities of whatever is distinctive. In that manner, the duality of knower and what is known is eliminated and the self becomes integrated with the inclusive world of its experience. This epistemological theory was a genuine contribution to empirical philosophy. [103].

James also revealed the weakness of a psychological rationalism. He saw that the method relies too much upon its own conceptual schemes in order to avoid experience. But James may have underestimated the authority which reason may have in the field of experience. Those who were critical of James pointed out that in comparing the values of different experiences we ultimately rely something other than what has been perceived. The stream of experience that passes before the attentive self does not contain within itself the concepts by which it is interpreted. There are moral implications as well. Our understanding of the virtues may arise out of experience, but the decisive meaning of good behavior cannot be found there. James became aware of these difficulties and, to discount the possibility that experience could be governed by imperious criteria of reason, he adopted a strategy of confession and avoidance.[104].

While admitting that non-empirical values can direct behavior into settled channels, James insisted on giving their influence a pragmatic significance. The authority of abstract goods was based upon the fact that they had been found to work in the past, and had therefore become part of the cultural heritage. In disputed matters of critical importance, however, James continued to defend the right of each individual to decide for himself what the proper course of action is. James' moral philosophy was consistent with his psychology. His basic premise was that moral relations do not exist in a vacuum. They give rise to claims and responsibilities as these are understood within the consciousness of particular human beings. Values have no objective status; they can only dwell within a mind that has feelings about them. [105].

What the individual feels is good is unconditionally good for him. His judgments are not reviewable. In James' ethical schema, the truth or falsity of personal moral decisions is irrelevant. Those who would bring the individual to account assume that there are standards outside of the individual life to which appeal can be made. But according to James, the individual is a "sort of Divinity" who is not accountable to any higher power. The self acts exclusively on behalf of its own existence. Its autonomy is similar to Emersonian ideals of self-reliance even though, unlike Emerson, James believed that our acts of will have much to do with who we are. [106].

To Peirce, this individualistic ethic is objectionable because it runs counter to the purposes of social existence. Peirce believed that there is a paramount need to bring unity out of diversity. This requires collaboration in the pursuit of truth. This aim is placed in jeopardy when the right to act is equated with the will to believe. For Peirce, the objective of ethics is to determine what is reasonable and that purpose is compromised when the good is decided by the vagaries of personal introspection. [107].

Despite their disagreements, Peirce and James were both committed to the central importance of practical life. For each of them, all ideas had to be related to some definite human purpose. They also agreed in another respect. Peirce thought that the dangers of arbitrary actions could be corrected by more objective forms of social inquiry. But his ultimate understanding of the nature of the good was as relativistic as that of James. For both Peirce and James the 'truth' of social consensus is subject to infinite revision because it does not have infallible foundations.

Peirce borrowed from Kant the expression 'pragmatic' to express the conditional purposes which are part of all modes of practical experience. In James' hands, pragmatism becomes more personal. As he understands pragmatism, it reveals the deeply individualistic character of the pursuit of righteousness and truth. The situation of each human being, with all his particular joys, sorrows, and perplexities is, for him, the decisive justification for any practical philosophy. As such, it must be able to assist each, with their irreducible differences of character and temperament, to chart his way through his experiences of life. [108].

Jamesian pragmatism affirms the relation between the practical life and the life of the individual. But for James, pragmatism is also meant to mediate between the extremes of rationalism and empiricism. The pragmatist is immersed in the experienced world but he is also alert to the world of values. These dimensions come together in the world of action. For James, man is what he wills. The serious person hopes to bring into reality whatever matches his desires for fulfillment. Under these conditions, truth is not an attempt to accurately represent an objective world. It is part and parcel of a creative adaptation to changing situations. And to the extent that these actions in the world yield greater personal satisfactions, the true is the good as well as the useful. [109].

All of this requires a certain personal orientation. The pragmatic individual must reconcile the need to reduce multiplicity to simplicity with the passion for distinguishing. The former tendency is universal; the latter will be found only in those few who have a natural desire to make complete acquaintance with the particulars, or parts, of any reality. James hoped to convince his public that only those who embrace both of these dispositions will really enjoy life to the full. Those who are willing to make the effort will find that they possess an authentic and inclusive philosophy. They will also have opened their minds to questions which had previously been under the jurisdiction of theology. James did not want to justify the ways of God to man, but he did want to make the thought of God useful to the human project.

The Search for a Higher Power

Like Henry Adams, William James was aware of the threat that a highly organized industrial system posed to the flourishing of the personal life. But James was not prepared to "throw in the towel". James rebuked Adams for his pessimism and criticized him for his failure to recognize the differences between material and human energy. The need, as James saw it, was to find ways to release individual moral capacities. This would draw him into a controversy between a materialistic and a spiritualistic understanding of the prospects for the future. For the materialists, the world just happens to be the way it is. The spiritual camp included all who believed that life on earth is governed by powers higher than those of reciprocal force. James allied himself with the anti-materialists. He approached the issues raised by this conflict with a pragmatic sensibility with its feeling for alternatives. The important question was: what different practical outcomes would there be if one or the other of the two views were true? [110].

While the materialists believed that the world can be no better or worse no matter what we try to do about it, those with a spiritual bent have deep hopes for improvement. They recognize a need to find support for our moral life in some form of eternal law. This reference to something higher attracted James' attention. It also fitted into his radical empiricism, that led him to look upon the world as unfinished. Bringing the greater reality to completion would require the help of a higher power. [111].

James' affinity with spiritualism was also aided by his interest in psychic phenomena. Such abnormal experience proved to his satisfaction that not all human behavior is subject to scientific explanation. He explored the subject in the Gifford Lectures which he delivered at the University of Edinburgh and which were subsequently published as *The Varieties of Religious Experience*. James argued that in the inner state of our being we may come to understand that our unique existence is engaged with a wider unseen universe whose order differs from that which is revealed to our senses. [112].

In *The Varieties* James explored the various dispositions that are parts of the pursuit by the individual of a harmonious relationship with whatever he conceives to be a god, or a god-like power. James recognizes the influence of the subconscious and analyzes the pessimistic as well as the optimistic modes of religious expression. He also reviews more fundamental qualities such as repentance and conversion, as well as the forms of mystical prayer. The difficulty in making these personal experiences part of a humanistic philosophy is that since they arise in solitude, they are to a large extent incommunicable. But James insisted that they are not frivolous or egotistical. To be religious is to have a serious state of mind. [113].

The experiential dimensions of religion had to be integrated with the principles of pragmatism. James wanted to show that pragmatism had a relevance to the most important issues of personal existence. He claimed that such a practical philosophy was useful to matters of ultimate concern as well as for more immediate purposes. In a full life there is a pursuit of higher as well as lower interests. Although he reserved to the individual the right to act according to his own feeling for the good, James also recognized that a desire for permanence of principle was rooted in the human heart. The essence of the good might seem to lie in the satisfaction of demand, but the noble attitude that we have inherited from the Transcendentalists is one that seeks for what is inherently right. [114].

Since he was always interested in the most inclusive ideals, James was willing to postulate a divine thinker who upholds a moral order that calls us to transcend our selfishness. But he would not concede supremacy to any Absolute whose powers could interfere with the initiatives that come from independent human action. To that end, he would give a sophisticated interpretation to the claims of free will that had originally unsettled the Puritan religious establishment. As we noted in the first chapter, the unorthodox search for reconciliation with a higher power had been expressed in Emerson's belief in a cosmic intellect. James agreed that a higher power makes itself felt in the sincere individual life, but he was not willing to follow Emerson's disposition to act with respect to higher things as if the ego did not exist. In this regard James' attitude was closer to that of Whitman. Like Whitman, James would not negotiate his encounter with divinity in a way that would endanger his own intense self- consciousness. [115].

While he was determined to preserve the inherent value of individual existence, James also wanted the self to have a relation with divinity. Striking an appropriate balance between these two objectives was difficulty enough in itself, but it was complicated by James' commitment to a radical empiricism. While he yearned for a spiritual happiness, his whole being was passionately engaged with the richness of temporal reality. These conflicting allegiances would lead him to resolve the decisive issues concerning God and man within an immanent frame of reference. William James had inherited from his father an aversion to theological doctrines which place an impassable barrier between the Creator and his creation. And being widely read in the relevant literature, William came to see that the whole of Christian theology, Catholic and Protestant alike, were dualistic in their maintenance of rigorous distinctions between the divine and the human. Such views offended William James because they excluded the human subject from the deepest realities of the universe. [116].

Like Channing before him, James was determined to correct all forms of religious understanding that keep us alienated from God. The Supreme Being would become the 'heart of our hearts' rather than the traditional Commander - in-Chief. But the road to the new ideal was strewn with the wreck of previous attempts to understand God in intellectual terms. This was especially true of attempts to reason to the existence of God from the recognition of design in the order of the natural world. The advance of evolutionary science had radically changed the relationship between man and the world within which he exists. James noted that it is now impossible to consider Nature as being either sublime or benign. A struggle for survival lies at the core of all living species; as a result, violence and ugliness are as prevalent as beauty and order. [117].

The modern mind could not ascend to God by contemplating the Natural world. Scientific cosmology was also not very helpful. If its mentality made room for an idea of God, it could only think of Him as the author of inflexible laws which take no account of individual reality. Such a God is in the wholesale rather than in the retail business of salvation. According to James, what the individual needs is the help of a higher power who, like the God of the Davidic psalms, is a living God; One who is full of "warmth, blood, and personality." [118].

Divine involvement in human affairs as recounted in the Bible became for James the paradigm of spiritual immanence. But he also had to deal with his father's peculiar attempt to reunite the Creator with his creatures. It will be recalled that for the senior James God is the creative principle within humanity en -masse. William, by contrast, wanted to vindicate the spiritual destiny of distinct, and different, individuals. To do this, he reinterpreted his father's theology so that it could be seen as a theory that made God the active principle in the general human drama, but which was flexible enough to satisfy the sensibility of those who cherished human solitude. [119].

William James resisted his father's teaching that divinity is found only in society, but he fiercely opposed all philosophies which held that personal existence is intrinsically dependent upon some ideal Absolute. James deeply believed that individuals are more than just objects for some All-knowing being. Everyone is a subject in his or her own right. Each has preference over any all. Essentially unique, each is not the atomic element of scientific materialism nor are they the generic types which abstract idealism imagines them to be. No existing human person in their full reality had ever existed before or will ever come again. James wanted us to understand that we cannot escape the burden of personal existence by pointing toward a greater abstract reality that supposedly sustains all in being. [120].

While James urged his public to renounce philosophies that do not respect our independent selves, he also reminded his audiences that we are all flawed and unfulfilled. To complete ourselves we must find something beyond the raw fact of our existence with which we can establish a real kinship. But we must not do so as a matter of contemplation but in terms of action. The world within which we live is a practical world and as we grapple with the distinct every day challenges of that world, we must have some support from a superior power whose Being can elevate our doings.

We all know that we are imperfect, yet something leads us on. The humanism that James was trying to develop rejects the notion that we are driven by an unknowable material energy, but it refuses to believe that our faults and sufferings can be relieved by submission to some ideal of timeless perfection. The important thing is for each to be faithful to his unique self while trying to connect its own existence with something which is wider and deeper than immediate experience. Since we are embedded in time, we must give our attention to the truths that come to us through our finite experiences. These existential realities –which include religious intuitions - do not point to anything beyond themselves. The world, like the self, is developed from within rather than from without. Time, space, and the self are brought together by the coordinating powers of subjective feeling. [121].

In this scheme of things, a religious belief is important because it is a conjunctive experience. It corresponds with our self -consciousness because it presents the universe to us in a personal form. For James, who hated the impersonal, the universe is to be understood as a 'Thou' rather than an "It". Since we are passionate beings, we cannot comprehend God as a stranger. Nor can he be totally distinct from whom we are. Such immanence encourages intimacy, but it also leads to pantheism. [122].

James would have to decide whether he could integrate the human and the divine in a way that respects the differences but rejects all definitive distinctions between them. An absolutist, or monist, conceives of divinity as a totality that excludes the complete and independent reality of the individual self. Pluralism holds to a distributive conception which assures the dispersion of discrete personal identities. If one cherishes the existence of oneself, and the right of each to be themselves, James thought that the pragmatic choice is clear.

The difference between an absolutist and pluralistic conception is also a difference between a timeless and a contingent understanding of all reality. James believed that in an unfinished world there are greater possibilities of intimacy with God than there is in a world which is understood to be a perfect whole. For when a Supreme Being is thought of in terms of absolute perfection, there does not seem to be anything outside of Himself which could cause Him concern. In the Jamesian creation, however, the world is full of distinct, but unfulfilled human beings who are caught up in pain and sorrow as much, if not more, than they experience joy and happiness. The gulf between their need and the source of their help cannot be infinite. Thus, James concluded, a God who can attract our finite love must be, like us, of an imperfect nature [123].

The useful divinity is a superhuman person who does not oppose us and who also calls us to cooperate with His purposes. He empowers us to add our own 'let it be' to his creative actions in the world. But James thought that our participation in the creative process must proceed without any guarantees of either success or salvation. As pragmatic conscience is determined to work out its own destiny, it does not concede the existence of irresistible grace. Yet while it affirms the power of the individual will, it will not adopt a Pelagian ethic.

James was not willing to assume that we all possess a natural power to be righteous. He understood that personal moral convictions, however strongly held, are always vulnerable. William James was also aware of how much independent individual action is constrained by the highly organized power of industrial society. The difficulty, as he saw it, was that while modern society has no motives for action other than those provided by technological imperatives, the individual has reserves of inspiration which he lacks the power to implement. He must depend upon a God who cares for him in his solitude. [124].

The quest for God varies in scope and intensity as the circumstances of individuals differ from one another. However, according to James, everyone who is sensitive to the dynamics of personal development will eventually reach out to some ultimate reality. Nonetheless, the pursuit will reflect that pluralism which, for James, is indispensable to an abundant humanism. If human nature were uniform, the total consciousness of the divine would be impoverished. The many would be dissolved in the One. The uniqueness of the singular would be annulled. The better course is for each to find the true significance of existence somewhere in the depths of his or her being. There, according to James, the self can make contact with a wider self which is distinct from, but not discontinuous with the individual. Such a mystical communion is our life in the making. It elevates individual purpose and helps to determine whether the world will be better or worse because of our deeds.[125].

James' reflections on religious experience are those of a passionately independent thinker. But they are also an extension of the revolt against the Calvinist hegemony that began in New England in the waning years of the Puritan experiment. As we have seen, the earlier rebellion, led by Channing, attempted to overcome the doctrines of Divine Sovereignty and human depravity which had been so forcefully articulated by Jonathan Edwards. While James' religious thought has some affinity with Emerson's romantic naturalism, James' emphasis upon practical action, and his affirmation of the freedom of the will, brings his views closer to the teachings of the Unitarians. To the Puritan mentality an inner corruption of the heart inclined the human will toward evil; moreover, a conversion to the Christian life would not enhance volition because the influence of grace transcends all natural human power. By contrast, the Unitarians believed that there is an innate goodness within each individual. When expressed in action, that inner integrity draws him into alignment with God. [126].

James' strenuous ethic is a continuation of the Unitarian belief in the limitless powers of the human will. However, in other respects, the relationship between James' philosophy and Unitarian teaching was more ambiguous. James thought that the attempt by Unitarian scholars to find a reflection of God in the natural world was untenable. And his attitude toward the problem of evil resembled more the beliefs of Theodore Parker than those of the Unitarian mainstream. Having thought long and hard about the problem of evil, James rejected Whitman's use of poetic license to avoid difficult choices between right and wrong. James also found the avoidance of the darker side of life in the religion of "healthy -mindedness" a mark of its shallow character. But James thought of moral depravity primarily as something in the external world that one must struggle to overcome. As was the case with Parker, James tended to externalize sin. [127].

For both William James and Theodore Parker, the presumption was that the will can act within relatively untainted motivation. Having overcome the burden of depravity, the individual, although weak and vulnerable, can still labor to improve his society in a partnership with the living God. However, like Parker, James did not fully appreciate the deeper propensities toward willfulness. In this respect, he was not as insightful as either Hawthorne or Melville. Nor could James escape the fragile quality of a personal identity which, according to his own psychological principles, is nothing more than what it is experienced as being. The inward flux that registers the encounter of the self with its external world is not drawn together by anything more substantial than the felt interests of the human subject. This highlighting of self-consciousness was also an unintended form of deification. In his attempt to comprehend the nature of human sensitivity, James was also trying to articulate an absolute conception of himself. The danger was of an inward recession into an inescapable emotional labyrinth. [128].

A radical subjectivity reflected James' agnosticism. He had a profound fear of ecclesiastical and social control. The individual right to believe, and to act upon one's beliefs, was of paramount importance. In James' humanistic psychology, beliefs could always improve one's life regardless of whether they were true or false. [129].

We have already observed that James' view of personal autonomy was challenged by Charles Saunders Peirce who, it may be recalled, considered James' version of pragmatism to be incompatible with the objective demands of modern life. James' theories were also questioned by a new philosopher, Josiah Royce. James used his influence to help secure for Royce a position at Harvard. While colleagues, they established a relationship of personal friendship and mutual admiration. Yet they had an unrelenting disagreement over fundamental issues.

To James, Royce was a philosophical Rubens: a mind full of color, boldness, and abundance. The fertility of Royce's abstract thought excused what, to James, was a lack of precision. Royce repaid the compliment by placing James in a class with Jonathan Edwards and Emerson. Royce believed that all three were thinkers of the first rank who had captured the spirit of their times and made a lasting impression upon the American mind. [130].

Royce admired James' pragmatism and profited from its concentration upon experience. But Royce thought that the radical individualism that it promoted led to moral caprice. Royce also believed that the relativism of James' perspective was incompatible with the demands of truth. To develop his philosophy, James had focused on the problem of regret. To combat the deficiency in James' epistemology, Royce concentrated upon the phenomenon of error. In Royce's constructive idealism an error was an incomplete thought of a finite mind. Correction requires a mental move beyond the ideas of the individual who holds a particular belief.

James agreed that the judgments of an individual thinking and acting alone might be erroneous, but he was confident that, over time, and through the exchange of ideas, truth would prevail. In responding, Royce based his rebuttal on the premise that an incomplete thought of a finite being cannot be corrected by consulting the minds of other finite beings. A whole community might believe that x is true, but still be mistaken. Royce insisted that the correction of error cannot be based upon any particular intentions. Reference must be made to a completed object. The failure of partial understanding can only be rectified from the standpoint of someone who possesses the whole truth of the subject in question. In Royce's theory of veracity this calls for a time-spanning consciousness, or Absolute Spirit, to whom all truth and error is know. [131].

In the early phase of his philosophic career Royce had been greatly influenced by Hegel. The young American thinker tried to comprehend the individual life as a particle in the progressive realization of an eternal mind. But as Royce matured, he shifted his attention from an intellectual conception of ultimate realities. He gradually came to the view that it is through the active will that we come into touch with our larger self and simultaneously approach the divinity that is within us. [132].

Like William James, Royce wanted to find a God who was not outside the world of finite agents. But Royce realized more clearly than his friend did that our hopes of divine possession are conditioned by our moral worth. Principle had to replace expediency. Royce could not abide ethical waywardness and he thought that he could improve upon pragmatism if he articulated a more elevated ideal of the good life. Royce also realized that he would have to resolve the antimony between absolutism and pluralism that was at the heart of the philosophical differences between himself and James. As Royce saw it, the need was to make a creative connection between individual existence and the life of humanity as a whole. This led Royce to conceive an idea of community that would be flexible enough to reconcile the tensions between the One and the Many. The philosophy of religion also had to be placed upon a deeper foundation. Royce wanted to bring inner spiritual dispositions into agreement with broader matters of doctrine and ritual. The aim would be to grasp the whole reality of things divine. To this end, individual deliverance would have to be coupled with a sense of corporate salvation.

James was concerned with the needs of an individual struggling to fulfill his unique existence; to Royce's mind, a complete religious outlook must encompass societal, as well as personal, existence. It had to draw the mind to the triad of being composed of God, man, and the cosmos. Inclusive inquiry would give us a clear understanding of the eternal spirit in which we live, and move, and have our being. Reflection upon ultimate matters would operate within a comprehensive framework. It would advance the modern project of finally overcoming the separation of God from His creation which had so long haunted the Christian theology. But creative thought could not avoid the stark realities of evil.

Royce agreed with the observations that James had made in *The Varieties of Religious Experience* concerning the limits of a "healthy-minded" attitude toward the problems of sin and suffering. Royce also rejected the simplistic view of the Incarnation as a confirmation of the natural divinity of man. In responding to these problems, he would develop a theory of Atonement which would be responsive to William James' more individualistic understanding of the need for salvation. Ironically, Royce's conception of redemption would be closer in spirit to the socially—oriented theology of Henry James Senior than to the religious sensibility of James' illustrious son.

Multiplicity and Unity

Josiah Royce was a child of the frontier. Born in California in 1855, he had youthful experiences of both a religious and a social nature that would significantly influence the development of his mature philosophy. Before moving West, his parents had been involved in Adventist Christian communities. These groups were committed to the belief that a sinless and ideal existence was attainable during one's earthly life. Royce eventually rejected the religious doctrines and practices of his parents, but throughout his life he held to the conviction that the eternal might intersect with time.

As Royce gradually became aware of the larger universe, he was troubled by the sense of spatial infinity and timelessness. He developed a desire for immortality. But he was also determined to resolve to his own satisfaction the complexities of real human experience. He tried to overcome an extreme sense of personal isolation by exploring the value of community. Having known the transient quality of particular affections, Royce longed for wider fields of attachment. The assassination of President Lincoln became a metaphor for the evil of disloyalty. Royce's own ethical theories would reflect the indelible quality of that national tragedy. [133].

The spiritual cast of Royce's mind led him to search for something beyond immediate experience that could explain the whole of reality. Something conceived in thought would have to replace the higher beliefs of the Christian tradition. Even though the possibilities of great comprehension were restricted by scientific naturalism, Royce retained a deep desire for unconditional, unseen truth. Metaphysics came to his assistance. Royce was immersed in German idealism, which held out the hope that some contact with the immortal could be realized within the depths of the self.

Kant revealed the ethical dimension of self-understanding in his works on the conscience and the absolute law that imperatively demands that you do your duty. This moral philosophy was attractive to Royce, especially in its assumption that as duty is done the self is enlarged. But he was not fully committed to Kant's outlook in matters of final belief.

While he shared Kant's judgment that the world of our experience is unknowable in itself, Royce was dissatisfied with the great philosopher's attitude towards the possibility of a supreme being. Kant treated God's existence as a postulate: a hypothesis assumed to be certain by a conscience that must behave as if there was a divine being. Royce's mind, and emotion, would require a greater certainty. In his own form of idealism he would try to work out a definite bond between God and man.

In his early publications, Royce sketched an intellectual conception of the Absolute as the ultimate source of truth and knowledge. However, he gradually moved toward a different conception of ultimate reality. Royce came to think of the will as the medium for working out the relationship between the self and the eternal. In self's search for an ideal, Royce saw the possibility of an intimate relationship being forged between the divine and the human.

Royce acquired the idea from post-Kantian thought that we become one with the Absolute Self to the degree that we are morally worthy to have such an affinity. He learned that the 'manly will', when it acts morally, comes to embody a portion of the divine personality. But while Royce was drawn to this subjectivism he was uncomfortable with its connections to Romanticism. In spite of his Western origins, Royce was somewhat of a Puritan. He was repelled by the ethical inconsistency of the romantic sensibility and its tendency to substitute emotional values for the rigors of moral righteousness. [134].

Royce was also troubled by an excessive reliance upon sheer will power within modern Germanic philosophy. He saw this arbitrary idealism as a leading contributor to the nihilism and pessimism that was beginning to inflict the modern world. Royce wanted to articulate a constructive idealism that could turn the energies of the will towards a more stable order of being. The need for a more comprehensive philosophy was not only propelled by the perversities of modern thought; it was also necessary to correct the deficiencies of American culture. Royce took issue with Pragmatism, which he saw as a generalization of the spirit of efficiency that animated the industrial economy. His central objection was that this disposition elevated expediency over principle. Royce absolved his friend William James from the general criticism because although

James had given philosophical sanction to the practical attitude he, like Royce, believed in the supremacy of the spiritual life. The real difficulty was the tendency of popular ethics. There were many admirable virtues, such as directness and diligence, within the American ethos. But Royce believed that there was too much reliance upon simple ethical maxims. The people were unpretentious, but they also avoided the complexities of moral thought. Even worse, Royce detected a tendency to expose the deficiencies of others while ignoring one's own personal failures.[135].

The practical wisdom of the American people was marred by a willfulness that could have tragic consequences. The people were self -reliant without being self -possessed. Being restless, their lives lacked firm foundations. According to Royce, they lacked a vision of wider ideals because they focused their energies upon immediate success rather than upon the wholeness of life. He was determined to correct that deficiency.

Royce realized that if he was to make a significant contribution to the American experience he would have to express the possibilities of improvement in a way that did not ignore the pressing realities of temporal life. He would not only have to reform the general quality of the national mind, but he would also have to take full account of the individualism that was so dear to James' heart. But Royce understood that something more than a dialogue with his friend was at stake. At one level, the objective would be to reconcile monism with pluralism; at another, it would have to be an attempt to overcome the deep antithesis between multiplicity and unity that had almost driven Henry Adams to despair.

As we have already observed, William James identified a fundamental tension between a monistic and a pluralistic understanding of experience. Out of respect for his father, he suggested that the two approaches could be reconciled. But he could not accept the idea that individuals are just objects for an all—knowing mind. For the son was certain that we are subjects in our own right. William James also objected to the idea that only a general form of humanity is worthy to receive divinity. He believed that the individual, standing alone, could also gain spiritual favor. For him, the infusion of infinity was likely to have biblical rather than metaphysical sanction. Even with these bold assertions concerning the relation between the divine and the human, James was concerned about the way these fundamental issues were dealt with by the idealists. Their Timeless Absolute seemed to be, all at once, completely what it is. Humanity, by contrast, is embedded in temporality. Could we share our ways of being? [136].

In James' mind, there was no perfect eternal Absolute at the heart of reality. He preferred to believe in the distributive interpretation of existence and he concluded that the "each" form of being human may be all there is. If Royce was to make an adequate response to the philosophy of his friend, he would have to show that particular and collective understanding could coexist. Royce had to prove that we could raise philosophy to a sense of unifying totality while, at the same time, respecting the time—bound quality of individual identity. To this end, Royce would build upon a framework provided by James' mature philosophy.

James dealt with the accusation that Pragmatism treats the immediately useful as the measure of human action by claiming that when Pragmatism is properly understood, it is a means of pursuing ultimate ends. He also asserted that superior minds do not limit their attention to short-range concerns. Remote perspectives and final things are equally important. The actions of the pragmatist seem to be rooted in present problems, but, according to James, they are actually leading him towards a more worthwhile future. [137]

The pragmatist does not assume that good will necessarily triumph over evil. James tried to delineate a middle way between those who think that salvation is impossible and those who assume it is certain. He did not think that the world either develops, or declines, in any predetermined way --so long as each, in his own way, adds his fiat to that of the Creator. [138].

James retained some of the traditional ideas concerning the distinction between the Creator and His creation. God was sufficiently different to be a powerful ally of James' ideals. Royce tried to eliminate this dualism by restricting the mysteries of creation to the boundaries of human thought. For him, the Divine is eternal, but he is not the First Cause of the human spirit. Royce thought that a conception of God in terms of omnipotence would destroy individuality. God does not create me just as I am; I am a work in progress.

In Royce's idealism, the connection between God and Man is manifest in an intimate bond between the ethical self and the divine will. The relationship is teleological, not causal. In me, God recognizes himself. The Absolute expresses itself in the concrete diversity of individuals whose deeds in time gradually form the willing of the world. [139]

Royce approached the problem of temporality from the perspective of the will, with its restless desire for satisfaction. [140] Our interest in life gives us a sense of direction that allows us to move from the past to what we hope is a better future. And, according to Royce, our ability to appreciate the succession of time is evidence of a deeper striving to unite the internal meaning of our personal existence with the external progress of the world as a whole [141].

The self lives out the connection of time with eternity. The completeness that is seeks is included in its striving. However, the wholeness is known only to the Absolute [142]. To make this point, Royce uses a musical metaphor. As one studying a score grasps a series of notes all at once, so does God grasp the entire time sequence of the world. He simultaneously takes in the past, present, and future of every individual who consciously wills his own fulfillment. In that sense, the real time of my consciousness is one with the real time of the universe.

The time relations within which acts of human will occur are the expression of what Royce calls a " World Will". That will is not foreign to my will. Rather, it is continuous with my willing. Thus it is that the world of real meaning is time-inclusive instead of timeless. .That is why, for the unsatisfied will, the present is a time of transition. The alteration is elusive. While doing a particular act, we are not fully aware of the true nature of our individuality. Constantly struggling toward ideals, we do not realize that our identities are something more than a succession of passing states of consciousness. [143].

According to Royce, it is only with deep reflection upon our inner meaning that we are enabled to see our doings as being both distinct and having a relation to the Absolute. We then become aware that our particular destiny is not shared with any other human being. Uniqueness is vindicated. Moreover, it has the potential of being one with the life of God. To realize this potential, we must have a unified conception of the moral life. [144].

Henry Adams believed that the disintegration of the medieval Christian unity was the greatest catastrophe in the history of the West. Royce thought that moral anarchy posed as similar danger in the modern world. It is not enough, he argued, for an individual to have fragmentary, but intensely held ideals. For though the conscience of an individual is uniquely his own, it is meant to direct him to his place in a universal moral order.

In Royce's ethics, true good cannot be limited to present experiences. James accentuated the difficulties of maintaining moral integrity when irreconcilable values solicit the will. Royce did not deny these complexities but he insisted that our overriding concern should be to discover the whole fabric of ethical meanings to which our particular experiences are connected. In Royce's metaphysics of the practical, it is necessary that we know the whole system of ethical truth before we can claim a legitimate place for our partial actions. The objective is to discern the overarching spiritual unities that constitute the deeper realities of the moral world. To approach these ideals we must be freely loyal to some cause. [145].

The duty of the individual is not just to be himself. Such an attitude ignores the nature of willing. The ethical will seeks to express the eternal and it can only do so in some comprehensive manner. For Royce, that unity is found in acts of loyalty. One who is loyal serves the whole. He is devoted to a way of life that transcends his own private concerns. Multiplicity and unity are reconciled in manifold acts of fidelity. Here, as elsewhere, Royce's vision was all -embracing. Surveying the moral landscape, he saw feats of devotion which ranged from the mundane levels of ordinary life to the heroism displayed on the field of battle. Like George Eliot, Royce believed that the good of the world depends as much upon unhistorical acts of loyalty as it does upon valiant deeds done in the public service. [146].

In Royce's philosophy of loyalty, devotion serves the interests of the individual even as it calls him to practice self-subordination. By choosing a cause to which he will be freely devoted, the individual gives to himself a unity that he would not otherwise possess. Life is harmonious because the individual is now a participant in a higher form of spiritual reality. Devotion to a cause draws one into a super-personal attachment through which many, who are otherwise unconnected, come together to share a common life.

Communal devotion is the only way to self-realization. According to Royce, ethical life has no meaning for an individual unless he is attached to a community. Loyalty is social and so is its virtue. When I perform my duties the community, in return for my services, confers upon me my substantial reality. [147].

Royce's emphasis upon the social gave his philosophy some resemblance to that of the Senior James and distinguished it from the radical individualism of William. Yet Royce was ambivalent about the value of the individual in society. He recognized that loyalty requires complete devotion but he also insisted that it does not lead to mystical fusion. The individual while subordinated, is not absorbed; still, he is only fulfilled in a common life.

For Royce the key to understanding the ontological relation between the individual and the group could be found within the deeper recesses of self-consciousness. The purpose of such introspection is not to open up the hidden resources of individual feeling, but rather to gain an abstract knowledge of a world that is valid for all. In the depths of inwardness the individual can grasp a meaning that is authentically his own but at the same time universal. He will realize his true grandeur. Although he does not have a substantial soul, the individual is nonetheless a part of the Selfhood of the human race. And humanity shares in the larger Selfhood which is the World -Will. [148].

In its raw state, self-consciousness is a series of fleeting experiences. Royce believed that the sources of its stability lay outside itself, because self-knowledge includes the comprehension of a larger whole. Paradoxically, what is most individual about the self will not appear unless there is a close connection between itself and something that transcends its own meaning. [149].

For Emerson, the necessary otherness was the world of nature. Royce thought that the universe in its wholeness expressed a meaning. But Royce also believed that the diverse reality of human existence was of greater importance. There was a social dimension to Royce's idealism . He maintained that that the individual self becomes what it is meant to be through its acknowledgment of other human beings who are different from himself and with whom he can have both contrasting and cooperative relationships. The existence of other human beings is a matter of wonder rather than of recognition. We are fascinated by the fact that others exist and we also come to see that their difference from ourselves intensifies their personal character. Like me, others have an inaccessible inner life. Royce insisted that although the reality of others is distinguishable from my own , all they think and do can enrich my own inner meaning. For my empirical self, in its isolation, is a longing without fulfillment.

Royce insisted that social formation must have a meaning commensurate with human dignity. Like James, Royce disliked impersonal collectivities. There must be real relations between individuals rather than external bonds holding them together. Human beings must come together in ways that are guided by ideal values rather than the compulsions of mechanical forces. [150].

Societies work through us .It is from them that we get our moral worth. Royce noted how from the family, to the nation, to humanity at large, particular attachments point beyond themselves to wider unities. There are various solidarities but all are guided by one Spirit. And, along the way of socialization, entities are created that are as real as the personal existence of those that compose them. [151].

The community, like the self, is a being with a past. But for both there must be expectation as well as remembrance. Present activity does not exhaust the time process for either the community or the individual. Just as the ethical individual does not find his reason for living in his momentary self, the need to look beyond is indispensable to the group. [152].

There can be cooperation without community . As Royce observed, individuals can loyally fulfilled the roles assigned to them without really knowing who they are or what are the purposes of the organization to which they belong. When this happens, they lose interest in ideal community and become like cogs in a machine. For societies to form, they must be meaningful. And to be meaningful they must be interpreted. The individual interprets himself to himself in the light of his past and future ideals. But if he hopes to be understood by others, and enter the full life of the group, he must communicate with them. To do this, he must enlarge his cognitive outlook beyond its formation in pragmatism.

The Jamesian pragmatism viewed life as the individual's perception of reality as it is guided by the conceptions he uses to increase his satisfactions. However, for individuals to exist as members of a community, they must exchange ideas, and for Royce, this requires ways of knowing that surpass those of seeing and conceiving. In social engagement we are not just connecting something that we immediately apprehend with some thought or value in our minds. In communication there is always some reference to another mind.

The relationship is triadic. It involves an interpreter, an object or event to be interpreted, and a person to whom the interpretation is addressed. This occurs inwardly when a present self interprets its past to its idealized future self. In society, the someone being addressed is another person or persons. The one making the address is interpreting some object to the one, or ones, being addressed. This is done through a sign or mental expression. The communication must be interpreted by those receiving the message. The process is practically endless. But Royce insists that that the process, however indefinite, has much greater human significance than anything that is of a purely self—referential nature. [153].

In interpretation there is no terminus in the object as there is with pragmatic perception. Nor is there the sterile contemplation of a general thought. Both perception and conception are self-limiting. James had railed against abstraction, but Royce argued that a consciousness restricted to the flux of experience is equally barren. Both miss that fullness of life that comes to one who has the will to interpretation that is, itself, the will to community.

As radical empiricism enriched the possibilities of experienced relations, so also does interpretation increase our understanding of the higher human functions of rational contrast and comparison. The advantages of idealism are evident. The greatest contribution that interpretation, so conceived, makes to humanity is that it unifies. For Royce, the ideal mind builds up community by communicative acts which clarify the ideas that we have of ourselves and of the communities of which we are a part. When that is done, what is dispersed, or fragmentary, is brought together. [154].

But what if men choose to stay apart; to prefer division over unity? Allegiance has spiritual significance, but there are always those who refuse to see the light. Much more so than Bellamy, Royce realized that the struggle between good and evil within the individual determines not only personal fate but also the prospects for social peace. And Royce had the courage to face these intractable issues . He did so not only with respect to their moral dimensions of the problem, but also with regard for the ultimate issues of freedom, grace, and redemption that had from the beginning troubled the American soul.

CHAPTER FOUR

From Beloved Community to Mass Society

The Transformation of Sin and Redemption

Royce did not share Bellamy's optimism concerning the prospects for general harmony and progress. Royce's sensibility was much closer to that of Hawthorne. Like the chronicler of Puritan culture, Royce was acutely aware the pervasiveness of moral wrong and its devastating effects upon community. In the works of Royce there is a strong sense of the tragic side of existence. A student of Schopenhauer, Royce learned from the German pessimist about all of the abundant misery and suffering that life in this world entails. [155].

Royce also shared William James' understanding of the precariousness of the individual life and the need for it to be secured by something beyond itself. As for the relevance of Christianity, both realized that it is something more than a moral system. From different perspectives both saw that the prospects for spiritual growth offered by the Christian faith transcended human volition. Yet, neither would allow the quest for salvation to cancel their ineradicable desire for personal independence.

James respected the Edwardian theologians who were willing to suffer eternal damnation if necessary for the glory of God. As a pragmatist, James was open to every ultimate eventuality, including the possible extinction of his unique self, if that was the unavoidable result of the pursuit of his ideals. Royce was also influenced by the Puritan mentality. He believed that we serve the majesty of God when we become the objects of His wrath. Royce's only fundamental desire was to struggle towards immortality while remaining indifferent to the prospects of either eternal reward or punishment. [156].

The principal distinction between Royce's philosophy of religion and that of James was that Royce focused upon its corporate dimensions while James' approach was essentially individualistic. Although James recognized that men must cooperate in the fight against evil, he insisted upon the 'eachness' of the campaign. Royce, on the other hand, felt that salvation was inherently social. These differences were accentuated by their fundamentally divergent views concerning the relationship between the temporal and the eternal dimensions of human existence.

James assumed that an isolated individual could be in touch with an ultimate power that can confirm the unique ideals by which he measures the value of his life. For Royce, the problem with this approach was that private ideals are too often the result of compulsive changes in individual thought and action. According to Royce, if we hope to be in touch with a power that is not really ourselves, we must transcend idiosyncratic desires and place our expectations upon a more stable basis.

Whatever is the object of ultimate meaning must also be available to all. Royce thought that James did not appreciate the significance of human solidarity to the quest for spiritual insight. Religion and fellowship are closely connected. Royce felt that there can be no unity of the spirit unless all are privileged to enter into the sacred precincts. In addition, the religious impulse must involve something more than the validation of our intimate feelings.

The more substantial expectation is one of meaningful self-possession. Everyone needs the assurance of a peace that can be experienced in spite of the turmoil of ordinary life. For Royce, the objective is an intimacy with one who knows our past, present, and future. For we seek to know even as we are known. [157].

Supreme insight requires powers of comprehension that are grounded upon philosophical, rather than psychological, premises. Royce kept insisting that we will not find the ultimate in the inner depths of our reflexivity. We need a broader vision of who we are. For Royce, this wider and deeper understanding is more rational than emotional in its content. For James, the deepest sources of religion were essentially experiential; to Royce, this approach is partially valid but ultimately irrational. To reach the potentials of reasonableness will require a reconstruction of what we mean by religious truth.

Royce thought that an analogy drawn from general experience proves that acutely personal religious feelings are too narrow in their range. We think of the rational man as one who can see many things together. Their wholeness, rather than their multiplicity, draws his attention. This conception of reasonable conduct cannot be ignored if we are trying to explicate the importance of religion to a fully human life.

One who thinks seriously about religion must use his powers of abstraction in a way that is not subordinated to immediate situations. Royce believed that abstract reason could establish connections between seemingly different religious experiences in a way that led to a broader understanding than could be obtained by an exclusive reliance upon either faith or feeling. To his mind, reason and religion were not opposed. It was only the blind and unreflective forms of belief that could not coexist with human thought. [158].

The interplay between reason and faith would lead us to higher unities. While satisfying individual need, the combining of belief and thought would also draw us to a way of life whose significance is superior to anything that we presently undergo. Royce believed that to do this, we must be open to the possibilities of religious insight that have not been verified by experience. This is difficult, if not impossible, so long as we think of the eternal as nothing more than an immediate presence in our lives.

As a pragmatist, James was open to religious beliefs that were accessible to individual feeling and when reliance upon them led to satisfactory doings. Royce agreed with his friend that all truth is practical and that any meaningful insight becomes a guide to personal conduct. But he also thought that James did not fully understand the full nature of morality or religion because he did not understand individual intention.

Royce believed that our actions are guided by ideals that cannot be reduced to purely human experience. Time intersects with the eternal. All of our endeavors, however practical they may seem, point towards an integral whole of life which brings us into the presence of the divine. This completeness was something that James could not comprehend. By confining meaning to what we experience from moment to moment, his reflections never pass beyond an empirical and fragile sense of personal identity. Royce was confident that we can establish who we are if we take a broader, more inclusive view. We can then judge life in a way that points to a higher reasonableness which is beyond whatever the singular individual undergoes.

A will poised for action is doing something more than evaluating practical consequences. Since when it decides, its deeds are irrevocable, volition must be guided by something that is absolutely true or false. If one has a good will, he must act in a way that he never has reason to regret the principle of his action. To achieve that purpose requires an integration of moral philosophy with religious insight. For Royce, this combination itself depends upon a reconciliation of the individual and communal aspects of human existence. [159].

James had excluded the social aspects of religion from his understanding of spirituality because he thought that they lead to what is conventional, and , even worse, the destruction of personal initiative. However, throughout the nineteenth century theologians were beginning to preach a new 'social gospel' which asserted that the individual was more likely to find salvation in some form of public activity than he or she would in solitary devotion. In its extreme form , this new vision limited the entire meaning of faith to some form of activism, in defiance of the traditional understanding that we must love God as well as our neighbor. Royce was torn between the venerable and the modern conceptions. His philosophical orientation gave primacy to the social. However, he also realized that if any experience of human togetherness was to have an ultimate meaning, it must suggest that a divine purpose is at work in the practical activity. [160].

In Royce's philosophy of religion the community, as well as the individual, longs for salvation. The shared need would, to a large extent, be satisfied by the realization of the virtue of loyalty , because loyalty benefits the group as well as the devoted individual. As loyalty raises the individual above his private concerns, it also binds many into one service. Royce's conception of loyalty not only fulfills the moral law; it also has a spiritual significance because it unifies all from above. [161].

The ideal is of a socially active person who freely chooses a cause to which he or she will devote his life. Such a person overcomes isolation and also furthers the loyalty of others who have their own particular mode of allegiance. Partial loyalty promotes general loyalty. In Royce's mind, a universal, but diverse, devotion to loyalty is not only the supreme moral good; it was also the means for bringing the Kingdom of Heaven to earth. [162].

Royce thought that personal loyalty has a spiritual purpose that is the equivalent of grace in the older theology. Divine grace took control of the sinner; so also does a social cause spiritually direct all who are loyal to its ideals. The essential difference is that while grace was considered to be irresistible, those who are loyal freely choose to live or die as their cause directs. The allegiance is not, however, to any purely human project. Devotion draws all who are loyal into a genuine relation with that higher unity of consciousness within which they all have their being.

In Royce's religious philosophy the mystery of loyalty transcends the powers of moral comprehension. There is an expectation of happiness for the one who is devoted to his duties, and the felicity cannot be understood in exclusively natural terms. A fulfillment of being awaits: a consummation that embraces our failures as well as our achievements. Unity comes from beyond ourselves. Royce postulates a superhuman but personal conscious life that is waiting to understand our needs and to complete our experiences. Being with us to the end, it brings a peace that surpasses understanding. [163].

Like all forms of grace, this spiritual experience will reveal the highest possible good. But Royce also insists that we are unlikely to realize that good if we rely exclusively upon our own efforts. As did our Puritan ancestors, Royce realized that the problem of salvation must eventually be resolved within the dialectic between grace and freedom.

Theologians such as Jonathan Edwards had taught that salvation cannot be earned by moral effort. Salvation comes from the Divine Redeemer who freely decides who is to be saved. The difficulty for Royce, as well as for James, was that those who think that they are saved too often go on a "moral holiday". They hope to get from grace what they were not willing to earn for themselves.

Then there were the moralists. Some, like Arminius, believed that we must actively cooperate with grace; still others would make the fulfillment of moral obligations a substitute for religion. It fell to Royce to try to reconcile these conflicting motivations. [164].

Royce thought that one can live in the spirit while vigorously devoting oneself to a chosen cause. The biographies of those who have led faithful lives prove that the highest moral devotion is within the reach of the loyal will. They also show that such heroic individuals have received a talent, or grace, which is , for them, their cause. These endowments make possible that justice and charity that are the fruits of the loyal spirit. [165].

The resolution of the tension between grace and freedom through loyalty did not, however, completely satisfy Royce's religious search. He was concerned that his position was too close to the "salvation by works" being espoused by the proponents of the social gospel. Royce saw the need to take more seriously the realities of sin and the prospects of redemption . As he engaged in deeper reflection ,he would look more closely as the basic doctrines of the major religions and, especially, at the inclusive claims of Christianity.

As we have observed, Royce did not look upon Christianity as just a repository of moral teachings. He saw that Jesus Christ was not simply a model of excellence; he was, more importantly, the Suffering Servant who had come to redeem the world. And Jesus atoned for the sins of all, not just for those who are isolated from society. These facts led Royce to reconsider some of the established religious beliefs and practices. The reliance upon the ethical gospel, especially among the Unitarians, was incomplete because it did not address the Messianic tragedy of Christ's life and death upon the Cross. The popular understanding of Christianity was also deficient. Most thought of their religion in terms of their inner private life. Royce, like James, saw this disposition as being similar to the attitude of mind promoted by Eastern religion.

For James, the detachment that these alien beliefs cultivated reflected a fear of the world of experience. Royce's analysis was similar but more subtle. He saw a similarity between Buddhism and Christianity. Both offered the possibility of universal salvation. But the Eastern belief directed human energies towards the impersonal essence of the universe. As we have seen, this approach to ultimate realities required a disciple to act as if his ego did not exist. Christianity, by contrast, was more attractive because it affirmed the intrinsic and infinite worth of every human being. [166].

Christianity was also preferred by Royce because it established a sacred union of the one and the many. Beyond individual salvation there lies a spiritual fellowship which is communal by nature. All who adhere to the Christian faith , no matter what their talent or status, are called to the participatory experience of the Kingdom of Heaven. To Royce's way of thinking, a recovery of that more embracing conception was indispensable if the Christian religion was to have a positive influence upon the fate of the modern world.

Henry Adams had believed that under the circumstances of modern life Christian unity had disintegrated beyond recovery. Royce thought that the proliferation of sectarian Christianity since the Reformation prevented the development of the Kingdom within the confines of organized religion. Beloved communities must be created anew outside of the boundaries of the established churches. But there must first be a reinterpretation of the basic themes of sin, grace, and freedom .

In his explorations into the core of personal identity, James followed the inclinations of the empirical ego towards various forms of inner satisfaction. Within the deepest levels of self-consciousness the search led to the hope for a redeemed inner nature. This " spotlessness from sin" in James' psychology constituted a pure form of egocentricity. In Royce's thought, the conquest of sin was an essential element of personal fulfillment. The overcoming was marked by a heightened sense of self -consciousness as the dissatisfied will's determines to move towards something better than its present condition. [167].

The resistance of temptation was an essential step in the development of personal integrity. Yet all fail. To Royce, inner moral correction was of greater humanistic importance than the condemnation of external evil. Like Henry James Senior, Royce conceived of individual reform as the shedding of self - centeredness. The purification will empower us to enter into relations of mutual love.

At a deeper level, Royce realized that he would have to recast the whole drama of sin and redemption if he was to make the Christian ethos intelligible to modern sensibilities. From the time of William Ellery Channing ,there had been a persistent effort to reconceptualize the problem of sin and to make it more compatible with human dignity. Royce inclined more to the traditional view of depravity, but he wanted to anchor his understanding of moral evil on empirical rather than on moral grounds. He would explain the fall from grace as something that arises out of the relationship between the individual and the community.

Like Freud, Royce saw individual discontent as a result of the progress of civilization. But for Royce the issues were more moral than erotic. To secure its political and cultural unity, every society must impose its laws and customs upon its members. The intrusions awaken self-consciousness. The more that we know of the social will, the more we become aware of ourselves. The paradox is that as society matures, so does the individual. As a result, tensions between the purposes of the group and those of the individual increasingly intensify. As social forces become ubiquitous, the personal will does not become impotent. Rather, it is aroused. Royce believed that external pressures cause the individual to become more deeply aware of his own inner being. He then starts to assert his independence in a way that clashes with the outward forms of civilized behavior. Since he wishes to give priority to his own will, the result is mutual hostility and potential general chaos. [168].

Hobbes had proposed to create order out of this unsociable condition by the power of the sovereign. Royce appealed to personal reformation. But for this to happen, the individual must realize that his inner being is divided. He is not torn between the elementary forces of good and evil within the soul, as traditional Christianity had taught; he is caught in the conflict between the demands of the social will and his own limitless desires for autonomy. For Royce, personal conscience is born out of the contest between individual self - reliance and the enforcement of social ideals and not, as Edwards believed, from any necessary inclination of the will toward evil. And the tension between the personal and social will is the cause of the moral calamities that inflict every civilized society. As the source is social, so is the remedy. Personal loyalty helps because, among other advantages, it advances the prospects for reconciliation. Yet Royce realized that something more is needed if there is to be a real healing of social strife. [169].

Just as he had reinterpreted the dogma of Original Sin to make it more relevant to modern conditions, Joyce also transformed the theology of the Redemption. In the Christian teaching on the Incarnation, Jesus Christ was born into the world to be the Savior and Judge of all humanity. Royce felt that the continuation of the messianic mission by the institutional churches had been compromised by their divisions and arcane mysteries. However, Royce realized that atonement for sin remains a continuing necessity for both individuals and societies . He set out to rescue the essential meaning from its sectarian distortions. He hoped to reconcile the idea of Salvation with the belief that God is immanent to human history. In his philosophy of loyalty, Royce tried to draw the meaning of grace out of the resources of his constructive idealism. Sensing the inadequacy of that approach, he now turned to biblical sources. Royce took from the Pauline epistles the idea that through conversion to Christianity the individual gains an elevated loyalty.

The religious attachment is not created in isolation. The conversion takes place when the individual becomes a member of the Christian community. Royce saw that this ideal, or beloved ,community is not just an aggregation of individual wills. Nor are its demands for harmony and peace alien to personal desire. Christian community could be reconciled with personal longing because the living together advocated by the Apostles is animated by a spirit of love.

Royce's meditations on Scripture led him to conclude that the antagonisms between the individual and society experienced in secular life can be overcome if the profoundest mysteries of Christianity are transposed to the conditions of modern life. The fullest understanding would come from the doctrine of the Trinity. Of the Three Persons that constitute divinity, Royce believed that the Holy Spirit had the most relevance to his mundane philosophy of religion. For the Spirit is indwelling in community. The presence of the Spirit is what opens up the possibility that the many may be one. Royce's hope was that this theological datum could be used to inspire the modern world to realize the brotherhood of humankind. [170].

The need for an infusion of grace into the life of modern society is evident from the persistence of sinfulness in the lives of every community. The virtue of loyalty exerts an influence over the life of the committed individual which, for Royce, bears some analogy with the effects of grace in the older theologies, but the possibility of disloyalty remains . Original Sin may be removed by grace, but acts of depravity are within the realm of possibility. History gives ample proof that a willful deed, done in full consciousness that it is wrong , can still occur. These are the empirical facts. A disloyal heart, preferring hate to love, can still shatter the order of the community. Unless there is some atonement, the rupture in the common life will never be healed. [171].

Calvinism taught that the sinner cannot be restored to holiness without divine favor and, if that is not forthcoming, the guilty one will suffer the penalty of endless torment. But modern humanism was beginning to dispel that gloomy prognosis. A growing sense of the inherent value of human dignity was offended by the vindictive retribution that lay at the heart of the Edwardian theology.

Modern man no longer believes in eternal punishment. Nor does he have a persistent sense of guilt. As the individual matures, he may become more aware of his faults but he is also more prepared to accept the consequences of his wrongdoing. Most importantly of all, if he commits a terrible sin with clear understanding of what he is doing, he will never forgive himself. Grace can erase the sins of the past, but the one who has received it is not predestined to persevere in saintliness. Arminius had it right. As long as the individual has a will of his own, he can reject the light. He can always be false to his ideals. In Royce's estimation, the result is not utter corruption. Yet the doer of the deed has condemned himself to what Royce calls the " hell of the irrevocable." [172].

In Royce's religious philosophy the traditional teaching on the endless punishment incurred by serious sin is re-enacted in the moral consciousness of modern man. The rebellious one knows that he cannot undo what he has done. The problem is that even though he does not feel that he is subject to the sanctions of an angry God, he will not forgive himself. Nor will allow for deliverance from above. For Royce, this resistance to supernatural help creates a central difficulty . If natural human societies are to be transformed into beloved communities, there must be some making of amends for the individual wrongs that disrupt the course of orderly and peaceful coexistence.

Saint Paul had taught that following forgiveness within the Church, the repentant sinner would experience a new liberty. For Royce, this option was closed. However, a different type of salvation could result from human initiative. It would be a refinement of the ideal of loyalty. Atonement would be something which arises within the natural human community. Within the group whose unity has been shattered by sin, some devoted servant will suffer on behalf of the offender. The prophetic image of the Suffering Servant is transformed into a modern narrative . There is no quasi-judicial satisfaction for sin; instead, a supremely loyal individual suffers for the faults of others. In his re-interpretation of the " felix culpa" of the Christian tradition, Royce sees s willful act of wrongdoing as the occasion of great social improvement. The sacrifice of Christ made the human condition much richer spiritually than it would have been if man had never sinned. Similarly, the innocent suffering endured by an individual who is acting on behalf of community can raise the life of human societies to levels of unity and peace that were unimaginable before treasonous disloyalty entered the fabric of human experience. [173].

According to Royce, sacrificial human loyalty parallels Christian charity. The results are equally universal. As the corrective acts of those who have not sinned renews the life of particular human communities, a sense of salvation begins to permeate the global consciousness. The world at large becomes, in effect, the true church. What institutional Christianity could not achieve because of its spiritual imperfections is supplied by the inclusive range of a constructive idealism that realizes through reason what was impossible to faith alone.

In the Christian tradition, the community of the faithful was meant to embrace the society of all mankind. Royce thought that his new prophecy was already being confirmed by the course of history. In the advanced nations, industrial development is gathering multitudes together into new forms of cooperation . There is a growing expectation of higher forms of unity. Royce believed that as humanity progresses, what Paul thought of as the saving mission of Jesus Christ is starting to become the Beloved Community of Mankind. [174].

The Primacy of Social Experience

In highlighting the importance of society, Royce opposed the individualism that William James had developed as part of pragmatism . By the end of the nineteenth century, new ideas were in circulation that would use a pragmatic attitude to advance the values of common life. The new approach would be called Instrumentalism . John Dewey was to be its secular prophet. Dewey was born in Burlington Vermont in 1859. His father, a storekeeper, had served the Union cause in the Civil War. His mother was a pious woman who had an active concern for the poor. John became a student at The University of Vermont where he came into contact with what has become known as Vermont Transcendentalism. [175].

At the University, speculation was directed towards a reconciliation of Christianity and philosophy. The leading evangelical thinker, James Marsh, tried to overcome the atomistic theories of Lockean empiricism by insisting upon the validity of innate ideas. Following Coleridge, Marsh taught that the Christian faith could be justified by introspection. When inwardly understood, faith constituted the perfection of human reason. And Christianity was rational because it was compatible with the universal laws of our being which we discern by reflective thought.

In the Vermont philosophy, the combining of reason and faith furthered the understanding of the organic interrelationship of all life. This sense of interdependence would lead Marsh and his followers not only to reject Locke's epistemology, but also much of the political thought of the English philosopher. Locke had held that political societies are composed of independent individuals who form governments in order to protect their individual rights. The Vermont thinkers , however, did not view societies as associations of fully realized individuals. Since all life was interconnected, authentic individuality could only arise out of association.

In 1829 Marsh published an edition of Coleridge's *Aids To Reflection*. Reading the work helped Emerson move beyond the limits of Unitarianism. But Marsh, unlike Emerson, saw in intuitive metaphysics possibilities of systematic thought that could provide general guidance for the conduct of life. Marsh wanted to develop philosophy in a way that avoided the transcendentalism associated with the culture of Boston, which Marsh felt led to sensuality and atheism. [176].

Marsh's successor at the University of Vermont, Joseph Torrey, was John Dewey's teacher and friend. Torrey's courses continued the efforts initiated by Marsh to make Christian piety compatible with modern thought. But tendencies toward pantheism were beginning to undermine the Burlington effort to reconcile faith and reason. Although Dewey was influenced by the Vermont philosophy , he began to take his inspiration from his studies of biology. He formed the idea that the organic interrelationships that were being inductively identified with the human body could be applied to the understanding of the functioning of society. During his graduate studies at Johns Hopkins, Dewey expanded his interest in physical reality. Developments in physiological psychology were yielding an experiential understanding of the human mind that would later be useful to Dewey's social philosophy. Dewey was also drawn to the discoveries of Charles Darwin. Dewey was particularly impressed by the way that that Darwinian principles of evolution moved modern thought away from speculation about ultimate origins and finalities and encouraged inquiry into the empirical conditions of actual life. For Dewey the humanistic implications were clear: we should use our minds to master the actual causes that affect our well-being rather than try to understand the universe at large. [177].

At Hopkins, Dewey's mentor, George Sylvester Morris, was working along the lines of thought that James Marsh had begun at Vermont. But now the reconciliation of faith and reason was inspired by an Hegelian philosophy that taught that The Absolute reveals itself historically through the medium of a collective consciousness. Morris interpreted the dialectic in a way that would lead to social engagement . Dewey was attracted to both the logic and the program. They were responsive to his craving for experiences of unity and his deep felt desire to overcome all dualisms and divisions. Yet although Hegel provided an ideal justification for Dewey's practical inclinations, the young American philosopher would set his mind against all assertions of absolute truth.

One of Dewey's earliest publications was a study of Leibniz. Leibniz held that the reality of the differences that we experience prevents us from postulating that all diversity is just the modification of a single substance. He also taught that the sufficient reason of whatever fills the universe must be outside of the succession of contingent particulars . For Leibniz, the ultimate meaning of facts was to be found in their relation to the Divine Intelligence. [178].

Leibniz's cosmic philosophy was sustained by his belief that we have an innate knowledge of necessary analytical truths, such as the principle of sufficient reason. Kant had a more humble conception of human powers. He thought that our knowledge was limited to the phenomenal world. In his philosophy , synthetic categories of understanding constituted experience as it is described. There is no need to reconcile efficient and final causation. Kant also held that the harmonies of our mental life are not derived from outside of human intelligence. They depend only upon the operations of sense and the inward categories of understanding. [179].

Dewey was influenced by both Kant and Leibniz. Kant's approach restored an immanence to both thought and activity that corresponded with Dewey's desire to get away from cosmological explanations and immerse himself in the real. Yet , over time, Dewey would incorporate into his own philosophy some of Leibniz's key ideas. This included the notion that substance was an activity measured by its ends and the idea that the world that we experience is permeated by interrelationships and continuities. Most importantly of all, Dewey would place Leibniz's conception of intelligence at the center of his own social philosophy. Reason, as active intelligence, would be organically connected to whatever it was trying to understand. [180].

Dewey's study of Leibniz and Kant prepared him for his critique of Royce's subjective idealism. Kant had restricted known reality to possible objects of experience. Royce thought that this was insufficient because for something to be really possible it had to be experienced by someone. His conception of Being included an ultimate reality that would provide the complete determination of all ideas and experiences. Royce thought that his view was confirmed by modern mathematics and logic, which pushed the notion of the true beyond actual human experience. The difference between Kant and Royce was that for Kant the real was sense determined by thought, while for Royce empirical discoveries could not reveal final meanings. Dewey's position was, in effect, an extension of Kant's . For Dewey, Royce's contrast between the contingent and the complete was unacceptable. If taken seriously, it would distract us from our natural inclination to comprehend experience as widely and as deeply as is humanly possible. [181].

Dewey decided that valid knowledge must be connected with life as we live it. As our search for truth is guided by the need to adapt to our circumstances, intelligence has a definitely practical quality. It is concerned with the potentialities of things that we hope to make real in concrete experience. This vital doing is so arduous that we should not have our mental energies diverted by a search for some higher justification. [182].

Royce's elaborate idealism, as far as Dewey was concerned, was nothing more than a reification of the experiential . Dewey was also convinced that our human dignity is offended if we are forced to think of ourselves as nothing more than fragments of some larger whole. Nonetheless, he realized that there was some relation between the ideal and the real., and, for that reason, he hoped to bring speculative reflection into closer contact with actual existence.

Following his graduate studies Dewey began teaching , first at Michigan, and then at the University of Chicago, where he was named Chairman of the Philosophy Department at the age of thirty-four. He established a laboratory school . There he developed an experimental curriculum that would implement his effort to establish that thinking and acting are parts of a single process. His work came to the attention of William James . James congratulated Dewey on his studies of Leibniz and Dewey returned the compliment by telling the senior scholar how much his psychology had influenced his own thought. [183].

In his later works, James recognized that Dewey, and others similarly disposed, were moving Pragmatism into new and uncharted territory . The developments would have humanistic significance. James saw that these new avenues of thought reflected some of the deeper changes in modern culture. They represented the shift away from theological to evolutionary explanations of experience as well as a rejection of aristocratic modes of social organization in favor of those of a democratic nature. [184].

James continued to defend the centrality of individual experience. As he aged, he reasserted his conviction that, as we move on, we must remain faithful to ourselves. However, he had come to realize that even as we pursue our own destiny we must be willing to accommodate our views to those of others. And he acknowledged that this need to adjust will require more social forms of cooperation . [183].

Like James, Dewey thought that our sense of human possibilities should be gleaned from experience. Dewey also pursued the possibilities of radical empiricism. The conjunctive aspects were more important to him that the disjunctive. His central conviction was that our lives are lived in association. For Dewey to adequately express this sense of relatedness would require him to distance himself from James' individualism. Dewey's separation from individualism was marked by his adoption of a distinctive mode of verification that came to be known as Instrumentalism. The expedient in thought and action should be determined by some collective procedure rather than by individual judgment. This shift from private to public concern reflected the influence of Charles Saunders Peirce.

For James, true ideas are those that we can personally assimilate as well as verify. One must have interchanges with the world, but they must be to one's ultimate benefit. But for Peirce, truth had to be something more than inward approval. He did not equate the right to act with the will to believe. He thought that James' outlook was similar to that of Emerson , both of whom, according to Peirce, saw themselves as independent individuals who did not have any organic connection with a larger society. [184].

Peirce believed that if the self is to have a coherent life, it must recognize something external to its own subjective world. This was the attraction of the natural sciences, whose successes came from the development of objective methods of observation and reasoning. For Peirce -and for Dewey- these impartial procedures should be the models for the search for truth throughout the whole social fabric of the modern world. They would enable us to mediate between the polarities of stability and change in matters of social conflict. Clarification of the values at stake would help alleviate disagreement and disciplined social inquiry would uncover the normative structure of the community suffering the antagonism. As differences were overcome, consensus would replace the proliferation of divisive private opinion. [185].

Intelligent inquiry would promote social peace, but whatever concord was achieved would be provisional. Dewey followed Peirce's view of the fallibility of meaning. They both assumed that experienced reality is inherently revisable. No beliefs are unchanging, no matter how deeply they may be held. [186].

A scientifically inspired pragmatism would give new significance to James' idea of an unfinished universe. But this socialization of meaning would require a reconstruction of individualism As Dewey pursued his studies of human nature, he developed a new understanding of the mind and will that would stress its corporate manifestations. Thinking could no longer be conceived as the majestic prerogative of isolated individuals. According to Dewey, it occurs within the evolution of nature and society.

Reflection is reactive. Intelligence is engaged when an unsatisfactory condition confronts us. As we then imagine promising possibilities, we pass from hypotheses into the world of doing. We make empirical observations of antecedents and consequences and we also weigh alternative modes of reconstructing the problematic situation. All who are interested can assent to an ultimate outcome. As we reconstitute the conditions, we recreate ourselves. [187].

In a social context, thinking is something much deeper than personal thought. And, as thinking is social by nature, so also is the determination of the good. For Dewey, the moral reasoning of separate individuals is not a source of public values. Personal moral sensibility is important, but only if it contributes to the reconstruction of values in common experience. A value must become valuable to all. [188].

Emerson believed that character was something complete in itself. It was not derived from experience. But for Dewey, individual character was the result of social formation. Its basic outlines come from education and the influence of subtler forms of public opinion. The objective of such shaping is to make a cooperative spirit the normal aspect of social relations. Science had made joint effort the key to the acquisition of relatively stable truths and, in Dewey's mind, the application of that spirit to social interaction would temper the centrifugal forces of individualism. The single one could no longer act in splendid isolation. But he would be enriched beyond his imagining if he would actively participated in the pursuit of a common cause. [189].

Dewey was intensely aware of how much modern life was essentially interdependent, and how much human progress depended upon effective communication. But his view of social exchange differed from that of Royce. As we have seen, Royce thought that as one participated in the dialogue of society one took from others what one thought would relieve one's dissatisfied will . Dewey thought that Royce's view of social communication was naive . It also was incompatible with the deeper objectives of solidarity.

The desire for personal autonomy was recognized by Dewey only on the condition that the individual adapted himself to the needs of the group. In the modern world, everyone had a role to play in some form of associated or corporate life. The ends pursued within all the disparate communities would remain private and particular, but they would be public, rather than secluded. And the objective of shared action would be the reconstruction of society rather than the salvation of the individual soul.

The rise of the social sciences had made a great impression upon Dewey. He was a friend of George Herbert Mead, and Dewey drew from that social psychologist the insight that selfhood was a function of one's relations with others. For the sociologists, the mind was not an independent faculty; it simply reflected the patterning of common thought that arises out of the development of human culture. [193].

Even the deeper sources of self-identity were not immune from newer influences. Emerson had held that the wisdom that comes from the eternal being of the individual was far superior to the judgments of society. But James had begun to undermine the metaphysical foundations of self -consciousness by making the empirical self of central importance. Dewey believed that when James reduced the knowing subject to virtually nothing other than a passing thought, he had practically eliminated the individual mind and soul from the arena of philosophical discourse. [194].

Dewey also thought that the ancient controversy over whether the self was the cause of its actions had been rendered irrelevant by scientific developments. It will be recalled that the question whether the individual could, by his own will, choose between alternatives had set the terms of the debate between Jonathan Edwards and the Arminians in colonial New England. For Dewey, the matter was passé'. The freedom of the will, as well as deeper matters of motivation, could be analyzed into identifiable sequences of specific, concrete conditions of observable action [195].

Like Henry Adams, John Dewey was well aware of how the public was becoming passive before the forces of modern science. But Dewey's analysis of the relation between technology and human existence was more nuanced than that of his predecessor. Dewey realized that the regimentation inherent in mass industrial society was adversely affecting the individual life, but he believed that retreat into a private world was not an intelligent option. At the same time, he insisted that one should not simply accept the impositions. Individual initiative, acting in a common context, could still redirect desire and imagination towards a better quality of life for all. For this to happen, there had to be a new understanding of the relationship between the individual and nature. For Dewey, the problem was to overcome the older dualism that saw humanity and nature as distinct, though related realms of being. Nature should not be something that we submit to for enlightenment, or shrink from in fear of its malignant powers. We must also reject the idea that nature represents an objective and independent order of reality. The conquest of nature by science had immense practical significance, but it also revealed something of greater importance about the evolution of life. According to Dewey, the progress of science had led to a deeper and more subtle adaptation of nature and mind to one another. Nature was now part of human experience, and nothing of value could be determined outside of that experience. [196].

Science had not only increased man's control over nature; it has also inflated the sense of personal independence. For Dewey, the reasons were in part historical. When the sovereignty of nature began to be challenged there was also a revolt, in the name of liberty, against established social and political institutions. The dismantling of all these governing authorities was necessary to the transformation of the West from a feudal society to a political democracy. But Dewey thought these changes also promoted the illusion that human existence was something wholly individual. [197].

The emergence of personal freedom led to the erroneous assumption that the individual could flourish in disregard of the social forces which surrounded him. Dewey saw the exaggeration of the rights of private property as being an effect of these changes. It meant that as new technologies developed, they would be concentrated in the hands of a minority who placed their selfish interests ahead of the public good. But the assertion of individuality had also promoted inflated conceptions of the human person that, to Dewey's mind, were an even deeper obstacle to social progress. From the time of the New England Transcendentalists , a strain of American thought had idealized a super-empirical ego that is conceived as being original, eternal, and absolute. The tradition thus honored a self set apart. To Dewey, however, whenever an individual distances himself from the realities of the social world he loses touch with that common experience that constitutes the new form of the natural. In Dewey's understanding of the human condition, the processes of industrial democracy, in all their spiritual as well as their material implications, constitute all the existence that modern men and women will encounter during the course of their lives. Interconnection is inevitable. The self, as a center of organized energy, must identify itself with something that has an external origin. For Emerson, that independent existence was Nature. For Dewey, it is Society. [198].

Like all the rest of nature, society can be transformed. Since the customs and habits that hold it together are provisional, they can be moved in new directions. The challenge is to turn the material that constitutes this "natural" social world towards a more equitable and stable form of common life. Dewey believed that the growth of the country would bring a new freedom, but it would be an empowerment extended to all rather than reserved for an elite few.

Early in his philosophical career Dewey began to articulate a more inclusive and organic understanding of democracy. After he moved from Michigan to the University of Chicago, he gained an acquaintance whose life and work gave him a new inspiration. Dewey came to know the social reformer, Jane Addams.

As the nineteenth century was drawing to a close, the influx of immigrants into the urban slums was creating a social crisis. The problems connected with these concentrations of population were compounded by labor unrest. Addams addressed the first problem by joining with a friend to start an educational settlement called Hull House. She addressed the second by taking an unpopular position with respect to a major labor-management dispute. In 1894 the American Railroad Union went out on strike against the Pullman Car Company. The conflict led to violent confrontations, boycotts, and criminal indictments. Addams' position deviated from that of those with whom she otherwise was sympathetic. Her view was that the antagonisms were unnecessary. Social conflict was nearly always based upon misunderstanding. Disagreements, she felt, were not really based upon objective differences, but rather were caused by the distortions of personal interpretation and bias.

When Dewey first heard Addams present her views he was not persuaded. he eventually concluded that he had overstated the extent of irreconcilable differences. Addams had encouraged him in his belief that intelligent social inquiry is the democratic way of reducing social divisions. [199].

Addams also reinforced in Dewey's mind the idea that democracy is a social as well as a political phenomenon. Dewey had learned from his mother that those of privilege must not disregard the needs of the unfortunate and Addams reaffirmed that sentiment. The problem was one of ethics as well as compassion. In Jane Addams' moral understanding, a purely private value system was irrelevant to the problems of modern coexistence. She agreed with Dewey that those who hope to have an influence upon the course of democracy cannot afford to live a life of isolation from the common world. Adequate motives for action must come from a vital contact with the experiences of the many. Addams also rejected out of hand the idea that we can legitimately limit our social relations to those whom we have already decided to respect. The essential democratic ideal, as she saw it, was one that recognized the interdependence of all and the infinite worth of each. [200].

Dewey agreed with Jane Addams that some form of associated living was necessary both to personal development and general progress. For him , the medium was democracy, not just as it arose out of experience, or even as a political theory. Dewey understood that the perfect conception of democracy had already been formed in the imagination of Walt Whitman. Recall that for Whitman human beings had an essential need to connect the culture that they fashioned here on earth to some mode of ultimate belief. In the medieval age, that relationship was formed by integrating human society with the doctrines and rituals of the Church. For Whitman, democracy would provide a framework for the future comparable to that which Christendom had given to the past. Democracy would inspire, and govern, every aspect of the coming collective age. Dewey's vision of democracy is an extension of this poetic insight. [201].

Dewey's conception, like that of Whitman, embraced multitudes. Hopefully, the people would not become a passive mass. Dewey expected that the American democracy would grow into a unified community within which each had the right to claim the quality of personality by his or her own efforts. In the broader struggle between pluralism and monism, Dewey sides with William James. The diversity of individuals is what gives vitality to a democratic society. But Dewey wanted to assure that distinctions did not become divisive. None can be set above, or below, others. Equality is the democratic ideal, not because it makes everyone the same , but because it assures that everyone can be as fully alive as they want to be. [202]

Democracy was an ethical ideal, but it had empirical qualities . As social life is experienced, one becomes aware that it cannot be transcended. The United States had become a technologically driven industrial society whose material dimensions were both inevitable and indispensable. Dewey would not ignore these realities. Rather, he wanted the benefits that this vital energy had brought to some to be extended to all. The hope would become a reality if the whole social and political process was sustained by the devotion of socially responsible citizens. The concentrations of power and organization that accompanied modern society had appalled James because he loathed all forms of bigness. Dewey acknowledged the dangers, but he also saw positive possibilities once the gross realities became subject to the authority of combined intelligence. Then what is can be changed into what ought to be.

The development of democracy had led to a de facto form of interdependent living. The combinations could be described in terms of the reciprocal forces of matter and energy. Dewey's appraisal was that the actual way of life was organic but not authentically social. He believed that a truly human society is one in which those whose activities are more or less automatically conjoined are raised to a new level through mutual communication . Only through true dialogue can the individuals within a social group understand the consequences of their activities and create the conditions under which that which merely happens be transformed and managed in a manner that is desirable to all. [203].

Dewey's communicative democracy bears some resemblance to Royce's idea of an interpretative community. Both sought to elevate routine cooperation into some form of shared meaning. But there were important differences. To Dewey, shared understanding is decisive. For Royce, as we have already noted, social intercourse always comes back to the individual will. In that sense, Royce's ideal was closer to that of Whitman who, while celebrating the commonness of democracy always yearned for individual completeness.

The communalism that inspired Dewey led him to insist upon the social nature of basic freedoms that are expressed in individualistic terms. Freedom of thought is fundamental, but it is not valued in isolation . Ideas are meant to circulate and become matters of common use. Dewey was sure that liberty and equality can be reconciled when individual initiatives are expressed in fruitful association with others and all benefit from the effects of common education and labor. [204].

As democracy comes into its own ,it will become what Dewey calls a Great Community. The human spirit will no longer be threatened by the forces of science and technology because the people will have assimilated all those powers to their own good use. Dewey hoped that as his Instrumentalism became socially effective, practical intelligence, inspired by both scientific method and the values of democracy, would bring equity and order to the vicissitudes of our fragile, but shared existence.

The Equalization of Life

In his utopian novel *Looking Backward* 2000 -1887 Edward Bellamy had imagined that the economy would gradually become subject to the principles of collective self -governance that were the political basis of the American Republic. At the time, in the late nineteenth century, there was a pressing need for change. The industrial development that followed the Civil War had brought increased prosperity but had done so under conditions of life and work that were becoming intolerable. Growth in the size and scope of the business corporation, coupled with aggregations of capital, were concentrating power in the hands of a few and, in addition, acrimony between labor and management was increasing the insecurity of millions who were struggling to survive.

Bellamy believed that the needs of all could be satisfied in a freely accepted form of collective social organization . Like Jane Addams, he thought that the discord within the economy was based more upon misunderstanding than it was upon natural enmity. He expected that as the country matured, self -interest would gradually give way to a non-Marxist form of socialism. In exchange for their services, all would be assured of the necessities of life through the efficient functioning of a single national organization that controlled the production and distribution of essential goods and services. [205].

With a single public corporation controlling the economy, Bellamy was convinced that the frenzy of buying and selling within the disordered society of his experience would give way to the peaceful coexistence of a fraternal civilization. But Bellamy's imaginative conception would not pass the test of reality. He had underestimated the extent to which laissez-faire principles permeated the national consciousness and he did not realize that economic freedom was a precious value for those who consume as well as for those who produce. More importantly, Bellamy could not have foreseen the degree to which, by the year 2000, the objective of equalized prosperity would be substantially realized by the expansion of free market capitalism.

Since the conclusion of the Second World War the revival of free enterprise, together with astonishing technological innovation, has led to a seemingly unlimited increase in the goods and services that have become available to the general public. In spite of financial uncertainties, by the end of the twentieth century the nation had experienced a prosperity whose abundance seems able to satisfy every conceivable material desire for acquisition and pleasurable use. And the tensions between labor and management that so disturbed Bellamy have been alleviated by the implicit understanding of all concerned that progress does not depend upon the clash of social forces. [206].

The modern system cannot be described as a form of socialism, but it has, nonetheless, its own techniques of total control. Consumers are encouraged to decide for themselves among competing products, but the pressures generated by modern advertising stimulate compulsive needs and desires that mock ideals of freedom of choice. Regimentation of behavior increases as standards of efficient organization and planning become more ubiquitous. The principles that led to the scientific conquest of nature have become the basis of the technological conquest of society. Abstract rationality reduces every multiplicity to a functional unity as systematic arrangements become the means of managing human and non-human alike. As administration replaces brute domination, coercion becomes more subtle and less obvious. State imposed order recedes, but the population becomes subject to the force of corporate bureaucratic power. In this " Brave New World" the aim of managers is to normalize the phenomenon of association by controlling all within a particular group and making them behave in a way that reduces social cost and friction [207].

With the expansion of democratic capitalism, life in common becomes increasingly under the control of an equalizing power. It becomes difficult for anyone to distinguish himself, or herself, from others. Social consolidation demands that the many be controlled by the few, yet all are directed by a compulsion rooted in the autonomous power of technology. Even those who are ostensibly in control are swept along by an inescapable destiny. As the whole progresses, the range of action is restricted. . The life prospects of the individual are determined by the polarities of work and unemployment. And the economy, politics, and culture, once thought of as mutually independent dimensions of society, are drawn together in a system that imposes its imperatives upon all. [208].

Liberty loses its value. As technological governance advances, the desire for freedom – which depends upon an awareness of servitude - fades from public consciousness. The vast majority are content with the benefits that are provided by the prevailing arrangements and they look upon the equalization of everything as a supreme form of liberation. Their subjection to the whole is an adequate substitute for them being unified within themselves. [209].

The coordinations of thought and action that characterize the modern economy are expressions of the emergence of mass society. Emerson was horrified by the rising population which he saw as exacerbating the existing tensions between the individual and society. Whitman's attitude toward the people en-masse was more benign because, for him, increasing immigration and urban expansion presented novel opportunities for the development of the democratic ethos. But what Whitman conceived as the future has now become a reality much more complicated than his innocent poetic vision could have imagined.

Mass society is essentially an anthropological, rather than a political, phenomenon. It is more encompassing than any numerical majority. And, it must be emphasized, it transcends all racial or ethnic distinctions. Mass society is a new form of human existence that has arisen because of general increases in population, the expansion of social opportunity, and the advent of a scientifically generated abundance. The masses are the multitudes who have risen from oppressive conditions, here and abroad, to enjoy the advantages of material civilization. [210].

The evolution of mass society completes the transition from an aristocratic to a democratic form of life. The distribution of offices, as well as goods and services , is shaped by the needs of the many rather than the aspirations of the few. The change from pioneering individualism to a new sense of commonalty is manifest in expanding educational and occupational opportunities as well as in rising standards of living.

In spite of its distributive imperfections, this material achievement has great humanistic value. Within the United States, and other developed nations, those who were previously marginalized by poverty and discrimination are experiencing a new sense of comfort and self-esteem. The dignity of work is affirmed, and the quality of labor is enhanced by the skills acquired in order to properly operate the new technologies . All this is to the good. And the demand for greater equality will make things better. Yet there is a darker side to the whole thrust toward material well-being that very few are willing to acknowledge.

If human dignity remains the standard, one must be willing to entertain the possibility that the changes are not entirely advantageous to either society as a whole or to the individual. Consider, for example, what has happened to the life of the mind. In the constitutional order, freedom of thought is a central value, yet the fullness of the ideal is rarely pursued. As the masses come into their own, they accelerate the homogenization of thought and feeling that is required by the interest in an expanding prosperity. In the circulation of ideas, the lowest common denominator tends to become the measure of meaning.

Technology affects the inward dispositions as well as the external circumstances of the many. The pursuit of noble ends is ignored as individuals become entangled in whatever is immediately practical and efficient. The actualities of the mundane replace faith in the invisible. As a result, any higher aspirations that might exist in the soul are deprived of concrete significance.

Some contend that the emergence of mass society evidences a decline in the biological quality of the human race. That proposition is debatable, yet it is obvious that many are content with their being of average ability. They know that remaining as they are they can obtain most of what they want. They are unwilling to develop their reason or their imaginative sensibilities beyond what is required for them to participate in the established routines of gainful employment or to experience a more refined enjoyment of the existing materialistic culture. [211].

The ordinary individual prefers bondage with ease to the strenuous pursuit of intellectual and personal freedom. As he becomes passive before the powers of industry and finance, he is also flattered by a popular culture whose offerings appeal to his emotional need to reduce the distance between thought and reality. At the same time that he is increasing his operational competence, the mass media is diverting his attention from deeper levels of reflection that, if pursued, might lead him to call into question the reasonableness of the established order.

The shift in the center of social gravity from the few to the many also modifies standards of accomplishment. The enlargement of social opportunities creates new prospects for self-fulfillment, but it also has made it possible for ordinary individuals, lacking distinctive talent, to gain positions of power and influence in every aspect of social life. Mediocrity is implicitly accepted .In spite of the rhetoric of excellence, there is no general expectation of personal growth and development.

The depth and quality of human relations has been adversely affected by the coming of mass society. Since utility takes precedence, individuals must relate to each other as embodiments of social functions rather than as distinctive personalities. The uniqueness cherished by William James is eclipsed. Most prize conformity and , being insecure, they are uncomfortable with difference. Individual independence of thought or action is looked upon as being socially divisive. [212].

In Royce's social idealism, the ability of individuals to communicate meaningfully with one another, in matters of difference as well as similarity, was considered to be essential to the creation of a civilized community. But as technology expands, the universe of substantial discourse contracts. Given the commercial imperatives of modern mass communication, thoughtful dialogue is replaced by a proliferation of words and symbols that are designed to manipulate the emotions rather than appeal to rational thought. Liberty of expression becomes a right to mislead. The hope of those in power is that a targeted audience will accept as self -evident something about which it would be more reasonable to suspend judgment. [213].

Corruption of language is found most prominently in the mass media, for it is there that the masses can most fully satisfy their appetite for distraction and superficial understanding. But the abuse of communication is a problem of the general culture. The use of words and symbols to nullify the distinction between truth and falsity can be found in literature and academic discourse as well as in newspapers and on television.

The expressive disposition to flatter or gain influence can be found wherever the mass mentality is operative. The mind -set of mass humanity is hermetic. Closed in upon itself, it concentrates upon a limited number of ideas that it is prepared to defend with great emotional force. At the same time, it resists any mode of thought that might endanger its unreflective self-confidence.

The fact that all have an axe to grind even influences higher education. Traditionally, universities were expected to have an unbiased openness to ideas. Intellectual vigor and independence set them apart from other forms of association. Increasingly, however, the integrity of speculative thought is sacrificed to some political passion. The academy becomes a venue for the use of language to chastise, or to intimate, those whose minds do not conform to prevailing political opinion. [214].

Walt Whitman was aware of the leveling of discourse that would accompany the development of mass society, but he hoped that a 'high average' of vibrant men and women would set the tone of the national character. He also insisted that collective tendencies had to be offset by a renewed sense of personal fulfillment. Whitman could not have anticipated the way that the rise of mass society would upset the fragile balance between equality and liberty. Nor could he have foreseen the antagonism that would develop between those who prefer the standardizations of common life and those who struggle to preserve a sense of personal distinction.

Most have no taste for the uncertainties that accompany the quest for a unique existence. They are more at ease with what is common, or can be expressed in some numerical formula. The great mass of men and women would rather be obedient followers than grow, within themselves, through the advancement of their own skill and daring. The general drift of the culture is toward a sameness that mirrors the monotony that is essential to the smooth functioning of the economy.

Although the individual may insist upon his privacy , he does not value solitude. He has an intense need to be something other than he is when he is isolated. Consequently, he looks for some corporate form of association that will provide him with social status. Adherence to the group relieves the individual of the burden of thinking for himself , as well as the need for personal moral decisions. Away from work, self-esteem may be sought through the images provided by television or by the adoption of the symbols of some celebrity or team that provide an emotional substitute for who he is by right of his own existence. [215].

These transitions from an individualistic to a collective way of life were anticipated by some of the philosophers whose works we have already examined. With some reservations, Royce welcomed the increase in interdependence that accompanied industrial development. To his mind, socialization would arouse deeper moral possibilities for the individual who aspires to live the ethical life. Group existence was to be inwardly sustained by personal loyalty and love. In reality, however, the social ethic does not depend upon individual devotion to maintain its normative power . As the tendencies towards cohesion accelerate, the social whole becomes of greater importance than the personal existence of any of its members. An unthinking attachment to the group, and its purposes, takes precedence over that deliberate allegiance that Royce identified as the summit of the ethical life In a mass technological society, there is less need for the subjective and free adherence of the individual will. The system seems to run itself. [216].

For William James, as for Emerson, the importance of the individual was not determined by his relation to the social world. Those who aspired to a full and independent existence could not be confined to the mundane. There was an eternal quality to their personal ends. Challenging the conventional opinion that none were distinguished, James insisted that everyone was irreplaceable. [217].

Although James saw society as a vast, undifferentiated desert that must be fertilized by individual initiative, he also taught that the creative individual should assert his own convictions in a way that makes genuine connections with others who are different from himself. For James, all ultimate realities-- those of time as well as those of eternity-- must be expressed as relations of one person to another. Unfortunately, the idea that individuals could be distinctive as well as interrelated has not withstood the pressures towards collective life.

In spite of his affirmations of the advantages of society , Royce had apprehensions that were similar to those of James. Royce was especially concerned about the pressures towards conformity that were being promoted by the media of his time. He also recognized the rise of a crowd psychology through which excitable multitudes were subject to the manipulative forces of commercial and political demagoguery. In his opinion - which was formed before the appearance of television - the trivialization of the mind was leading the nation into a new kind of servility. All were becoming the servants of powers too strong for them to resist and swept along by events too complicated for them to understand.

The solution to the force of conformity that Royce advocated was an interesting mix of ethics and geography. Continental collectivism was the disease; regional renewal was the remedy. To avoid the contamination of mass opinion, the individual should bring his self -consciousness into alignment with some particular part of the country. An attachment to a specific place could, according to Royce, relieve the sense of homelessness that was spreading across the nation. For the individual to experience distinctive possibilities, he should become more deeply connected to wherever he spends most of his life. As an active participant in a community with unique ideals and customs , the individual would find an enrichment that surpassed the more inclusive, but bland sense of togetherness promoted by the mass media. [218].

The provincialism advocated by Royce reflects the general truth that an authentic human life can only be fully lived by way of a deep engagement with a limited, but distinctive community. But the impersonal nature of mass society creates needs for intimacy whose value is more dubious. Royce could not have foreseen how small social structures would develop that lacked any geographical anchorage. The multiplication of communications technologies illustrates the difficulty. Vast numbers of "media communities" have been created through the Internet . These cater to narrow interests and provide the individual with the opportunity to reinforce his egocentric values.They also allow him to avoid the actual company of others. Such micro-grouping validates the individual in a limited circle of virtual encounters while they protect him from the dissimilarities inherent in more inclusive, and realistic, social arrangements. [219].

Dewey agreed with Royce on the humanistic dangers of mass society, but he thought that proper education would draw the masses into the wider encounters that are necessary to the solution of public issues. If trained in critical analysis as children , the masses would be intelligent problem -solvers as adults. The theory was inspired by realities. At the time of Dewey's maturity, the major social problem was the Great Depression. Dewey was confident that if the people acted cooperatively they would master the economic crisis. Unsatisfactory situations could be redesigned in such a way that the reasonableness of the solutions proposed would solicit the consent of all concerned. [220].

Dewey insisted, over and over again, that liberty cannot flourish in detachment from association. He recognized the way that gross materialism was destroying the spiritual values of personal life, but he rejected the idea that general improvement was dependent upon the antecedent renewal of the individual life. To Dewey, the restoration of any form of individualism was divisive, even if it included social responsibility as an aspect of personal flourishing. [221].

In Dewey's social philosophy the individual can only be fulfilled when the dominant energies of the larger democratic community become as essential part of his mental and moral outlook. The pursuit of public ends and the realization of communal values demanded that the externalities of society be admitted into the inner world of sentiment and affection. The internalization of corporate ways of thinking would eventually replace the fruitless search for private meaning.

Transformation would occur when the individual grew to the point where he could harmonize his subjective feelings with the objective conditions of his existence. Having once thought of liberty as a license for unlimited acquisition, the reformed person would work with the community to assure a more equitable distribution of material and cultural goods. Dewey had faith that with everyone sharing in the basic values of education, opportunity , and enjoyment, a common social satisfaction would start to outweigh solipsistic dreams of independent fulfillment. [222].

Dewey did not neglect the value of personal initiative. He recognized that those whose personal interests were constrained by the forces of social democracy might be tempted to retreat. Dewey reminded them that the situations in which they found themselves were, although unavoidable, not permanent. The conditions of coexistence are problematic and they can be changed. As human aspirations evolve, what is established is bound to be judged to be unsatisfactory. Frustration might be expressed by solitary protest, but Dewey believed that the better course was for the individual to join with others to intelligently frame better outcomes.

Although the provisional nature of social arrangements was essential to Dewey's understanding of democracy, he was equally committed to the view that change should not be directed by any higher order of values. Nor should it come about because of pressure from any spiritual institution. Social realities must be developed according to their own intrinsic potentials. For Dewey, all values were part of human experience and nothing of importance could be determined outside of that experience. [223].

According to Dewey, the meaning of truth was inseparable from the consequences of action. .The premise reflects his insight into how human association shares in the organic quality of all forms of evolution. But on the plane of moral reflection the idea is unpersuasive. It ignores the fundamental conflict between power and authority. Without standards that to some degree transcend experience, one cannot reasonably decide if a particular outcome is morally legitimate or just practically effective. Nor is there any basis for distinguishing between just and unjust pressures to conform. By reducing knowing to doing, Dewey avoids the distinctions between thought and action that empower the individual to make independent judgments of right and wrong . They prevent him from deciding between what is righteous and what is merely useful. Dewey affirms a working intelligence through the refinement of logical methods of disciplined and critical inquiry. But as practical rationality is enhanced, the power and range of reason, in itself, is diminished. It becomes simply one item in the operations performed by individuals as they try to make a satisfactory adjustment to their changing social environment. Left to its own resources, the practical intelligence at the heart of Dewey's philosophy becomes, unwittingly, the servant of the will to power. [224].

Dewey's social pragmatism marvelously advances the accomplishment of immediate ends. But it is incapable of directing the will to more inclusive ways of knowing that can, at least indirectly, positively influence the course of practical life. Like the science that it imitates, this philosophy of the mundane eliminates all consideration of higher purposes or causation. As a result, it does not grasp the possibilities of living well or living better that are the aims of any civilization . [225].

The widespread use of practical intelligence was expected to transform de facto interdependence into authentic community. But like Comte, whom he admired, Dewey would only allow the masses to possess that degree of inductive understanding needed for them to function efficiently as workers and as citizens. Fatally, Dewey assumed that the human spirit would flourish once it made the methods of science its own. However, like Royce and James, Dewey underestimated the forces that would make the nation a mass society. The conception of the rational at the heart of his philosophy is weaker than the powers of leveling and conformity with which it must contend. [226].

The resources of reason in the general culture are not wide or deep enough to counterbalance the relentless powers of a technologically driven mass society. The individual is offered unlimited opportunities , but his distinctive existence is no longer recognized . As the individual becomes increasingly assimilated to a world of objects, he loses his sense of inner being. He is also unable to see the fully human reality of others whose fate is no different from his own. [227].

The development of technology testifies to the abstract greatness of human creativity, but it has not led to the creation of a higher civilization. Material advantages become accessible to all, but our hopes for a reconciliation of personal desire with common destiny have been disappointed. As we begin a new century, we may finally be willing to recognize that neither the individual, or the community, is perfectible from within. Once those unpleasant truths take hold, we may then have the wisdom to reconsider not only the balance between the one and the many, but also that deeper relationship between the divine and the human to which our ancestors were so faithfully committed.

CHAPTER FIVE

Toward a New Christian Humanism

Religion and Democracy

Early in his career, John Dewey struggled with the apparent antithesis between religious faith and the world of experienced reality. He concluded that traditional Christianity must accommodate itself to the scientific progress and democratic aspirations of modern life. While he reached these decisions on his own initiative, they were deeply rooted in post- Edwardian theology.

The Unitarians had begun to close the gap between the dogma of Creation and the realities of human nature. They thought of the relation between God and man in terms of one personality with another; the qualities that distinguished them being more a matter of degree than of kind. The hope was for a new solidarity between the divine and the human that would assure a fulfilling future here on earth. Other theologians were entranced by the idea of historical progress. They began to look for signs of ultimate value which were not attributable to the Christian belief in the Redemption. High Calvinism had rejoiced in God's vindictive justice, but the newer currents of thought believed that the Supreme Being took delight in human happiness. [228].

There was also an attempt to eliminate the distinction between grace and nature. Channing and his followers had affirmed the basic moral goodness of the individual, and others were gaining deeper insights into the freedom of the will. There was a growing awareness that accountability depended upon real options of choice. Although there was little thought of absolute autonomy, most were convinced that the individual had a greater capacity for self-determination than orthodoxy was willing to admit.

During the last half of the nineteenth century, attention was directed more to the religious significance of social life than to questions of individual destiny. The Darwinian discoveries, as elevated by German Idealism, saw the fundamental issues of being human as turning upon interdependent, contingent relationships. Everyone had to face his or her problematic situation in a social environment that was becoming the modern form of the natural world. Social solidarity was in the air and amateur theologians, such as the senior Henry James, were trying to inject a divine element into the communal developments. [229].

Dewey welcomed the innovations that rejected any distinction between nature and humanity, and he was attracted to the proclamations of the social gospel. But philosophy was his primary interest. Studying the works of Leibniz, Dewey came to understand the importance of interconnected activities. He was also drawn to Hegel's insights into the social dynamics of antagonism and reconciliation. While he was careful to separate his own philosophical position from the collectivist implications of Hegelianism, Dewey hoped to complete Hegel's metaphysical effort to transfer the understanding of human destiny from a transcendental, to an immanent, perspective. Dewey would try to tie ideal values to the actualities of social interdependence. [230].

Just as the personal and the communal could not be completely separated, neither, in Dewey's mind, should there be any alienation between God and man. But reunion would not be found in the pursuit of absolutes. For Dewey, experience was the new ultimate. Consequently, final intelligibility was not manifest in the contemplation of a priori being, but in the observation of everyday existence. Throughout his long life, Dewey struggled to overcome the subordination of the temporal to any higher realities. To reconcile Christianity and humanism, he expanded the idea of Revelation to encompass all the diverse meanings of life that were unfolded in the course of history. Dewey wanted to expand the range of human cognition beyond the confines imposed by religious doctrine And, since the Kingdom of God is a call to spiritual brotherhood, he thought that the fraternal possibilities must not be restricted to the boundaries of formal religious association. [231].

To Dewey's mind, religion had for too long been thought of as something that illuminates those concerned with their soul's salvation. When an individual is preoccupied with a future life, he loses interest in the life that he is actually experiencing. Dewey wanted Christianity to overcome this distancing of spiritual interest from reality by drawing the believer's attention to the social dimensions of existence and the responsibilities for the good of others that it entails. [232].

Dewey's personal experiences did not give him reason to hope that the Christian Churches would welcome the new epiphany of life on earth. It seemed to him that institutional religion did not want to have anything more than a tentative and superficial relationship with the emerging democratic society. The difficulty, as Dewey saw it, was that the established faiths could not accept this world on its own terms. Even worse, they were determined to reduplicate in time values that they thought had a transcendental source. Moreover, he felt that those who think of themselves as being religious look upon human interdependence as either a source of evil or nothing more than a means to their eternal destiny. [233]..

As Dewey gradually withdrew from formal religious affiliation, he developed a hostility towards all modes of religious doctrine that looked for meaning beyond what is experienced. In the spirit of Whitman, Dewey placed his faith in the flourishing of Democracy. He thought that he would find the criterion of truth, and the decisive standards of conduct, within the shared activities of those who are devoted to the cause of liberty, equality, and fraternity. [234].

A shift to the secular realities would put an end to the dominance that the Christian churches had exercised over human culture. The transformation would be personal as well as institutional. Prescientific medievalism had fixed the dramatic center of existence in the ultimate destiny of the individual soul, and this approach to the meaning of life had been sustained by the obedience of frightened men. Now, as fear of final retribution recedes, Dewey expected that a preference for public values would take precedence in the minds of men over any concerns they might have with personal salvation.

The demands made by religious doctrine must be tested by their consequences for human well-being. Dewey was sure that the methods of pragmatic verification coincide with basic political principles. According to these empirical tests, the traditional teachings could not be reconciled with democratic ideals of tolerance and diversity. They also did not meet the standards of egalitarian satisfaction, because they presumed to provide a complete understanding of the vagaries of human life. By contrast, the vitality of a democratic community depends upon the circulation of a plurality of meanings that arise, under contingent circumstances, from diverse and incompatible points of view. [235].

Dewey also believed that the distinction between good and evil that is essential to the moral mission of Christianity is also incompatible with the objectives of a democratic society. He honestly thought that, in its uncompromising form, the distinction is diabolical. An insistence upon the difference between right and wrong was not only intolerant; it also destroyed the consensus that is the foundation of social unity and peace. [236].

The self -centeredness connected with the idea of sin has no place in a sociological understanding of the human condition. For Jonathan Edwards, the depths of depravity were revealed through a study of the motives for action. For Dewey, the causes of social troubles were to be found in an objective examination of pre -existing conditions.

Although Dewey resisted the doctrinal intrusions of established religion, he did not want democracy to be nothing more than a secular humanism. William James had taught him that an interest in religion plays a significant role in the formation of the human personality. This affirmation resonated with Dewey's hope that life in association could develop in a way that reconciled the ideal and the actual. The inclination towards the absolute was also politically useful, even if could not mean, as Royce had hoped, that God would be identified with the doings of finite wills. Dewey's expectation was more modest. He thought that if citizens would approach the collaborative projects of common life with a deep faith both they, and community, would flourish. Dewey wanted to encourage a religious attitude toward the concerns of public life. While he realized that such a disposition might be influenced by doctrinal factors, Dewey believed that a religious interest in temporal affairs is more likely to arise out of the experience itself. For him, what one does in collaboration with others is a good that does not depend upon anything outside of itself.

James had defended the power of the will to modify social conditions that it found to be offensive to its own ideals. Dewey distanced himself from that conception of action. In his social psychology, the individual does not unify himself by his own subjective determination. Rather, the self finds meaning when it is directed beyond itself to all the natural and social realities that it encounters . These must be integrated into the imagination . According to Dewey, once they are brought together they can form the basis of a modern religious sensibility. When we reconcile ourselves with our world, our emotions are no longer suspended between heaven and earth. Now they are supported by inclusive ends, drawn from experience. Such integration of the self and the temporal enriches our understanding of what it means to be religious. [237].

Dewey's conception of a religious approach to life took account of much more than was conventionally understood as a 'moral' outlook. An authentic spirituality of the mundane would be actively engaged with all that was happening in a changing world. To Dewey's way of thinking, anyone who was truly religious would be alive to all of the positive values that were arising out of the scientific, cultural, and political activities of the expanding democratic society. [238].

The flourishing of democracy requires unities of action within a pluralistic society. Dewey realized that such a gathering must have a durable emotional base. Under the circumstances of divergence, cohesion can occur only through the constant integration of ideals within the minds of those who do not share a single view of ultimate ends. Still, the pressure for some ultimate anchorage persists. Dewey tried to express a new idea of supreme reality that would not only overcome the dualism of the divine and the human, but would also protect Democracy from an aggressive atheism.

Even though religion and atheism were antagonistic, they shared the view that man can never find ultimate meaning within temporal existence. To contend against this strange alliance between belief and unbelief, Dewey suggested that a religious attitude--as distinguished from adherence to a religion-- was indispensable. The one who gives his allegiance to Democracy needs to have some sense of final support for his efforts. According to Dewey, as one assimilates the ideals of civic friendship he is not, as Royce thought, being loyal to himself; he is becoming attached to all the various aspects of truth and beauty that are the accomplishments of a vibrant civilization.

To participate in a meaningful way in the accomplishments of democracy, it is important that the citizen not understand himself in any mechanical or servile way. But he should not feel that his intrinsic dignity is tied to some supernatural source. Dewey would remind him that what he is to be will not be found within the depths of his soul, but from what he does as he becomes more aware of his connection to society [239].

For social activity to be religiously inspired in the manner recommended by Dewey, it must reflect a passion for social justice. Like Theodore Parker, Dewey had an acute sense of the injustice that occurs whenever the lives of many are subject to the selfishness of the few. The 'Old Adam' was still at work in the minds of those who tried to evade the need to submit their private desires to a common interest. By avoiding their social responsibilities, he pointed out, the rich deprive the masses of the essentials of a dignified existence. In Dewey's moral perspective, the struggle against this oppression has to do with time, rather than eternity. It concerns the urgent interests of daily life, rather than the remoter values of the religious traditions. [240].

The pursuit of justice leads to a new sense of historical finalities . For Dewey, the modern individual can gain a better idea of God than he received from the Christian tradition once he discovers the ultimate values that lie within the interstices of social experience. Then, a spirituality will be nurtured by a piety toward the actual. Love of neighbor was the one Christian ideal to which Dewey remained sincerely attached throughout his life. He seemed to believe that if the passion for social righteousness gained priority over the desire for personal sanctity, the full meaning of the Reformation would become apparent in the daily life of the democratic society. But what Dewey saw as progress, would be interpreted as a falling back by many within the Protestant community.

Dewey's reconstruction of Christianity would have saddened Jonathan Edwards. The great Puritan theologian thought that there could be no meaningful brotherhood among men unless it was secured by the antecedent, and paramount, love of God. Love of neighbor was, of course, an essential part of the Christian life, but it depended absolutely upon the higher allegiance. Edwards was certain that no one could generate a deep and lasting fraternity by his own efforts. It was impossible to bring the Kingdom of God to earth unless the sovereignty of the Divine was first acknowledged. The theology endorsed the active life, but only in subordination to the will of the Creator and the demands made upon the soul by the coming of the reign of Christ. Without this orientation, love of man remains a form of self -love, albeit on a large scale. In addition, a concern for the welfare of others can be quite as well an expression of the will to power as an outpouring of Christian charity. [241].

Adherence to Divine Sovereignty was a matter of hope as well as memory. American Protestantism looked back to the Revelation of God in Christ and forward to the final redemption in grace. Its. premise was the freedom of God, rather than the liberty of man. In the dialectic of the divine and the human, all the initiative came from above. But while dogma focused upon divine reality, in the order of experience the kingdom being proclaimed was as much one of darkness as of light. The central teachings were those of Predestination and the natural depravity of man. Especially in its Calvinist form, God was conceived as being an angry deity, always threatening his creation with destruction. In addition, orthodoxy took a hostile, or indifferent attitude towards human independence, and preached no confidence in anything that exists this side of eternity. [242].

As the nineteenth century progressed, American Protestantism entered into a liberal phase. It began to look upon historical experience as being as much a sign of man's goodness as it was proof of his propensity toward evil. These changes affected the general culture as much as they influenced social philosophers such as John Dewey. The divine was becoming one with social experience. Excessive individualism was being replaced by social solidarity. The Social Gospel movement took advantage of the insights of the rising social sciences that recorded the exploitation of human labor by the expanding capitalism. As a result, Christian values were brought closer to the sufferings of those subject to the forces of industry. But these theological changes were also beginning to blur the distinction between the church and the world. Within the American consciousness there was a widespread conviction that all tradition should be swept aside so that we, as a people, could confront life on original terms. Hope for the future was no longer inspired by a remembrance of the Incarnation. The Protestant congregations had once thought of themselves as a chosen people with a unique spiritual mission. They were beginning to think that the land of promise had become the promised land. The realization of the Kingdom was becoming the time-bound belief in the superiority of the nation. [243]

Henry Adams understood what was happening more deeply than most of his contemporaries. As he expressed it, the Dynamo had replaced the Virgin as an object of veneration. The shift to American Supremacy that would eventually transform international relations was, for Adams, a form of self-worship expressed through the deification of American Democracy. The changes were a profound threat to Adams' sense of personal integrity. Unlike Royce, he could not affirm a creative tension between the individual and collective consciousness. Nor would he have been able to find subjective satisfaction in the social collaborations advocated by Dewey. In the world of Adams' experience, all the externalities were more powerful than himself. The genie was out of the bottle. Interrelatedness was ascendant and it was not consensual. Since there was no escape from the new Absolute symbolized by technological democracy, one had to make the necessary adjustments while witholding ultimate loyalty. All that remained for Adams was a reflective search for whatever unities that he might find within himself. [244]

Developments in the twentieth century both challenged and confirmed Adams' pessimism. There were heroic moments in battles abroad and in the conquest of discrimination at home. A wider circle of humanity was gaining access to the necessities of life and millions found fulfillment in the pursuit of the ordinary occupations of the economy. But, at the same time, there was a growing sense that life in common had an inauthentic quality that could not be reconciled with the search for personal identity. The more reflective could no longer identify the good with the goods. Nor were they satisfied with an instrumental pragmatism that satisfied the instinct for survival but frustrated their desires for a more complete understanding of themselves and of their world. More acutely than Henry Adams, they felt that they lacked the essential elements of personal self -possession.

Dewey was well aware of the adverse effects of corporate life upon the individual, but his mental outlook could not comprehend the deeper unsettling feelings. For him, the meaning of individual existence was not a matter of philosophical importance. Social impositions might be onerous, but they could be offset by collaborative acts that would endow the democratic ethos with a religious significance. Dewey could not appreciate the extent to which the forces of consolidation and conformity would deprive the social process of any decisive value for those concerned with who they were and where they were going. [245].

At the time of Dewey's death there were great expectations that democratic experience would provide a complete a fulfillment of all reasonable aspirations. By the time that the twentieth century drew to a close, the mood had changed. Sensitive individuals found themselves incapable of deep loyalty to the general community, nor did they appreciate the value of conjoined activities as much as Dewey had anticipated. A new division began to develop among the population at large. It was separating the mass who were satisfied with the prevailing social system from those who wished to preserve a meaningful sense of personal identity. The rebellious minority would resist the subordination of the individual to collective mediocrity . They would also refuse to allow the community to be a representative of the self. But the resistance was balanced by a resignation to the socialization of public life. They would no longer try to change conditions through the personal initiatives recommended by William James. The restructuring of society would be abandoned in favor of the intimacies of personal self-creation. The post-modern retreat would be different from the withdrawal of the Transcendentalists from conventional life. The new private man could not recognize the substantiality of his own existence. Now there was nothing of a timeless nature upon which the self could draw in its quest for authenticity. Contingency reigns. The self, like language and community, is a product of time and chance. [246].

As the consensus concerning the purposes of temporal existence begins to break down, there is no parallel effort to connect the self with any higher sense of being. The attempt to reconcile Christianity and humanism is exhausted and, as a result, there are no secure foundations from which the individual can bring a positive attitude to life in community. The resulting vacuum is filled with a psychological understanding of human nature that only reinforces the existential loneliness.

With the advance of technological civilization , the belief that human life is subject to a divine sovereignty loses its influence over individual life. But the oversight of a Superego persists. The State exercises control over its citizens by exaggerating their feelings of insecurity, while the mass media strive to orient the life of the masses around the imperatives of production and consumption. Separately or conjoined, these two forces attempt to discourage the ego's illusion that its destiny is in its own hands. The self , having eluded transcendental authority, remains in the hands of something more powerful than itself. [247].

Those who are trying to retreat from the artificial construction of social reality cling to the Freudian belief that even as the ego is repressed by external forces, it can still take charge of itself. This renewal of the self is not marked by a return to a metaphysically sublime will, nor does it involve a return to the sacred . Ironically, the strengthening of individual existence is expected to arise out of the revelation of the irrational. The probing of the unconscious lays bare the random desires that ferment deep within the individual psyche. The adherence to principle that had distinguished Royce's moral philosophy is discredited. Idealization is seen as a mask that covers a previous trauma. As the psychological understanding of individual life becomes more prevalent, the standards of the rational mind are discounted. Many come to believe that general understanding of what is reasonable is unnecessary and dangerous. . As personal existence becomes autobiographical, the only imperative is to learn to cope with, and overcome, one's past experiences. The self that is trying to escape the pressures of mass society is encouraged to cultivate itself and to do so, as far as possible, in isolation from the crowd. A narrow circle of family and friends becomes the limits of meaningful association. The reconstructed self does not oppress others, and he has a genuine sympathy for those who suffer. But he has no desire for constructive engagement with any wider society, whether it be of a secular, or religious, nature. [248].

Rethinking Human Nature

The making of the idiosyncratic the measure of meaningful life obstructs the realization of Dewey's ideal of fulfillment through association. It has also diverted our attention from some of the more elevated conceptions of personality that are an important part of our cultural history. For example, the shrinking of the range of self development bears little relation to Whitman's understanding of the complete individual, who shapes himself, or herself, into a significant separate whole while still being an active member of democratic society.

The new introspection does have some attributes of an Emersonian individualism, especially in its contempt for the crowd, but it lacks the master's comprehension of the roots of personal independence. The Sage of Concord took contingency as seriously as any contemporary thinker, but he was also aware of deeper powers. For Emerson, the soul was not a compensation for the failures of living, but a life in itself. Only it really is, because it has within itself the original source of authentic being. [249].

The decline of interest in the fate of the individual soul began, oddly enough, with the Puritans. Their great theologian, Jonathan Edwards, insisted that everyone is ultimately accountable to a severe final judgment, but he was so impressed with the sovereignty of God that he was unable to attribute stable qualities to individual human existence. This attitude was reinforced in the devotional life of the colonial period. Calvinist conceptions of the saved soul did not allow for the independent value of the distinct human being. Like the rest of the Reformation, Puritanism shifted the ground of personal identity from institutions to the individual, but it also rejected the humanists' affirmation of the primacy of the singular person. For the reformers, the only identity worth having was one that the individual could not attain by his own power. Authentic life was to be achieved through submission to a transcendental absolute. The objective was to internalize faith in a way that reproduced within the individual the life of the Saviour. In that context, selfhood was a condition to be overcome rather than cultivated. [250].

As the New England theocracy began to lose its preeminence, its basic conviction that the self was detestable continued to influence the development of American thought. Particularly hateful were the antisocial tendencies rooted in individualism. Like his Presbyterian ancestors, the senior Henry James thought that the essential moral question was one of salvation rather than self-development, but for him salvation would not come through a return, in faith and humility, to a transcendent and remote deity. Society was to be the redeemed form of man. To become truly human, the self would have to give up its egocentric pride and identify itself with a common destiny. For reformation to occur, the once sinful self must become a social being . He must also understand that humanity en masse was to be the venue for the reconciliation of God and man. [251]..

While respectful of his father's ideas, William James resisted the paternal attempt to subsume personal identity into the undistinguished lump of humanity. As we have seen, William sought to defend the unrelated freedom of the real me from the collectivist tendencies of his time. However, he was not able to anchor his psychological existentialism upon any unshakable foundations. William James recognized the traditional understanding of the human soul, and he respected the related belief that personal identity was a matter of immortal importance. But James thought that the principle of substantiality was satisfied by the discovery that an internal power enables us to bring together our particular perceptual experiences. Beyond that, it was for each individual to decide what he thinks of himself and of his world. [252].

For James, the essence of the individual life consists of the unique, and voluntary, responses that each makes to his or her particular situation. Josiah Royce tried to refine that recognition of the value of the individual will by probing the depths of self-consciousness. His objective was the unity of personal and universal experience. But Royce, like James, excluded the existence of a substantial soul from his philosophy. Royce assumed that the final expression of the self might be found in a different form of consciousness, but he thought it was enough, for the purposes of living, to identify the self as part of the Selfhood of the human race. In Royce's idealism, the task was to integrate self-consciousness with social consciousness in a way that preserved the individual's desire for personal meaning. Social communication would help him move past the transitory aspects of his isolated self-awareness. Transactions with others would be mutually enriching, but they would acquire a special, and inaccessible, significance within the separate self. Through his encounters with others, as well as with the surrounding universe, the single one would unite his individuality with the Absolute that is God. [253].

Royce tried to make the particular human being significant by inflating the value of the individual will. Unfortunately, this invocation of subjective infinitude was no match for an emerging way of knowing that was equally determined to objectify the self. The rising social sciences would not interpret the communications of common life in terms of individual destiny, nor would they permit the encounters of diverse selves to be taken as opportunities for separate fulfillment. Social intercourse was becoming the means of making the individual conform to the interests of that 'generalized other' that constituted the substance of the whole community. Ironically, the individualistic and collectivist perspectives had a common premise. Socialization denied the value of personal independence but, like its opposite, it was determined to find humanistic meaning in a way that takes no account of the substantiality of the human soul. The positions strangely converge. For those who favored society, as well as those who defended the individual, the self had no ontological status.

[254].

With the ascendancy of the social sciences, those who favored subjectivity began to withdraw their deeper feelings from the arena of organized life. Like William James, they would not allow their quest for personal fulfillment to be determined by external forces, but, unlike James, they did not feel responsible for the unfinished condition of the universe. For such a sensibility, as we have noted, freedom is not to be found in acts of collaboration with others, especially when others' interests are different from one's own. As social conformity becomes more and more abhorrent, the sense of self-determination begins to form itself into the defiant attitude of the *ego contra mundum*. [255].

In this new understanding of self-realization, the individual is not obliged, in conscience, to choose one way or another of directing the course of his existence. Creating meanings at the pleasure of his freedom, he becomes the cause of who he is. His actions have no permanent register, because there is no inner depth, or unity, to cultivate. But as we have seen, at an earlier time in our history those who pursued an independent path had a genuine confidence in their own inner being. They also had a firm sense of objective value. Although the Transcendentalists detached themselves from Puritanism, they retained its sense of the importance of moral righteousness. For them, as for their ancestors, ideals were superior to empirical facts. They also stood by the principle that what is wrong in itself cannot, for practical reasons, be turned into a good. [256].

Earlier American humanists believed that the center of their souls needed external support, but they would not relieve their inner indigence by drawing upon the resources of organized religion. Established beliefs provided no solace because, in addition to being joyless, they paid too much attention to the end of time. The solution was a form of pantheism. The transcendentalists thought of themselves as becoming divine, but the ascent would be within the confines of this world. The aim was to create a natural man who was pure of heart. Henry Thoreau was their representative figure. Thoreau called upon his fellow men to reject materialism and rejuvenate themselves through an immersion in the natural world. Humanity would be elevated by the reenactment within the soul of the rhythms of death and renewal that are manifested in the changes of the seasons. According to Thoreau, if man would only get in touch with the vast resources of nature, the burdens of economic necessity would be lifted and they would begin to experience life in its fullness. [257].

Nature was enriching, but its allurements were ambiguous. Some thought that they could enjoy the sensate world with an innocence similar to Adam before the Fall. Emerson was aware of the dangers of such enthusiasm, but his ardent desire for spiritual perfection led him toward an absorption of the conscious self in a cosmic whole. The impersonal ideals that he relentlessly pursued began to engulf the very self-identity that he hoped to preserve. [258].

Like the transcendentalists, Emerson thought that truth had its origins in the depths of the soul. It is there that one perceives the elements of absolute being. Emerson also thought that personal character was substantially complete from the beginning of individual existence. Since who he was did not depend upon experience, he could remain as far as possible from the actual course of common life. Others, such as Hawthorne, took a different sounding and realized how much our actions among our fellow men and women make us what we are. But it was Herman Melville who made the decisive shift away from the transcendentalist point of view.In his mature novels, Melville delineated the character of the idealist and imaginatively identified the tragedies that await those who are foolish enough to pursue absolute ends. Such individuals excuse themselves from any common understanding of the human condition. They also hate the inscrutable laws of the universe that seem to allow evil men to turn human possibilities to ignoble ends. As dissatisfaction intensifies, the idealist begins to lose his psychological security. He finds himself afloat within himself. Overruling experience, he depends upon principles that displace prudence. As seen by Melville, such an individual cannot integrate the general aspects of a fulfilled life with qualities of personal character that might sustain such aspiration. [259].

Melville would sink his soul into an abyss, but it would be of man rather than of nature. In his imagination, humanity becomes the unplumbed strength that restores life to itself. This anthropocentric turn did not completely exclude a higher vision. In spite of his disappointments, Melville remained attracted to Christianity. He was particularly drawn to the personality of Jesus Christ, whom he saw as the supreme symbol of that which can never be completely defeated.

As Melville aged, he became more interested in the fate of humanity as it endures the trials of history. Acutely aware of the tragic dimension of life, he assumed that the contest between good and evil is an indecisive struggle that neutralizes the vitalities of human nature. His goal became serenity rather than salvation. Ahab, the central character in *Moby Dick* , abdicates the crown of his personality and becomes one with the physical forces of the universe. Melville renounces himself so that he could achieve organic solidarity with all other human beings. To his mind, this was the way to a more sorrowful, but more significant, life. The necessary yoke was the only alternative to a ruinous obsession with absolute ideals. Melville's essential message is that the meaning of life is to be found in man rather than in God. In extremity there is a faint hope of redemption, but the fundamental idea is that human reality is something that must be completely hammered out upon the anvil of time. History records the alternations between depravity and righteousness, and there is no escape from the inexorable ebb and flow of contingent being.[260].

The philosophy of Melville is honest and realistic, but it implies too much resignation to evil. In the past century, we were exposed to horrors that happen whenever men, like those who condemned Billy Budd, give their ultimate allegiance to the commands of other men. And more recent history has taught us that humanity cannot survive, much less flourish, without some perspectives upon the nature of life on earth that are not reducible to the will.

Within our culture, we have a need for the understanding of an ideal order of being that overlaps with, but is distinguishable from, that conceived by our transcendentalist traditions. We must recover a sense of moral life that values experience, but has principles that are not governed by contingencies. Such a philosophy must also reaffirm the great truths of the Christian tradition -- of Creation, the Fall, and Redemption -- and do so in a way that is not a threat to the fundamental integrity of the human being. To begin such a recovery, we shall explore what it means to be a person.

One cause of the confusion over the nature of the self is the doctrine of original sin that was developed within the Protestant Reformation. If one assumes, with the Puritans, that a deep and indelible depravity lies at the heart of human existence, it is impossible to appreciate the full nobility of what it means to be a distinct human being. Subsequent attempts to replace the idea of radical corruption with images of total innocence merely restate the problem rather than provide a solution. If we are to understand the nature of the human person , we must reexamine the premise of initial corruption, as well as the relation between God and man. However, philosophical considerations are of equal importance. The initial task is to make some meaningful distinctions between the different qualities of human existence, and to develop an understanding of these differences that calls forth a metaphysical, rather than a theological, mode of reflection. At this point it will be helpful to make some reference to the Catholic philosophical tradition. That venerable way of knowing makes a critical distinction between the individual and the person and, while doing so unambiguously, it does not treat the two aspects as completely separate realities. The basic idea is that every human being is an individual because of the material aspect of his, or her, existence, and a person because of the spiritual dimension. [261].

Much of the confusion surrounding the question of what it means to be a human being comes from a failure to recognize the coexistence of individuality and personality . For the materialist, humanity, like the rest of the cosmos, is composed of nothing more than empirical particles. From this perspective, the meaning of anything pertaining to the human can be determine exclusively by the methods of the natural sciences. For the idealist, to be human is to be essentially a spiritual being; one whose distinctiveness is revealed to introspection or to intuitive modes of thought. Neither the materialist, nor the idealist, sees that every human being has both spiritual and material dimensions. They also do not realize that both of these aspects must be taken into account if the nature of human existence is to be fully, and realistically, understood.

As an individual, every human being has an actuality that flows from the simple fact that he, or she, exists. In that sense, individuation is rooted in matter, and as such, it is subject to all the determinations of the physical and biological world. Generically, the individual self is a fragment of the human species. Through self -consciousness the individual is aware of the existence other human beings, but he cannot help expressing his unique reality in distinction from them. This elementary quality leads, on a natural plane, to a narrowing of the ego. Excluding from itself all that others are, the individual is prone to be anti-social. It is this aspect of individuality that the Senior James found to be so offensive, not only in its acquisitive expressions, but also because it failed to appreciate the positive good of human fellowship.

Individuality is also the basis of Royce's 'original sin' of social division. When self-understanding is, in this sense, individualistic, it is irresistibly ego-centric. The more his awareness of himself intensifies, the more the individual resists external pressures to conform to the normative order of society. The difficulty is that although the singular self wants to avoid the company of others, he has fundamental needs that can only be satisfied through association. At this level of common life, the good of society is nothing more than an aggregation of individual goods. Furthermore, whatever unities are achieved among the members of a group are always precarious. Multiplicity and dispersal are ever present dangers, and the potential fragmentation goes beyond the normal diversity that constitutes a healthy pluralism. Henry Adams saw with terrifying clarity that as material differences accelerate, all are left in their isolation to the mercy of those who possess technological and political power. [262]..

As we saw earlier in these reflections, tendencies towards selfish dispersal have been met by vigorous attempts to define the individual as an essentially social being. All of these efforts contain important insights into the importance of collaborative association , but the comprehension is imperfect. Such conceptions of society simply transfer the problematic of individual existence from the private to the public plane. Within the social group the individual, qua individual, is no different than he was in his independent state. His dignity may be politically affirmed, but for social and economic purposes he is a part, and nothing more than a part, of a larger and more meaningful whole. Deeper qualities that flow from the spiritual dimension of his unique being are irrelevant to the imperatives of practical life. Such restrictive views eventually lead to some form of dissociation. As the individual realizes that he is replaceable, he tries to escape the social totality.

Is the determination to have a substantial existence independent of group life necessarily anti-social? John Dewey obviously thought so. There was some truth in that view, because the desire to define oneself apart from others can be exacerbated by the evil that lurks within the recesses of every human heart. But resistance to absorption in society can also be based upon an authentic desire to be a person. In this respect, William James' rejection of his father's social humanism is of critical importance to an understanding of the complexity of what it means to be a human being.

William James' philosophy is generally understood to be a defense of 'individualism,' and in some respects it is, particularly in its emphasis upon existential diversity. But James also tried to protect the more profound dimensions of our shared existence. In his mature reflections, James tried to articulate the various elements of an effective liberty that not only resists prevailing power, but also tries to surpass itself in its thrust towards ultimate satisfaction. The project of James' life was in the direction of a fulfillment that preserved his unique existence. He wanted to assure that his being, and his perfection, were his own. He also wanted to be in touch with a higher power that could affirm his deepest longings. These two tendencies were not fully integrated within his psychic life. . While he recognized the existence of a moral order ordained by God, James was convinced that he must develop himself in a way that was intrinsic to himself. He would determine his own destiny , regardless of the consequences in time or for eternity. [263].

William James had a predominately emotional disposition. His intense subjectivity was nourished by his artistic inclinations and his deep-seated interest in human psychology. His inability to reconcile a radical inwardness with objective reality was noticed by friendly critics such as Peirce and Dewey, whose preferences were for external modes of scientific verification. But James' basic attitude raises the more interesting question whether one can understand what it means to be a person according to measures of comprehension that are essentially self-referential in nature. One of the characteristics of modern life is that its purposes are no longer determined by reference to a transcendent order of meaning . Freedom becomes a matter of unmediated self-direction. For some, this situation leads to self-indulgence as well as a relativistic attitude towards questions of ethics. But the subjective outlook is not entirely arbitrary. For being in touch with oneself is, of itself, a moral value. [264].

The dilemma for the Christian is that the authority of the human subject cannot be the sole standard of what is right and what is wrong. Each may have an original way of being, but cannot be the sole source of what guides his destiny. At the same time, however, one must be attracted to, and freely accept, the standards of the good and righteous life. If one is to be a person, and not just an individual, one must choose for oneself what one is to be. There is further complexity. If we rely entirely upon ourselves, we not only become socially isolated; we also lose touch with who we really are. If the desire for unconditional autonomy becomes the dominant motive for action, there is a turn toward selfishness that is also a turning away from reason. The rational becomes nothing more than a means for the realization of self-centered goals. The total effect is that the self relies wholly upon itself, and its imaginings, as motives for action. [265].

The desire for unconditional self-determination has various causes. Among them is the lingering influence of a Puritanism that, with its pessimism over human possibilities, stressed the impotence of the intellect. While asserting the absolute power of God, the theology disconnected the individual from any intermediate order of being that might be discerned by the powers of the mind. Morality was the expression of the will of the divine sovereign; it had nothing to do with the created order of existence. When the divine sanction failed, it was inevitable that the will of the individual would become the ultimate arbiter of good and evil.

In the Catholic tradition, the proper exercise of reason leads to an understanding of human nature that, in turn, governs the exercise of the will. But the Reformation theology assumed that human nature was ruined by the corruption of primal sin and that conviction led to a vacuum in the realm of being. Within that framework it is understandable why Emerson and the Transcendentalists were attracted to the enhancing qualities of the natural world . If they were to affirm their being fully, they had to find an alternative external source of personal enrichment. Those who rebelled against their Calvinist inheritance were not only attracted to the loveliness of the fields and skies of their New England; they were drawn to everything that existed before man acted upon it. This confidence in the restorative powers of the nature world was undermined by the ascendancy of science and technology. Then, when the source of being symbolized by nature lost its value, there was a deeper retreat into self-consciousness. Within our philosophical culture, this led to Royce's conception of a metaphysical ego that manifested the will's desire for absolute meaning. Both natural and human existence would be integrated within the wholesome power of reflexive self-consciousness. The ideal method elaborated by Royce had many admirable features, but in promoting the inflation of the will, his philosophy was unable to reach the foundations of personal decision. His humanism not only distorted the relation between reason and volition; more significantly, it could not properly account for the roots of action.

Self -consciousness brings to awareness all that the self has done, or suffered. While it is debatable how successfully such cognizance eludes the influence of the sub-conscious, the more important point is that experiencing oneself as the subject of one's actions is not the same as the action itself. Stated differently, doing is different from remembrance . Nor is it the same as the awareness of what might be. Making a choice involves something more than a movement in consciousness that is expressive of the will. When a person acts, elements of the good are involved that implicate the self, but the values being affirmed also have an independent existence. [266].

An adequate conception of the person acknowledges the operations of the self-conscious will, but also respects aspects of being that are extra-mental in their nature. In explicating these ontological qualities, the objective is to identify potentials of human nature that are simultaneously interior to each and the shared property of all. When seen in that light, the subjective and objective dimensions of what it means to be human become at least potentially reconcilable. Recognizing that the good does not originate with the self, one also affirms that the self, in its freedom, must assent to the values that come from beyond his own existence.

Catholic philosophical understanding affirms the external order of human nature, yet it respects the positive role of the human subject in the realization of that order. But it does not make either dimension an absolute. The dogma of Creation protects Catholic thought from making the subject completely autonomous, and it also protects the self from being engulfed by an external order of being. For this Christian theology, God is the ultimate cause of both human nature and personal existence.

The integration of philosophy with revelation was not feasible once the Protestant Reformation came into conflict with the humanism of the German Enlightenment. As Protestantism turned away from the natural law tradition, it sought to discover a supreme authority in the scriptural foundations of ethics. However, the humanists were anxious to avoid the subservience of the mind or will to any form of transcendence. To advance that goal, they attributed a primacy to reason. Leibniz, for example, respected the laws of human nature and celebrated the power of the human intellect to discern them, but he thought that this order revealed an ultimate structure of the universe that was binding upon God and man alike. The significance of this development may be seen by contrasting it with the Catholic philosophy , which holds that although human reason knows the natural law, it does not bring it into existence .The classical Catholic view also holds that the natural law is not a burden upon the autonomous subject. The reason is that the measure of the law is one of congeniality. The intellect sees as good what is consonant with human nature and it judges as evil what is not in harmony with that nature. That discernment is made through the ethical awareness of specific human beings. In other words, while Catholicism affirms the general range of the natural law , the good of the species is not its paramount objective. In light of the Last Judgment, only the particular person has a destiny that is of ultimate importance. Only a specific he, or she, can make choices that have eternal significance. [267].

Catholicism sees the natural law as something that enhances personal existence but insists that the dignity in question remains that of a created human being. It follows that although ethical decisions guided by reason incorporate an a-temporal good into the substance of one's being, they do not put the self in touch with the eternal. Nor are such choices immune from the distortions arising out of the subconscious or the dispositions of the heart. The essential problem of depravity remains. Here the balance of Catholicism is of great importance. The tradition holds to the conviction that at the core of human existence there is neither absolute corruption nor primal innocence. Rather, the teaching insists that a dramatic struggle between good and evil is constantly enacted within the soul of every human being. The outcome determines, for better or worse, what kind of person he, or she, shall be. [268].

According to the view that we are trying to explain, the person is formed by free decisions that reflect principles of reasonableness which are the property of all of humanity. It may be objected, however, that every human being makes himself by actions that express his or her uniqueness. The perception of originality inspired William James to defend the infinite value of each, and it is obvious that he was trying to protect that part of ourselves which is spiritual rather than material in nature. In this sense, 'individuality' may be thought of as having a deeper value than personality.The person is the abstract subject of juridical, or moral, rights and duties By contrast, individuality manifests, in a profound manner, all that distinguishes one human being from another. From this perspective, personality expresses what one has; individuality determines what one is. It would seem, therefore, that the distinction that we have attempted to draw between the person and the individual cannot be sustained at the most important levels of human existence [269].

The difficulty may be resolved by returning to the question of the existence of the human soul. As we have seen, various American philosophers have tried to comprehend the nature of the person in ways that avoid, or ignore, the traditional Christian view that every human being has an immortal soul. But excluding that premise from the effort to understand the core of our existence leads to a confusion over the substance of who we are. It is important, therefore, to have some knowledge of the deepest underpinnings of human identity, if the concepts of the person and the individual that we have been exploring are not to be hopelessly intertwined.

When the concept of the soul is introduced into reflections upon human existence, selfhood gains a deeper meaning. It now implies something that is not limited to the constraints of time, although, on the premise of Creation, it suggests something less than the particularization of an eternal will. The traditional view is that each human soul has an immortal quality that integrates the carnal and the spiritual dimensions of being human. The particular soul has a carnal aspect because it has a substantial relation to a particular body and it is spiritual because it is the inmost source of unity and freedom. This provides a deeper understanding of the somewhat contrasting ideas of personality and individuality.. The soul makes the human being something more than a composite of animality and reason. At a level deeper than the subconscious, it sustains the inner life and gives the person a principle of unity and development. The existence of the soul breaks the continuities of biological evolution, and gives the person a degree of self-possession that, in its orientation to the eternal, surpasses all the collective ends of humanity. Yet, as we shall see, such an elevation does not entitle the person to use its independence to avoid the sufferings of the world or to refuse to contribute to the positive well -being of the communities within which he shares both an eternal and temporal destiny. [270].

Societies Secular and Sacred

As an individual, the self is preoccupied with itself and with its own well-being. Societies that are based upon this tendency expand entitlements to acquisitions, emphasize rights of privacy, and, in general, seek to protect the individual from the intrusions, and the burdens, of others. Individualism has had a substantial influence upon political theory because it provides a practical way of minimizing social obligations while, at the same time, maximizing individual liberty. Competing visions of life in common exaggerate the importance of shared interests and attempt to reduce the range of personal freedom and initiative. In their extreme forms, the two positions express the opposition between liberalism and all forms of political totalitarianism. Some are certain of the final victory of the liberal ideal; yet, in spite of such expectations, collectivism remains a threat to all communities that as civil, as well as political, societies, must strike a balance between the polarities of the one and the many.

To gain a better understanding of the basic tensions of social existence, it will be well to pursue the distinction between the individual and the person, even though, as we have indicated, both aspects inhere in every human being. It may be said that the more a human being experiences himself as a person, the greater is the inclination toward substantial self-determination. As anyone becomes aware of his uniqueness, they resist being a fragment of the whole and start to develop the exclusive power that they have over themselves. The assertion of personal independence should not be confused with the willfulness that Royce identified as the source of social division. One who is beginning to be a person resists external impositions, but is not necessarily trying to make his own freedom an end in itself. Yet there will remain some distinction between the self and others. If a person is trying to determine for himself who he is, -- beyond what others tell him he should be-- he must set his own ends for himself. These particular purposes may not be the same as those of the surrounding society. Nor will they be limited to immediate or practical concerns. In the search for personal identity the most profound desire of the self is to relate itself to the transcendental realities of truth, beauty, and goodness. Moving in such a direction takes the person beyond the horizons of the common life. Depending primarily upon oneself, he or she struggles to becomes a whole that can face the ultimate absolute that is God. [271]

Self-determination is a matter of action as well as contemplation. An authentic person is someone who is seeking the experience of being good through the self-mastery of his passions and the positive assimilation of all that is valuable in the world that surrounds him. Unlike the individual, the person is not preoccupied with himself and his own well-being. Dewey feared that a substantial degree of personal independence meant withdrawal from the life of association. He did not understand how much personality requires external expression. The distinctiveness of the person lies in the interior growth of knowledge and love, but these qualities naturally overflow. They are meant to be shared with others who possess the same expansive powers. [272].

The dialogue between persons is most intense in situations of intimacy, but it reaches the widest, as well as the narrowest, experiences of community. In all phases of life, a person requires society because of his dignity as well as his need. One is dependent upon society for all the moral and cultural resources it can provide, but also needs the company of others because association gives each person an opportunity to manifest his own deeper nature. As an individual, the self is related to society in a dynamic of immersion and retreat; a person values his solitude, but he is prepared to sacrifice his comfort in order to contribute to all that constitutes the good of living together . To be willing to be fraternally generous , while at the same time retaining the integrity of self-possession, is an essential attribute of personality.

Persons know, however obscurely, that they subsists in a singular, but fragile existence. They may be tempted to renounce their specific identity so that the precarious selfhood may be secured within the immensity of some larger whole. For Emerson and the Transcendentalists, that larger whole was Nature. They looked to the natural world to reinforce their own uniqueness and simultaneously lessen their dependence upon human society. They did not understand the need that each person has for communion with others. Those who have an intense need for human companionship can make a comparable mistake. They are inclined to substitute a social identity for their own existence. As those who overvalue life in common are unwilling to assert their personal independence, they become absorbed by the life of the community. [273].

Striking a proper balance between singular and shared life is not easy. The difficulty is reflected in the mystery of personality , because it involves a subordination to, as well as the transcendence of, society. A person has a spiritual destiny that surpasses temporal existence, yet he remains subject to the common good of the actual communities that he inhabits. Thus, in any form of association, there is always some loss of independence. Private interests may be legitimately subject to public interests; private judgment to public decision. As a matter of legal justice, every persons owes many obligations to the community and, in extreme situations, may be called upon to sacrifice his life for the common security.

As societies become more interdependent, the status of the person tends to be expressed in terms of duties to the group. But in its deepest significance, what it means to be a person in society can be best understood in terms of rights. As morally comprehended, such entitlements transcend all ideological preferences. As persons, human beings are entitled to conditions of shared existence that are compatible with their dignity and enhance their freedom. The measure of the quality of any society is whether it ennobles, or degrades, human life. All depends upon whether those who compose community are treated as persons and not just as individuals. In a civilized society, access to goods and opportunities is not provided just to keep individuals functioning within the established social system. Distribution is governed by considerations of inherent human worth. Personal entitlement to the fundamentals of the good life is most evident in tangible matters such as employment, health care, and social security, but material well being, while indispensable, is not the sole standard of living well. The effort to enhance everything that is human touches all social policies that implicate the spirit, including the expansion of religious freedom, the pursuit of liberal education for all, and the moral tone of the general culture.

In our democracy, the concrete rights that one possesses are derived from the Constitution, as well as from legislative, administrative, and judicial modes of law-making. Some rights are considered to be inalienable. However, while there is a natural tendency to make essential rights part of the legal order, it would be a mistake to restrict the moral understanding of the rights of the person to what is legally enforceable. A deep sense of the ontological roots of personal entitlement can legitimately influence the development of the juridical order, but it is important to realize that what is at stake applies to all situations where personal integrity is threatened by some form of either civil or political power. If democracy is to be a society of persons and not just an aggregate of dispersed individuals, the higher ideal must influence all aspects of human interaction.

To be a person one must determine one's own destiny. The prerogative has public as well as private implications. Dewey prized liberty and despised conformity but he also feared that disunity produced by independent judgment might obstruct the formation of a general consensus. And while he respected dissent, he preferred that personal dissatisfaction with existing arrangements should be ameliorated through collaborative responses to problematic situations.

Dewey's insistence upon the necessity of cooperation to the success of democracy reflected a profound truth about the nature of the common life. However, he did not fully understand how strongly the personal dimension of co-existence must persists even as life in association becomes more interdependent. Dewey did not appreciate that even while deeply involved in common affairs, one must have one's own reasons for acting. It is a basic humanistic truism that those who collaborate with others experience a greater fulfillment than they would have if they tried to make their way alone. As a family member, a neighbor, a fellow worker, or as a citizen, one who joins with others in trying to find solutions to common problems will gain much personal satisfaction for his pains. But for authentic cooperation to occur, each participant must bring to the tasks at hand the resources of his own reason, will, and imagination. This creates an unavoidable tension between shared inquiry and personal originality. Hopes for social unity inspired Dewey to recommend that the impartial methods of the natural sciences be applied to the resolution of social controversies .He thought that the rigorous use of inductive logic in problematic situations would modify preconceived opinion and draw the participants towards a solution that all could at least provisionally accept. Dewey was not sufficiently aware of the fact that those involved must personally assess the value of what has been discovered. Nor did he realize the extent to which the participants must judge for themselves the merits of what is proposed as a solution to the perceived difficulty [274]..

The Darwinian discoveries and the emergence of the new science of sociology led Dewey to assume that all important values have their source in historical experience. He reached the further conclusion that in matters of doubt about the public good society is empowered to be the decisive representative of the self. Shared understanding was meant to overcome the dualism of self and society. The difficulty was that Dewey did not appreciate the value of legitimate self-love. He could not understand that the one who is trying to be a good citizen is also trying to be a good person. While having significant social responsibilities, a person must also be concerned about his own proper perfection. While it may seem paradoxical, Christianity does not assert that an authentic person lives exclusively for others. Altruism is not an absolute. [275].

The preference for the socially normative in matters of value conflict implies that the community is the proper subject of action. Democracy is imaginatively conceived as something more real than those who compose it. And it is true that every political or civic association modifies the lives of its members as well as the quality of their being together. All must, to some degree, do what is expected of them. But if there are to be responsible relationships between human beings, everyone involved in community must determine within themselves the nature and extent of these bonds. Each person remains independent in thought and judgment even when acting in the service of values that are held in common with others. [276].

Liberalism emphasizes the separate rights that one holds in opposition to others but authentic personal freedom is public as well as private in nature. The more the possibilities of social participation, the greater are the real liberties. That is why access to all processes of communication is of great importance to the flourishing of both personality and democracy. . But such engagement has negative as well as positive aspects. One may, and at times must, object to what others believe to be desirable.

Allegiance can be expressed through disagreement. When a person is striving for the realization of value, he will not accept the view that there is nothing good, or evil, itself. Nor does he consider that every action, communal as well as self-regarding, is never anything more than a means to a practical end. One who has a sound conscience will not directly advance any political or social goal that he judges to be intrinsically immoral . In addition, he will not support any distributive project that he considers to be inconsistent with the common good.

Courage is an indispensable civic virtue. One must be prepared to dissent with respect to a broad range of social issues, embracing everything from the protection of the poor and the innocent to passing judgment upon the justice of the nation's foreign policy. The actual is more provisional than Dewey imagined. But it is important to note that the disposition to challenge is firm but not fanatical. In lived experience, one who is brave may have to bear with some of the practical consequences of political and social evil, without giving them his personal endorsement. [277].

Dissent is not an expression of disloyalty so long as the dissenter is sincerely pursuing a common good and is not just arbitrarily asserting his or her own liberty. As long as disagreement is not violent or coercive, it must be respected. That is why freedom of thought and expression has a value that surpasses what the law can compel. The community, including those with effective power, must gives to those who object reasonable means for making their views known. Nonconformists must also be given opportunities to work within the relevant group to promote change. These wider obligations are reciprocal. Those supporting the status quo must be willing to have a constructive engagement with those who disagree, while those in opposition are obliged to collaborate with persons of good will to constructively overcome division by way of peaceable, and reasonable, dialogue. No matter how strong his convictions, the objector can never impose his views on others. [278].

Although it is important to protect the right of disagreement, its value should not be exaggerated. The freedom of the person in society may be manifest most dramatically in dissent, but that is but a small part of the dynamic of participation. Each member of every social or political group has the responsibility to positively promote the good of the whole in whatever manner the circumstances and his talents allow. One must never be content to sit in judgment.

It is discouraging to see persons who are otherwise morally conscientious deliberately avoid the ordinary social responsibilities that are an inevitable part of every form of communal life. The great value of Dewey's social philosophy is that it convincingly demonstrates how much all aspects of common life depend upon willing cooperation for their maintenance and flourishing. Those who seek to fully understand the relationship between the person and society must not ignore his insights.

To have a deeper sense of dedication, and a willingness to do more than the law demands, requires the development of that intangible generosity that we have already identified as a central quality of being a person. Some have tried to identify the ultimate grounds of such inspired responsibility. Royce explained the moral basis of civic duty in terms of the virtue of loyalty, and he wrote eloquently about the depths of sincere devotion to a common cause. Dewey added a religious dimension to the effort to unify the ideal and the real. Dewey's interest in avoiding a purely secular form of humanism led him to articulate the relevance of a religious attitude towards the problems of life in common. He tried to distinguish such a personal disposition from an adherence to a particular faith. He also hoped to make the attitude as dependent as possible upon the experience of living with others. [279].

The spirituality that Dewey sought to promote would be another aspect of the integration of the self with the community. The effort to connect subjective belief with objective social experience was unsuccessful, but the issue that Dewey raised deserves to be more fully explored. Contemporary political thought has begun to take the relation between religion and public life seriously, and the matter is of great practical importance. But an inquiry into the relationship between religious belief and secular existence cannot be limited to its implications for constitutional order. Forms of communal experience of a spiritual nature must also be taken into account if the significance of religion is to be fully comprehended. We should see if the cultivation of a devoted attitude toward the problems of living together can be fully articulated without taking into account the possibility of personal adherence to a religion. [280]..

In *Looking Backward* , and his other writings on society, Edward Bellamy imagined that by the end of the twentieth century the nationalization of production and distribution would bring economic equality to the citizens of the United States and other advanced countries. The transformation from private to public purposes was expected to raise the general standard of living, but the ultimate objective was not limited to an improvement in the material conditions of life. Bellamy believed that , over time, the people would recognize the limits of affluence and technology. Realizing that the more they had, the less they would need, they would use their prosperity as a foundation upon which they would build their spiritual life. Once the transition had been made to a collectivized economy, material development would come to the aid of moral evolution. [281].].

In Bellamy's conception of imagined progress, concern with higher matters would arise out of the aspirations of the people rather than through the influence of organized religion. The Temple was gone. The spiritual religion that Jesus had promised to the Samarian woman would have become a social reality. The public would develop a great interest in matters of human nature and destiny. As their intelligence became elevated, they would no longer tolerate mediocrity. In matters of importance they would look towards those who had the largest souls. Only those who had an ennobling message would find an audience that was receptive to their claims of leadership. [282].].

In the social utopia envisioned by Bellamy, individuals would no longer be subject to the arbitrary will of others . The emancipation of women would herald the end of all social, as well as domestic, servility. Artificial uniformities would disappear and independent action abound. In the public sphere, traditional imbalances, such as those between industry and agriculture, would be corrected. Harmonies once thought to be unattainable would be miraculously realized. All these transformations would become possible because of the advent of universal love. The dialectic between unity and discord would be resolved as mutual affection extended its gentle sway to relations between nations as well as those between individuals. Humanity would become conscious of its oneness with God. The people would experience a real sharing in divine life that would lead to a happy acceptance of death. Like other American thinkers, Bellamy was influenced by a Hegelian philosophy which postulated the unifying power of an immanent spirit that brought a modern equivalent of The Kingdom of God to earth. But Bellamy was also haunted by the residue of Puritanism that was part of his family ancestry. In everything that he wrote, he sought imaginative ways to counter or avoid the principle of original corruption. In *Looking Backward* the transformation from private to public capitalism is peaceful because everyone comes to understand that the evil lies in the existing economic arrangements rather than in the hearts of men.

The premise of peaceful change is not implausible. After all, near the end of the last century, we saw the Soviet Empire make such a transition from socialism. But whatever may be the form of the economy, it remains true that material evolution has not brought the spiritual development that Bellamy had hoped for. Rather, as we have shown, it has led to a technologically governed mass society whose fundamental goals are inhospitable to spirituality. Nor has prosperity removed the deeper evils that persist in all forms of human relationships . Even if the production and distribution of goods is arranged in a way that insures the greatest amount of freedom, malice, envy, and greed will continue to have their destructive influence upon every form of shared life. Moral disharmonies may be provoked, or intensified , by systemic factors, but they are ultimately traceable to the evil that lurks within the recesses of every human heart.

At the beginning of these reflections we observed how the earliest period of our history was marked by the severe insistence upon the doctrine of utter depravity, and how the reaction to that teaching was manifest in various theories of inward innocence. Some assumed that in this new world, men and women would eventually be free of all moral corruption, and that ideal influenced Bellamy's idea of what our common life would be like at the end of the twentieth century. .

The expectations of natural spiritual growth, while uniquely American, also had their roots in the philosophies of the European Enlightenment. Pascal was one of the first to identify the modern indifference to questions of personal evil and redemption. Pascal was influenced by the Jansenist school of Catholicism that, like the Puritans, thought of the will as being essentially corrupt. Many Christians shared the belief that depravity turns the mind away from what it does not want to see. For Pascal, this was the principal reason for the decline of the influence of the Catholic Church. Embarrassed by his moral imperfection, the modern man resists any authority that reproves him and calls him to repentance [283].

The resistance to the correction of personal evil was reinforced by wider developments in thought. For Pascal, it was the heart that experiences God; for Leibniz, it was reason. Leibniz expanded the powers of human thought so that he could bridge the divide between God and man . However, in making divinity the quintessence of the human, Leibniz blurred the essential distinction between the natural and the supernatural. In the rationalism of Leibniz, grace does not restore creation. Nor does it, by its own power, elevate the natural order of existence. Charity was, in one sense, the mercy that God shows to the contrite; in another, it was the wisdom that manifests the perfection of reason. In Liebnizian theology the Revelation of God in Jesus Christ becomes subordinated to the authority of a universal reason. .

As for moral reform, Leibniz thought that improvement was possible so long as it conformed with divine omniscience. The 'complete' concept of the individual as known by God must include the possibility of such correction.[284].

Kant rejected this metaphysical reasoning because it was incompatible with his idea of the full actualization of the autonomous will. Kant thought that if we are to be the exclusive authors of our actions, we must have within ourselves the decisive principles of moral determination. Kant was , however, acutely aware of the problem of evil. Seeing the malice and violence that span all of human experience , Kant realized that if his moral philosophy was to be complete, he had to uncover the subjective grounds of evil. He concluded that malice was rooted in the inward struggle between self-love and respect for the moral law . The ultimate positive outcome was not in doubt. Good will eventually triumph because the principles of morality imply that man is capable of doing what he ought to do. Such a capacity logically requires a predisposition within human nature upon which it is impossible to graft anything that is fundamentally wrong. According to Kant, within the depths of personality there lies the equivalent of an autonomous good will. The Christian doctrine of Original Sin could not alter this ethical optimism. Kant felt that those who assume an innate corruption have allowed the contingent events surrounding the Fall to obscure the potentials of rational freedom under the moral law. Whatever the extent of depravity, a good will remains at the heart of every human being. [285].

Kant also opposed the dependencies implicit in the Christian doctrine of Grace. Undue emphasis upon the need for divine assistance was incompatible with the value of independent action. Grace implies that we are unable to do what we ought; morality insists only that we do what we are capable of. For Kant, each individual makes ethical progress by fulfilling the duties that he commands himself to observe by his own injunctions. [286].

Kant's rational theology had an ambiguous relationship to Puritanism. Innate corruption and the related doctrine of predestination were rejected because they assume that some are naturally unworthy of blessedness. Yet although Kant's God, like that of Channing, is not a tyrant, His Judgments are severe. When God decides who is worthy of ultimate happiness, there is little pity or forgiveness. His benevolence is limited by His Justice. [287]..

Kant's views are not completely individualistic. Religion had a social as well as a personal dimension. In his reflections on the social contract ,and in his Project For Perpetual Peace, Kant recognized that morality and community were interdependent. He further believed that above all legal and political regimes, there should be an inclusive ethical commonwealth within which all could rally who love the good . This ideal corporate worship would not resemble the traditional Christian churches , with their humiliating distinctions between clergy and laity. Nor would there be any dogma of Atonement that relieved the members of their own moral responsibilities. Nonetheless, Kant's acknowledgment that there is a need for an assembly of a people of God, united in tasks that cannot be completed by men acting alone, is of permanent value to any study of the relationship between Christianity and humanism. [288].

The recognition of a corporate dimension to religious experience resonates with our own historical experience. In post-Puritan New England, an attempt was made to translate the spirit of the Reformation into an indefinite expansion of personal freedom. One within the transcendentalist circle saw the need to go past that objective. The decline of Calvinism had left Orestes Brownson dissatisfied with the humanistic alternatives. He concluded that, however conceived, Protestantism was essentially a critical religious movement, that could not satisfy the deeper human need to worship together in concord and peace. To Brownson, this deeper desire for unity could only be satisfied by a stable and universal religious organization, and for him, that spiritual authority was the Roman Catholic Church. [289].

Brownson's choice was a singular act of religious freedom. From the perspective of democratic theory, that is the decisive meaning of any faith conversion. Interestingly, such an appraisal is not as inconsistent with the teachings of the Catholic Church as one might imagine. Catholicism insists, even more vehemently than secular thought, that no philosophy or single rule of faith can be imposed by the State and that one can only freely choose a religion. Yet even as she respects the diversity of religious belief, the Church constantly calls all to share in the sanctifying gifts that she has to offer . Moreover, with great courtesy, she asks everyone who think seriously about such matters to carefully weigh her bold claim that the fullness of the Christian life can be realized only within the sacramental order that she has developed and constantly struggles to preserve [290].

A concern over the basic options was not alien to the minds of those who have been the subject of these reflections. Melville realized that the fundamental issue had become something more profound than the conflict between Protestantism and Catholicism. He sensed a developing contest between the forces of atheism and the diminishing possibilities of a fully Christian life. For Henry Adams, the growing tension between belief and unbelief was manifest in the reverence being accorded to industrial and technological advances. William James tried to fashion a personal response to the growing chaos. James sought to combine a pantheistic conception of divinity with a subjective quest for spiritual fulfillment. He wanted to have intense communion with a saving power while remaining faithful to the various facets of his own unique being. The project was hopelessly subjective. The self that James wanted to affirm lacked the substance needed to sustain an independent existence. Moreover, while his spiritual interests were serious and sincere, he overvalued religion as a psychological therapy. It was useful for relieving the terrors that tormented the soul rather than for providing truths that set one free. The something higher with which he hoped to be in touch did not exist in itself, independent of the inner need to believe. [291].

James' existential approach to matters of ultimate belief was opposed by the more communal disposition of his friend Josiah Royce. The basic divergence, here as elsewhere, was between an individualistic and a societal conception of the purposes of human existence. For Royce, religious experience, like the rest of life, should be comprehended in terms of some form of wholeness rather than as a matter of separate and immediate satisfaction. For a religion to be humanistically appealing, it had to offer a salvation that was open to all . To Royce, it was the universal and inclusive quality of Christianity that made it distinctive. Its message was general, but it did not call for the absorption of the ego into some impersonal substance. Christianity offered a meaningful self-possession that could be realized in association with others who accepted the same faith, doctrine, and discipline.

The Unitarian rejection of the Trinity was also unacceptable to Royce. By reducing the relation between humanity and divinity to the individual's dialogue with God the Father, Channing and his followers failed to explain how the many could become one. Royce insisted that the Kingdom of Heaven is an authentic community, and he saw, most perceptively, that peace and unity among its members cannot be assured without the indwelling of the Holy Spirit.

Royce's understanding of Christianity was much closer to classical Catholicism than was true of most other American religious thinkers. Like Kant, Royce saw the importance of the communal dimension to matters of ultimate belief. But in Royce's philosophy of religion, humanism trumps Revelation. A beloved natural community would compensate for the ineffectiveness of the established churches. Redemption becomes one of the tasks of the suffering that is an integral part of human history. In the modern world. Atonement for sin would be the work of man rather than that of the One who was both God and Man, Jesus Christ. [292].

Royce did his most important work on the meaning of Christianity prior to the outbreak of the First World War, and although he was alive when that calamity began, he never experienced the full horrors of the twentieth century. He was part of a generation that had high hopes for the spiritual as well as material progress of the human race. Nevertheless, his theory must be tested for its truthfulness. We should be willing to believe, with Royce, that particular acts of loyal sacrifice, in ways beyond counting, do actually make up for the sins of others. However, there is no doubt that his general thesis cannot pass the test of experience. The belief has not be verified by the realities. Indeed, it has been contradicted. Like Bellamy, Royce thought that natural human societies would become imbued with the deepest religious values as a matter of natural development. Both believed that the essential questions of sin and forgiveness can be resolved conclusively upon an anthropological plane. A similar flaw vitiates Dewey's understanding of the relation between religion and human progress, particularly in his insistence that as democracy evolves, social experience will be the primary source of spiritual inspiration. These failures point to the need for a humanism that makes the love of God,-- and a looking towards Him for redemption, --compatible with an intense love for human fellowship.[293].

But such a revival must not repeat the mistakes of the past. Our history has been haunted by a theology that preached the alienation of God from man. Puritan Christianity thought that in order to properly worship the divine, it was necessary to belittle the human . As we have seen in these reflections, the opposition that would honor human dignity would also marginalize religious faith and worship. As the influence of organized religion declined, it came to be widely believed that the human being, acting alone, or in association, could achieve the supreme objectives of fulfillment, happiness, and peace. As the secular spirit spread, the powers of the will were restored, but volition was set above grace. Men would either deny the evil within themselves or assume that they could resist it by their own power. Holiness remained an ideal , but it would be gained by entering into the spirit of nature or by uniting the self, and its destiny, with the temporal objectives of a capitalistic democracy. [293].

The humanism of the American experience has not provided an adequate ground for human dignity, nor has it been able to protect the individual person from the intrusions of technological, economic, and political power. But the nobility of its objectives cannot be denied. If we remember the historical conditions out of which our humanism arose, an authentic Christian response can not afford to take an adversarial stance towards its fundamental purposes. The hope must be for a theology of the Incarnation that no longer humiliates man but rather rehabilitates him in God. Such an understanding of Christianity will no longer set the liberty of Divine initiative against the freedom of man. It will preserve our desires for righteousness without eliminating the constant need for Divine Mercy .

Even to imagine these possibilities requires great humility. The central American temptation is willfulness. Our most perverse desires do not arise out of materialism or licentiousness; they are rooted in a yearning to act as power, rather than reason or grace, should determine. The overcoming of this primal fault will require a profound and authentic conversion. For a free people, these are hard sayings. Catholic Christianity demands a recognition of something that is above, as well as within, the self. It calls for an honest acknowledgment that we are not gods, but creatures and, without exception, both noble and perverse. Catholicism also challenges the singular conception of religious experience that expects a direct relationship between the self and God, for it insists that longings for divinity must be mediated through a sacramental order, common modes of worship, and the teachings of religious authority. Yet it also offers to everyone who accepts its doctrines the prospect of an authentic participation in the life of God.

The incompatibility of Catholicism and Democracy is a staple of our ethos and we are still working out the proper boundaries between the sacred and the secular within the realm of public law and policy. But the questions raised by these reflections are of a more personal nature. Anyone who desires to have a full Christian life should ponder how else, except through membership in the Universal Church , he or she might find the lasting happiness that, in their heart of hearts, they hope to possess. As James observed, religion is a serious business. Catholicism can only attract those who sincerely want to harmonize life in this world with that of the world that is to come. Within the Church, they will discover a reconciliation between the polarities of grace and freedom that have vexed our cultural history. They will be enabled to affirm their unique personal selves as well as the human nature that they share with others. Here one's hope is for a deliverance that is not an escape from God nor a retreat from the journey of temporal existence. One who is experiencing the fullness of the Christian life maintains a relation to the world that neither surrenders to its powers nor abandons it in its need for love and justice. [294].

Roman Catholicism must also question itself if it hopes to become more relevant to the spiritual challenges implicit in the historical development of the United States. The position of the Church is difficult because the American experience threatens its corporate integrity even as it rouses its pastoral mission. There are balances to be attained that are more arduous than is commonly realized. Religious authorities must respect the autonomy of the secular world without abandoning their obligation to pass judgment on its values. They must demonstrate a genuine belief in personal liberty, even as they uphold the demands of the objective moral order. And while it must not adapt the Gospel to the culture, Catholicism must not distinquish itself by being nothing more than a counter-cultural influence. Those with appropriate responsibilities must encourage as well as admonish. Above all, they must be constantly affirming the infinite value of every human being, especially those who are in any way poor or helpless.

Notes

1 Jacques Maritain, *Integral Humanism Temporal and Spiritual Problems of A New Christendom trans. Joseph W. Evans; revised by Otto Bird in vol. 11 The Collected Works of Jacques Maritain)* Notre Dame, Indiana: *University* of Notre Dame Press, 1996) 147-336. Romano Guardini, *The End of the Modern World* (Chicago: Henry Regnery Company, 1968).

2 *The Renaissance Philosophy of Man, Selections In Translation* ed. *Ernst Cassirer, Paul Oskar Kristeller & John Herman Randell, Jr.,* (*Chicago: University of Chicago Press, 1948)*; Reinhold Niebuhr, *The Nature and Destiny of Man* A Christian Interpretation (New York: Charles Scribner's Sons, 1949). Book I Ch. 3, III> See also, Guardini, op. cit. Ch. Two.

3 Nicholas Rescher, *The Philosophy of Leibniz* (Englewood Cliffs, N. J. : Prentice Hall 1967); Herbert Wildon Carr, *Leibniz* (London: E. Benn Ltd., 1929). See also: *Leibniz, A Collection of Critical Essays,* Harry B. Frankfurt, ed., (Garden City, N.Y.: Anchor Books, 1972). For the general cultural developments, see Ernst Cassier, *The Philosophy of the Enlightenment* (Princeton: Princeton University Press, 1951) and Carl C.Becker, The Heavenly City of the Eighteenth Century Philosophers (New Haven: Yale University Press, 1932).

4 See the authorities cited supra.

5 " Now what could precede the will and be its cause" Either it is the will itself, and nothing else than the will is the root or it is not the will that is sinful. Sin…cannot rightly be attributed to anything except to him who wills it. I do not know why you should look for anything further. Augustine *The Problem of Free Choice* (De Libero Arbitrio) Bk. Three, 17, 49. Dom Mark Pontifex, trans. (Westminster: The Newman Press, 1955).

6 Augustine " Retractions", *The Problem of Free Choice Ch.* 8. "*Pelagianism in its extreme form asserted that in part at least man is able to live a good life by the aid of his reason…He has by nature both the will to good and the power, and* all that religion needs to do is to add some measure of revelation to the knowledge already possessed to show man what is right and what is wrong. Then it remains for man himself to follow the light as indeed he is well able to do." A. Dakin, *Calvinism* (London: Duckworth, 1945) at 36.

7 *Summa Theologica* I, II, Q. 109, Art. 1-4

8 Martin Luther, " The Freedom of A Christian Man" (1520) *Luther's Works* 31, 3-28 " The will, therefore, is so bound by the slavery of sin…that it cannot excite itself, much less devote itself to anything good…man sins voluntarily…with the bias of his passions, and not with external compulsions. there is no impropriety in affirming that he is under the necessity of sinning." *A Compendium of the Institutes of the Christian Religion By John Calvin Hugh t. Kerr, ed., (Philadelphia: The Westminster Press, 1964) Ch. XI. See also Dakin, op. cit. and John T. McNeill, The History and Character of Calvinism (New York: Oxford University Press, 1962).*

9 Suarez's view will be found in his *De Legibus*, Bk. II, Ch.6.

10 Andrew DelBanco, *The Puritan Ordeal* (Cambridge, Mass & London: Harvard University Press, 1989); Ralph Barton Perry ,*Puritanism And Democracy* (New York: The Vanguard Press, 1948); Herbert Schneider, *The Puritan Mind* (1931) (Ann Arbor: The University of Michigan Press, 1958); Vernon L. Parrington, The Colonial Mind Bk. I, Part I in *The Main Currents of American Thought* (1927) (New York & London: Harcourt, Brace, Javonovich, 1954). See also Paul Conklin, *Puritans And Pragmatists*, Eight Eminent American Thinkers, (New York: Dodd, 1960) and Henry Bamford Parkes, *The American Experience* (New York: Alfred Knopf, 1955). The influence of Puritanism upon modern commercial development is described by Max Weber in his *The Protestant Ethic and The Spirit of Capitalism* Talcolt Parsons, trans., (New York: Charles Scribner & Sons, 1958) Ch. 1.

11 The important challenge to strict Calvinism was the claim of Arminius and his followers (who included Grotius) that the Atonement was meant for all, and that although man needs grace he can resist and even lose it. For a more extended discussion see Frederick D. Kershner, *Pioneers of Christian Thought* (1930). (Freeport NY: Books For Libraries Press, 1958) Ch. XIV. Arminianism in America is explained in Conrad Wright, *The Beginnings of Unitarianism In America* (Boston: The Beacon Press, 1955). See also Bruce Kuklick, *Churchmen And Philosophers From Jonathan Edwards to John Dewey (New York & London: Yale University Press, 1985). A similar problem concerning the concurrence of grace and personal freedom arose in Catholicism with the Molinist controversy.* See Anton C. Pegis, " Molina And Human Liberty" in *Jesuit Thinkers of the Renaissance* (Milwaukee: Marquette University Press, 1939). As for Jansenism, see R. A. Knox, *Enthusiasm A Chapter In The History of Religion with Special reference to the XVII and XVIII Centuries (Oxford, At The Clarendon Press, 1950).*

12 " A Careful And Strict Inquiry into the Modern Prevailing notions of that Freedom of the Will, which is supposed to be essential to Moral Agency, Virtue, and Vice, Reward & Punishment, Praise and Blame" (1754) . The text appears as vol. 1 of *The Works of Jonathan Edwards Freedom of the Will* ed., Paul Ramsey (New Haven & London: Yale University Press 1957) and in A Jonathan *Edwards Reader John E. Smith, Harry S. Stout, and Kenneth P Minkema, ed., (New York & London: Yale University Press, 1995). See also and Perry Miller, Jonathan Edwards (New York: William* Sloane Ass. 1949). For a fierce criticism of Edwards by an eminent nineteenth century New England humanist see Oliver Wendell Holmes, *Pages From An Old Volume of Life* (Boston : The Riverside Press, 1891). More general studies include, Parrington, The Colonial Mind Bk. II, Part I , II, ii.

13 " The Great Christian Doctrine of Original Sin Defended" (1758) *vol. 3, The Works of Jonathan*

Edwards Clyde A. Holbrook, ed., (New Haven & London: Yale University Press, 1970) and in A *Jonathan Edwards Reader.*

14 " The Beauty of the World" (1725) and "The Nature of True Moral Virtue" (1765), which includes the beautiful as an aspect of moral virtue, in *A Jonathan Edwards Reader.* " The Nature of True Virtue" appears in *vol.8 of The Works* as Dissertation II.

15 Edmund Morgan , *Benjamin Franklin* (New Haven: Yale University Press, 2000); Alfred Owen Aldridge, *Benjamin Franklin And Nature's God* (Durham: Duke University Press, 1967).

16 The moderating influences are traced in Kuklick, op.cit. Ch. 2&3 and Herbert W. Schneider, *The Puritan Mind* Ch. VI, VII. See also Mark A. Noll, *America's God: From Jonathan Edwards To Abraham Lincoln (Oxford & New York: Oxford University Press, 2002).*

17 " The Moral Argument Against Calvinism" (1809) in *The Works of William E. Channing* D.D. (Boston: The American Unitarian Association, 1875) pps. 459-468. Basic studies of the life and work of Channing include Andrew Delbanco *William Ellery Channing An Essay On The Liberal Spirit in America* (Cambridge: Harvard University Press, 1981); Madeleine Hooke Rice, *Federal Street Pastor, The Life of William Ellery Channing (New York: Bookman Associates, 1961); Arthur W.* Brown, *Always Young For Liberty, A Biography of William Ellery Channing (Syracuse: Syracuse* University Press, 1956); David P. Edgell, *William Ellery Channing An Intellectual Portrait* (Boston : Beacon Press, 1955); Jack Mendelsohn, *Channing, The Reluctant Radical* (Boston & Toronto: Little Brown & Com;pany, 1991). Channing is also discussed in Perry Miller, *The Transcendentalists* (Cambridge: Harvard University Press, 1966) 21-25 and in Kuklick, op. cit. Ch. 6.

18 " Introductory Remarks" (1841) in *The Works of William Ellery Channing* 1-11. In the earlier " Moral Argument Against Calvinism" Channing argued that " ...God, in giving us conscience, has implanted a principle within us which forbids us to prostrate ourselves before mere power, or to offer praise where we do not discover worth... He rests his authority on the perfect coincidence of his will and government with those great and fundamental principles of morality written on our souls. He desires no worship but that which springs from the exercise of our moral faculties upon his character..." *The Works* at 465 See also " Unitarian Christianity (1819) in *Three Prophets of Religious Liberalism: Channing, Emerson, Parker* Intr. Conrad Wright (Boston: The Beacon Press, 1961).

19 If God should bring to life creatures which are "...utterly depraved and then pursue them with endless punishment we should charge him with a cruelty not surpassed in the annals of the world." " The Moral Argument Against Calvinism" in *Works* 467-68.

20 See the sources cited at note 16 , above.

21 The moral sentiment is an "insight into the laws of the soul" while the religious sentiment, which is "our highest happiness" is the way that the soul knows itself [as something] divine and deifying." " The Divinity School Address (1838) in Vol 1, *The Collected Works of Ralph*

Waldo Emerson Intro. Robert E. Spiller, (Cambridge: The Belknap Press of Harvard University Press, 1971) 76-93, 77. The text can also be found in Ralph Waldo Emerson (The Oxford Authors) ed., Richard Poirier, ed., (Oxford & New York: The Oxford University Press, 1990) 53-67. Basic studies include F. O. Matthiessen, *American Renaissance Art And Expression In the Age of Emerson And Whitman { London & New York: Oxford University Press, 1941);Stanley Cavell, Conditions Handsome and Unhandsome (Chicago & London: The University* of Chicago Press, 1998); Robert D. Richardson, Jr., *Emerson, The Mind On Fire* (Berkeley: The University of California Press, 1995); Donald Yannella, *Ralph Waldo Emerson.* (Boston: Twayne Publishers, 1982); Van Wyck Brooks, *The Life of Emerson* (New York: E. P. Dutton, 1932); Regis Michaud, *Emerson The Enraptured Yankee* George Boas, trans., (New York & London : Harper Bros. 1930); George Henry Woodberry, *Ralph Waldo Emerson,* (1907) (New York: Haskell House, 1968). See also Harold Bloom, *Figures of Capable Imagination* (New York: The Seabury Press, 1976) Ch. 3.; *Ralph Waldo Emerson, Modern Critical Views* Harold Bloom, ed., (New York: Chelsea House Publishers, 1985), and *Emerson, A Collection of Critical Essays Milton R. Konvitch * Stephen E. Whicher, ed., (Englewood Cliffs, New Jersey: Prentice Hall Inc. 1966).*

22 "… A man never sees the same object twice: with his own enlargement the object acquires new aspects. Does not the same law hold true for virtue? It is vitiated by too much will. He who aims at progress should aim at an infinite, not at a special benefit. The reforms whose fame now fills the land…fair and generous as each appears, are poor bitter things when presented for themselves as an end. …The imaginative faculty of the soul must be fed with objects immense and eternal…" " The Method of Nature" (1841) in *1 The Collected Works1*17-137,132 -133. See also " Intellect" (1847) in Poirier, pps. 176- 185. Santayana noted that Emerson could be active in defense of freedom and in fighting against oppression, but that "…[H]is contemplative nature held him back from a full engagement with the life of the world. ." in *Emerson, A Collection of Critical Essays,* 31-38.

23 " Good is positive. Evil is merely privative, not absolute. It is like cold, which is the privation of heat" " The Divinity School Address" in *The Collected Works* at78. It has been pointed out that Emerson's removal of evil takes away the tension from human life. "… There is no drama in human character because there is no tragic fault ." Allen Tate, *Collected Essays* (Denver: Allen Swallow, 1955) 200-201.

24 See the criticism in Santayana, op. cit., note 22 above.

25 " The Method of Nature". In " Experience" (1844) Emerson asserts that "…the great and crescive [growing] self, rooted in absolute nature, supplants all relative existence and ruins the kingdom of mortal friendship and love…" Poirier, 216-234; 230. Similar ideas can be found Thoreau and in Holderlin who , with joy, affirms that "…the fullness of the living universe feeds and satisfies my starving being with its intoxication…" *Hyperion* at 22. By contrast, Jonathan Edwards insisted that God is other than the world itself, and that man, as dependent being, must work out his destiny within the created order. See Perry Miller, *Errand In The Wilderness* (Cambridge: Harvard University Press, 1956) Ch. VIII.

26 For Emerson, ecstacy is both the cause of nature and represents the wise man at his best. " The Method of Nature".

27 Referring to his Calvinist ancestors Emerson asks "…And what is to replace for us the piety

of that race? We cannot have theirs; it glides away from us day by day, but we can also bask in the great morning which rises forever out of the eastern sea, and be ourselves the children of the light. I stand here to say, Let us worship the mighty and transcendental Soul" " The Method of Nature" in *The Collected Works*, at ; Poirier, at 95. See also Emerson's essay "The Over-Soul".

28 Averroes, the great Arabic philosopher, thought that the world was an eternal reality endless moved by a self-thinking mind. He postulated an eternal being in order to account for the complete realization of intellect within the human race. See Etienne Gilson, *Dante And Philosophy* (New York: Harper & Row, 1963) Ch. 3.

29 Compare the observation of Tocqueville: " The idea of unity so possesses man …that if he thinks he has found it, he readily yields himself to repose in that belief. Not content with the discovery that there is nothing in the world but a creation and a Creator he is still embarrassed by this primary division of things and seeks to expand and simplify his conception by including God and the Universe in one great whole… *Democracy In America* Vol. II, First Book, Ch.vii. (1840). Tocqueville thought that such a false unity should be resisted because it destroys individuality. The truth of his challenge will be seen in the reflections that follow in the present study.

30 " In the woods…all mean egotism vanishes. I become a transparent eye-ball; I am nothing, I see all; the currents of the Universal Being circulate through me; I am part or particle of God. . " Nature" (1849) Ch. I. Similar expressions appear in Emerson's other essays, as they do in the writings of Thoreau. These dispositions have their roots in the Eastern Religions whose doctrines were familiar to Emerson. Siddhatta Gotama, the Buddha, who refused to affirm the existence of a supreme being, thought that freedom from the suffering of the world could be found within himself. He searched for the absolute reality of Brahman, the impersonal essence of the universe. This was an immanent presence within all that lived. Self-discipline was to discover the presence of that reality at the core of one's being. It would be identical with one's own deep Self (Atman). To attain that state of consciousness, Buddhists are to behave as though the ego does not exist. Karen Armstrong, *Buddha* (New York: Lipper/ Viking, 2001) at 25. See further, Ch. IV, I, of the present work where the influence of Buddhism is appraised by the American philosopher Josiah Royce.

31 " Society everywhere is in conspiracy against the manhood of every one of its members… The virtue in most request is conformity. Self-reliance is its aversion. It loves not realities and creators, but names and customs. " Self- Reliance" (Essays First Series, 1857) in Poirier, at 133. See also the excerpt from " Society And Solitude" (1870) in Poirier, 419-424 and Maurice Gonnaud, *An Uneasy Solitude: Individual And Society in the Work of Ralph Waldo Emerson trans. Lawrence Rosenwald, (Princeton: Princeton University Press, 1987). The attitude of Thoreau was similar .See his "Walking" (*1862) in The American Transcendentalists Ch. Four.

32 Theodore Parker, *The Transient And The Permanent in Christianity* George Willis Cooke, ed., (Boston: The American Unitarian Association, 1900). Biographies include Henry Steele Commager, *Theodore Parker* (Boston: TheBeacon Press, 1947) and R.C. Albrecht, *Theodore Parker* (New York: Twayne Publishers, 1971). See also *The American Transcendentalists, Their Prose And Poetry* ed., Perry Miller, (Doubleday, 1957). Chapter Three.

33 Parker believed that Channing represented a new stage in Protestant ascendancy, greater " not only than Luther but of Jesus himself". With Unitarianism a new positive religion had arisen that had a deeper and broader range than the Calvinism it replaced. The ideas were

novel: religion would now be identified with the normal use of all our faculties of body and spirit ; every power that we possessed would have eternal as well as temporal significance. The purpose of religion would not be to prepare us for what lies beyond the grave; it would empower us to make a heaven of the here and now. Theodore Parker, *The World of Matter And The Spirit of Man* (Boston: American Unitarian Association, 1907) Ch. VII.

34 Delbanco, *William Ellery Channing* Ch. One. Emerson also had some reservations about the zeal of the reformers. The fierceness of Parker's social criticism appears in his writings. He attacked the corruption of Boston, within clerical circles as well as with laymen: "...There are a great many bishops who have never had a cross on their bosom, nor a mitre on their head, who appeal not to the Pope at Rome, but to the Almighty Dollar, a pope much nearer home. Boston has been controlled by a few capitalists, lawyers, and other managers, who told the editors what to say and the preachers what to think. " *The World of Matter And Spirit at 370.*

35 Vernon Parrington, *Main Currents of American Thought* Vol. 2, Bk. III, Part IV, II; F. O. Matthiessen, *American Renaissance*, Book Two; Yvor Winters, *Maule's Curse, Seven Studies in the History of American Obscurantism* (Norfolk, Conn.: New Directions, 1938) 3-22; Roy R. Male, *Hawthorne's Tragic Vision* (New York: W.W Norton & Company 1957). See also Henry Bamford Parkes, *The American Experience* ch. IX.

36 Arlin Turner, *Nathaniel Hawthorne, An Interpretation* (New York : Barnes & Noble Books, 1998).

37 See the introduction by Paul Montazzolini to *Nathaniel Hawthorne, The Scarlet Letter* (1850) (New York: Barnes And Noble Books, 1998).

38 " The symbolism of Moby Dick is based upon the antithesis of the sea and the land: the land represents the known, the mastered in human experience; the sea, the half-known, the obscure region of instinct, uncritical feeling, dangers and terror." Yvor Winters, *Male's Curse* at 53.

39   *Male's Curse* 65-66 Compare, Matthiessen, *American Renaissance* Book Three, X. and Tyrus Hillway, Herman Melville (Boston: Twayne Pubishers, 1979) III William Ellery Sedgwick, *Herman Melville, The Tragedy of Mind* (Cambridge: Harvard University Press, 1944). See also Hershel Parker, *Herman Melville, A Biography* Vol. I, 1819-1851 (Baltimore & London: The Johns Hopkins University Press, 1996); Vol 2, 1851-1891 (2002). Henry Bamford Parkes observes: "...In Melville's Ahab the drive of the American will is carried to its furthermost limits. For him, as for Poe, there is nothing higher than the will, yet the will must go down to ultimate defeat. Man cannot conquer nature, nor can he destroy evil, either within or without. *The American Experience* at 202.

40 Merlin Bowen, *The Long Encounter, Self And Experience in the writings of Herman Melville* (Chicago & London: The University of Chicago Press, 1961). Compare: A. N. Kaul," The Blithedale Romance and the Puritan Tradition" in *Nathaniel Hawthorne Modern Critical Views* Harold Bloom, ed., (New York: Chelsea House, 1886) 59-70.

41 " He is no longer protesting the determined laws as being savagely inexorable. He has come to respect necessity. " F. O. Matthiessen, " Billy Budd, Foretopman" in *Melville, A Collection of Critical Essays* Richard Chase , ed., (Englewood Cliffs, N. J. : Prentice -Hall, 1962). Matthiessen also observes that Melville's notes indicate that Captain Vere was modeled on Jonathan Edwards, as one who was severe but righteous. See further: *Twentieth Century Interpretations of Billy Budd* Howard P Vincent, ed., (Englewood Cliffs N.J. : Prentice -Hall,

1971).

42 Lewis Mumford, *Herman Melville* (New York: Harcourt Brace & World, 1962) Chapter Twelve. Compare Vernon Parrington's assessment of Melville's final days: "…Life could not meet the demands he made on it. .the malady lay …in the futility of life itself; and so, after pursuing his dreams to the ends of the seas, the rebellious transcendentalist withdrew within himself awaiting annihilation. There is no other tragedy in American letters comparable to the tragedy of Herman Melville. " *Two, The Romantic Revolution in America,* Book II, V. III. Melville was influenced by Schopenhauer. In his studies of pessimism the German philosopher developed ideas about creation that are reflected in Melville's stories. For example, in an essay entitled " On The Sufferings of The World" Schopenhauer claims that evil is a positive force that makes its existence felt. He was also hostile to any idea of benevolent creation : " There are two things which make it impossible to believe that this world is the successful work of an all-wise, all-good, and, at the same time, all-powerful Being; firstly, the misery that abounds in it everywhere; and secondly, the obvious imperfection of the highest product, man, who is a burlesque of what he should be. … the grevious sin of the world has produced the grevious suffering of the world." *The Essays of Arthur Schopenhauer*, T. Bailey Saunders, trans., (New York: Willy Book Company, n.d.) II, 13.

43 " Well reason they, who from the birds and flowers/ would prove that God is all a God of Love; / For feelings, that transcend e'en reason's powers,/ To all mankind the same doctrine prove/ Thus Nature with the Scripture doth accord,/ For God's Love declares the Sacred Word." " Nature Teaches Only Love" (1888) in *Jones Very, The Complete Poems* Helen R. Deese, ed., (Athens & London: The University of Georgia Press, 1993). The introduction contains important insights into Very's life and poetry. See also " Jones Very and Ralph Waldo Emerson: Aspects of New England Mysticism" in *Maule's Curse* 125-146. For a more general study of the tension between the demands of religious discipline and the poetic inclination in colonial New England, see Jeffrey Hammond, *Sinful Self, Saintly Self; The Puritan Experience of Poetry* (Athens & London: The University of Georgia Press, 1993).

44 See the introduction to Walt Whitman's *Leaves of Grass*, The First Edition (1855) Malcom Cowley ed. (New York: Viking Press, 1959). In his later years Whitman wrote that Leaves of Grass was intended "…to express in literary or poetic form, and uncompromisingly, my own physical, emotional, moral, intellectual, and aesthetic Personality, in the midst of, and tallying, the momentous spirit and facts of its immediate days, and of current America-and to exploit that Personality, identified with place and date, in a far more candid and comprehensive sense than any hitherto poem or book." " A Backward Glance O'erTravel'd Roads" (1888) in *The Portable Walt Whitman* Mark van Doren ed., (New York: The Penquin Group, 1973) 296-312, at 298.

45 See the poem " One's Self I Sing" (1867) in *The Portable Walt Whitman* 252. The tensions between individualism and democratic fellowship are explored in "Democratic Vistas" (1871) in *The Portable Walt Whitman* 317-382. Important studies of Whitman include : Jerome Loving, *Walt Whitman, The Song of Himself* (Berkeley: The University of California Press, 1995); Paul Zweig, *Walt Whitman, The Making of The Poet* (New York: Basic Books, 1984); Roger Asselineau, *The Evolution of Walt Whitman* (Cambridge Mass: The Belknap Press of Harvard University,1967); Gay Wilson Allen, *The Solitary Singer: A Critical Biography of Walt Whitman,* (New York: The MacMillan Company, 1955); Henry Seidel Canby, *Walt*

Whitman, An American (New York: Literary Classics, 1943); Richard Chase, *Walt Whitman Reconsidered* New York: William Sloane, 1855). See also F. O. Matthiessen, American Renaissance Art And Expression In *The Age of Emerson And Whitman*, (New York: Oxford University Press, 1941) Part Four.

46 " The presence of the greatest poet conquers...Now that he has passed that way see after him! There is not left any vestige of despair or misanthropy or cunning or exclusiveness or the ignominy of a nativity or color or delusion of hell or the necessity of hell...and no man thence forward shall be degraded for ignorance or weakness or sin." *Leaves of Grass*, Preface in *The Portable Walt Whitman* 5- 27 , 10. In the poem " To A Common Prostitute" (1860) the poet invites her to " Be composed-be at ease with me- I am Walt Whitman/ liberal and lusty as Nature/ Not until the sun excludes you do I exclude you"/...*The Portable Walt Whitman* 205. See further, R. B. Lewis, " The New Adam" in *The Americanness of Walt Whitman* Leo Marx, ed., (Boston: D.C. Heath & Company, 1960).

47 " Never was there, perhaps, more hollowness at heart than at present, and here in the United States. Genuine belief seems to have left us....The spectacle is appalling. We live in an atmosphere of hypocrisy throughout. The men believe not in the women, nor the women in the men...I say that our New World democracy, however great a success in uplifting the masses out of their sloughs, in material development, products, and in a certain highly deceptive superficial popular intellectuality, is, so far, an almost complete failure in its social aspects, and in really grand religious, moral, literary, and aesthetic results. It is as if we were being endowed with a vast and more and more thoroughly appointed body, and then left with little or no soul." " Democratic Vistas" in *The Portable Walt Whitman* 325-326.

48 " Viewed today...the problem of humanity all over the civilized world is social and religious, and it is to be finally met and treated by literature. The Priest departs, and divine literatus comes..." " Democratic Vistas" at 320-321.

49 " Democratic Vistas" at 332-337.

50 "I submit, therefore, that the fruition of democracy on aught like a grand scale, resides altogether in the future...when it, with imperial power, through amplest time, has dominated mankind"- has been the source and test of all the moral, aesthetic, social, political, and religious expressions and institutes of the civilized world.- has begotton them in spirit and in form, and has carried them to its own unprecedented heights....has fashioned, systematized, and triumphantly finished and carried out, in its own interest and with unparalleled success , a new earth and a new man. " Democratic Vistas" 344-5.

51 See " The Great Unrest of Which We Are A Part" in " Specimen Days" (1882) *The Portable Walt Whitman* 387-640, 635. The quotation in the text is from " Out of The Cradle Endlessly Rocking" (1859). See further, Richard Chase, *Walt Whitman Reconsidered* Ch. III.

52 *The Portable Walt Whitman* 275-284. For a discussion of Whitman's concern with death, see Paul Zweig, *Walt Whitman*. Compare the comments of D.H. Lawrence: " It is the American heroic message. The soul is not to pile up defenses round herself. She is not to withdraw and seek her heaven inwardly, in mystical ecstacies. She is not to cry out to some God for salvation. She is to go down the open road, as the road opens into the unknown, keeping company with those whose soul draws them near to her...the soul in her subtle sympathies accomplishing herself along the way. D.H. Lawrence, " Whitman The American Teacher" in *The Americanness of Walt Whitman*, 89, 96. See also Alfred Kazin *God And The American Writer* (New York: Random House, 1997) Chap.5.

53 " Camerado, I give you my hand!/ ...Will you give me yourself? Will you come travel with me? / Shall we stick by each other as long as we live? " " Song of the Open Road" .15 (1876) in *The Portable Walt Whitman* 156 -167, 167 . Whitman also observed that " Leaves of Grass is avowedly the song of Sex and Amativeness , and even Animality - though meanings that do not usually go with those words are behind all, and will duly emerge; and all are sought to be lifted into a different light and atmosphere. ... Difficult as it will be, it has become, in my opinion, imperative to achieve a shifted attitude from superior men and women toward the thought and fact of sexuality, as an element in character, personality, the emotions, and a theme in literature...The vitality of it is altogether in its relations, bearings, significance - like the clef of a symphony." " A Backward Glance O'er Travel'd Roads" (1888) at 309.

54 Whitman was sure that all reflections on democracy came down to a single self, the "thought of identity-yours for you, whoever you are, as mine for me. The quality of Being, in the object's self, according to its own central idea and purpose, and of growing therefrom and thereto - not criticism by other standards, and adjustments thereto - is the lesson of Nature..." " Democratic Vistas" in *The Portable Walt Whitman* at 348.

55 This tendency of Whitman's has been compared to Emerson's fundamental disposition. See, for example, Quentin Anderson, *The Imperial Self An Essay in American Literary And Cultural History* (New York: Alfred A. Knopf, 1970) Ch. I-III.; James Loving, *Walt Whitman*, Ch. 10; James Dougherty, Walt Whitman And The Citizen's Eye (Baton Rouge & London: Lousiana State University Press, 1993) Stephen Whicher, *Freedom And Fate An Inner Life of Ralph Waldo Emerson* (Philadelphia: The University of Pennsylvania Press, 1953). Others have seen Emersonian characteristics in the lives of other poets " .The claim of this self is more radical, more absorbing, potentially more excluding, than other civilizations...American individualism was such that a man could be shut up in the solitude of his own heart. Eliot could not permit social ties to invade his solitude. He could not love...as did other lesser gifted men...Lyndell Gordon, *T.S Eliot, An Imperfect Life* (New York & London: W.W. Norton & Company, 1998) at 416.
While love seemed to be the driving force in Whitman's life, his affections were more generic than specific. He was gregarious, but he did not understand other distinct human beings: " For to understand people is to go much deeper than they go themselves; to penetrate into their characters and disentangle their inmost ideals. Whitman's insight into man did not go beyond a sensuous sympathy..." George Santayana, " The Poetry of Barbarism" in *The Americanness of Walt Whitman* 74-82, 81. See also, *Walt Whitman Abroad* Gay Wilson Allen, ed., (Syracuse, New York: Syracuse University Press, 1955).

56 *The Education of Henry Adams* An Autobiography (1919) D. W. Brogan, ed., (Cambridge, Mass.: The Riverside Press, 1961) Ch. XXII. Compare the poem " Song of the Exposition" (1871) in *The Portable Walt Whitman* 262-272.

57 Paul C. Nagel, *John Quincy Adams, A Public Life; A Private Life* (New York: Alfred A. Knopf, 1998); Lynn Hudson Parsons, *John Quincy Adams* (Madison, Wisconsin: Madison House, 1998); William H. Seward, *The Life And Public Services of John Quincy Adams* (1849) (Port Washington, New York: Kennikat Press, 1971). See also the study of John Quincy Adams in John F. Kennedy, *Profiles In Courage*. Henry Adams had recognized the importance of the Unitarian reform.: "Under the influence of Channing, and his friends, human nature was adorned with virtues hardly suspected before, and with hopes of perfection on earth altogether strange to theology. The Church then charmed. The worth of man became under Channing's teaching a source of pride and joy". *History of the United States of America*

During The Administration of Jefferson And Madison Abridged Edition. Ed. By Ernst Samuels (Chicago: The University of Chicago Press, 1967) at 377. See also " Boston" (1848-1854) in *The Education of Henry Adams* Ch. II. For a general study of this remarkable family see Richard Brookhiser, *America's First Dynasty The Adamses 1735- 1918* (New York: The Free Press, 2002).

58 See the introduction by Brooks Adams to Henry Adams, *The Degradation of the Democratic Dogma* 1919 (New York: Peter Smith, 1949).

59 Louis Auchinloss, " Henry Adams" in *Makers Of American Thought* An Introduction to Seven American Writers Ralph Ross, ed., (Minneapolis: The University of Minnesota Press, 1974); R. P. Blackmur, *Henry Adams* (New York & London: Harcourt, Brace, & Javanovich, 1980); George Hochfield, *Henry Adams, An Introduction And Interpretation* (New York: Barnes & Noble, Inc. 1962); J. C. Levenson, *The Mind And Art Of Henry Adams* (Cambridge: The Riverside Press, 1957); Robert A. Hume, *Runaway Star An Appreciation of Henry Adams(Ithaca New York: Cornell University Press, 1951). See also: Andrew BelBanco, Required Reading: Why American Classics Matter Now (New York: Farrar, Straus & Giroux,* 1997) Ch. 5; T. J. Jackson Lears, *No Place of Grace, Antimodernism and the transformation of American Literature* And Culture (New York: Pantheon Books, 1981); Lewis Mumford *The Golden Day A Study Of American Literature And Culture* (Boston : Beacon Hill Press, 1936) Ch. V.See also : New Essays On The Education of Henry Adams John Carlos Rowe, ed., (Cambridge: Cambridge University Press, 1996).

60 See Lears, op.cit. and Henry Steele Commager, *The American Mind, An Interpretation of American Thought Since The 1880's* (New Haven: Yale University Press, 1950) Ch. II.

61 " He cannot think of life as having meaning apart from a goal that is outside of and larger than the individual. This is the most fundamental and omnipresent manifestation of his Puritanism... The Absolute might be a political ideal, an historical order, or a cosmology; whatever its nature, at various moments in his intellectual career, its presence or absence determined the intelligibility of life for him. ..." Hochfield, *Henry Adams* at 32.

62 *Democracy And Esther Two Novels By Henry Adams* Ernst Samuels, intro., (Gloucester, Mass: Peter Smith, 1965). There are good analyses of the two novels in Hochfield, Ch. 7, Hume, *Runaway Star* Ch. V and Lears, *No Place Of Grace* Ch. 7.

63 The poem is discussed in Hochfield, Ch. 7 and Hume, Ch. V. See also, Henry Adams, *Letters To A Niece and Prayer to The Virgin of Chartres* (Boston & New York: Houghton Mifflin Company, 1922). This work includes a memoir by the niece, Mabel La Farge.

64 Henry Adams, *Mont Saint-Michel & Chartres*, (Boston : The Riverside Press, 1905) Ch. XVI. Adams eventually transferred his conception of Divine Providence to his understanding of Nature. In both cases, the convenience of the creature was not part of the plan. " Nature's way is rather that of absolute and irreversible legality; like St. Thomas' God, it is pre-eminently just and not merciful..." Hochfield, *Henry Adams* at 132.

65 According to Adams, in the Middle Ages, veneration of the Virgin Mary was a great source of hope because " ....She alone represented Love. The Trinity were, or was, One and could, by the nature of its essence, administer one justice; must admit only one law. In that law, no human weakness or error could exist. *Mont Saint Michel & Chartres,* at 250. See further, Alfred Kazin, " Religion as Culture; Henry Adams's Mont-Saint Michel and Chartres" in *Henry Adams and His World* David Contosta & Robert Muccigrosso, eds., (Vol. 83,

Transactions of the American Philosophical Society Pt. 4) (Philadelphia: The American Philosophical Society, 1993) pps. 48-56.

66 *The Education of Henry Adams* Ch. XXXIII. In Esther a conversation between the heroine and Professor Strong, a character who is thought to be the alter ego of the author, is revealing. When Esther questions him about his religious views, Strong replies: 'There is evidence amounting to a strong probability of two things…mind and force. *Esther*, Ch IX.

67 " The Tendency of History" (1894) in *The Degradation of the Democratic Dogma* 125-133, 131.

68 " Logically, the religious solution is inadmissible -pure hypothesis. It discards reason. I do not object to it on that account; as a working energy I prefer instinct to reason…" Letter from Henry Adams to Henry Osborn Taylor, 15 Feb., 1915, in *The Selected Letters of Henry Adams* Newton Arvin, ed., (New York: Farrar, Straus, & Young, Inc. 1951) 268-270. Adams characterized his early beliefs as a 'mild deism'. He left the Unitarian Church but regretted the total loss of faith: " The religious instinct has vanished and could not be revived, although on made in later life many efforts to recover it. …"Boston" (1848-1854) in *The Education of Henry Adams* Ch. II.

69 " Every man with self-respect enough to become effective, if only as a machine, has had to invent a formula of his own for the universe, if the standard formulas fail…One sought no absolute truth. One sought only a spool on which to wind the thread of history without breaking it… "Vis Nova" (1903-1904) in *The Education of Henry Adams* Ch. XXXII.

70 " The Grammar of Science" (1903) in *The Education of Henry Adams* Ch. XXXI. Adams was emphatic in his belief in the predominance and inclusiveness of the Second Law of Thermodynamics. While the law of conservation left room for religious belief, modern physicists most hold that the law of Entrophy includes God, Man, and the Universe. " A letter to American Teachers of History "(1910) in *The Degradation of the Democratic Dogma* 136-129, at 209.

71 " A Dynamic Theory of History" in *The Education of Henry Adams* Ch. XXXIII. While Adams treasured reason, he reluctantly abandoned belief in the independence of thought: " As a force it must obey the laws of force; as an energy it must content itself with such freedom as the laws of energy allow; and in many cases it must submit to the final and fundamental necessity of Degradation…" " A *Letter to American Teachers of History*, at 208. See also Henry Wasser, *The Scientific Thought of Henry Adams* (Thessaloniki, Greece, 1956).

72 With the steady degradation of solids, energy becomes nothing more than potential motion in absolute space. The revival of mathematics facilitates levels of abstract thought that allows all conceivable phases of immaterial motion to merge with the hyper-space of the mind. " The rule of Phase Applied to History" (1909) in *The Degradation of the Democratic Dogma* 267—311, at 273. Although the power of abstraction gives a superior intensity to the mind, Adams insisted that every mental activity is subject to the laws that govern all forms of energy. See " *A Letter to American Teachers of History*" 220-221.

73 "Chicago" (1893) in *The Education of Henry Adams*, Ch. XXII.

74 The laws of civilization extend the forces of society in a way that is unfavorable to individual forces: " …The individual, like the crystal of salt, is absorbed in the solution, but the solution does work that the individual could not do…" " *A Letter to the American Teachers of History*" at 211.

75 Adams was not persuaded that the mere prolongation of life is a sign of progress, The real need is for an increase in social energy, and this requires a tension between individual and social forces." " *A Letter to American Teachers of History*" Ch. II.

76 See the alternative " Prayer to the Virgin" and " Prayer to the Dynamo" in Adams, Letters to a Niece And Prayer to the Virgin of Chartres.

77 Auguste Comte, *Positive Philosophy* 2 vols. Harriet Martineau, trans., (New York: W.Gowans, 1868). As we shall see, Comte had a significant influence on John Dewey. Other philosophers were more critical. See, e.g. John Stuart Mill, *Auguste Comte And Positivism* (Ann Arbor: University of Michigan Press, 1961); Jacques Maritain, *Moral Philosophy* (New York: Scribners, 1964) Part II, Ch. II. ; and Isaiah Berlin " Historical Inevitability" in *The Proper Study of Mankind An Anthology of Essays* Henry Hardy & Roger Hausheer, ed., (New York: Farrar, Straus and Giroux, 1997). I discuss Comte's influence upon international thought in my *Theories of World Governance* (Washington: The Catholic University of America Press, 1999) Ch. 4.

78 *Henry James Senior, A Collection of His Writings* Giles Gunn, ed., (Chicago: American Library Ass. 1974); *The Literary Remains of the Late Henry James Senior* Ed. William James (Boston & New York: Houghton Mifflin Company, 1884); DwightW. Hoover, *Henry James Senior and The Religion of Community* (Grand Rapids: William B. Erdsman Publishing Co. 1969); Frederick Harold Young, *The Philosophy of Henry James Senior* (New York: Bookman Ass. 1951). Van Wyck Brooks was of the opinion that James was a 'mystical democrat' " He once remarked that a crowded horse-car was the nearest approach on earth to the joys of heaven." *New England : Indian Summer 1865-1915* (1940) (Chicago and London: University of Chicago Press, 1984) at 135. For a comparison of the elder James' personality with that of Emerson, see Ralph Barton Perry, The Thought And Character of William James (Cambridge: Harvard University Press, 1948) Ch.II. See also R.W. B. Lewis, *The American Adam: Innocence Tragedy And Tradition In The Nineteenth Century.* (Chicago: University of Chicago Press, 1955) Ch. 3.

79 " Society The Redeemed Form of Man" " (1879) in *Henry James Senior A Collection of His Writings. Ch. 2.*

80 See: *The Literary Remains of The Late Henry James Senior*, 296-297.

81 Ibid.

82 Wilfred M McClay,*The Masterless Self And Society in Modern America* (Chapel Hill & London: The University of North Carolina Press, 1993) Ch. 3. A similar idea of the collective appears in *Looking Backward.* While watching a military parade in Boston, the time-traveler, Julian West, thinks that " Here at last were order and reason, an exhibition of what intelligent cooperation can accomplish…" He also hopes that the crowd watching the march will grasp the incongruity between the " scientific manner in which the nation went to war with the unscientific manner in which it went to work…" Edward Bellamy, *Looking Backward* 2000-1887 John L. Thomas, ed., (Cambridge, Mass.: The Belknap Press, 1967) Ch. XXVIII.

83 *Looking Backward*, Ch. V.

84 For general assessments, and summaries of the literary criticism surrounding Bellamy's work

see Lewis Mumford, *The Story of Utopia's* (1922) (Glouster, Mass. : Peter Smith, 1959) Ch. Eight, sec. 4-6 and Vernon Parrington Jr. *American Dreams: A Study of America's Utopia's* Second Edition (New York: Russell & Russell Inc. 1964) Chapters Eight and Nine. We shall return to Bellamy's utopian thought in Chapter Five of the present work.

85 Arthur E. Morgan, *The Philosophy of Edward Bellamy* (New York: Kings Crown Press, 1945).

86 Ibid. See also the introduction to *Looking Backward* above, note 39.

87 The story is "Miss Ludington's Sister". See the discussion in Morgan, op.cit., pps. 58-66. Bellamy's approach to the problem of past guilt should be compared with that of Dr. Oliver W. Holmes. Holmes, the father of the great Supreme Court Justice, was a scientific rationalist as well as a man of letters. Like Bellamy, Dr. Holmes dealt with the problem of sin, and its effects upon personality, but for Holmes bad habits were just matters of bad ancestry He would reject the myth of the Fall in a new anthropology guided by science that would lead to the formation of individuals who were innocent and happy. See R.W.B. Lewis, *The American Adam* Ch. 2.

88 See also Wilfred McClay, op. cit.

89 " The Philosophy of Solidarity" (1887) in Morgan, *The Philosophy of Edward Bellamy.*

90 See generally, Louis Menard, *The Metaphysical Club* (New York: Farrar, Straus, & Giroux, 2001). The influence of Hegel upon Walt Whitman is evident in the themes of " Democratic Vistas" In a section of Specimen Days (1882) entitled " Carlyle From American Points of View" Whitman reviews the influence of German Idealism upon the intellectual life of the United States. The appraisal is generally positive, but Whitman notes that the whole development, from Kant to Hegel, is unsatisfactory from an emotional point of view. *The Portable Walt Whitman* 602-621.

91 " The Religion of Solidarity" Pt. III.

92 See the discussion of tendencies toward oneness in " The Religion of Solidarity" Pt. IV.

93 William was born in 1842. He was the eldest child. William had three brothers: Henry, who was to become a famous novelist, Wilkinson, and Robertson, as well as a sister, Alice. Basic biographies include: Guy Wilson Allen, " William James" in *The Makers of American Thought* ed., Ralph Ross, (Minneapolis: The University of Minnesota Press, 1974) 49-84; George Cotkin, *William James, Public Philosopher* (Baltimore & London: The Johns Hopkins University Press, 1990); R. W. B. Lewis, *The Jameses, A Family Narrative* (New York: Farrar, Straus & Giroux,1991); Ralph Barton Perry, *In the Spirit of William James* (Bloomington: Indiana University Press, 1958); *The Thought And Character of William James* (Cambridge: The Harvard University Press, 1948). See also George Santayana, *Character And Opinion In The United States* (New York: Braziller, 1958) Ch. III. The destructive consequences of the modern economy were the subject of a book published by Henry Adam' brother, Brooks Adams, *The Law of Civilization And Decay, An Essay On History* (1896) (New York: Alfred A. Knopf, 1943).

94 Henry James Senior, *A Collection of His Writings* Giles Gunn, ed., (Chicago: American Library Association, 1974) Ch. 1,2. *The Literary Remains of Henry James* (1888) Intr. William James, (Upper Saddle River, N.J.: Literature House, 1970); Austin Warren, *The Elder Henry James* (New York: The MacMillian Company, 1934); Dwight W. Hoover, *Henry James Senior*

And The Religion Of Community (Grand Rapids:, Michigan: William B. Erdman's Publishing Company, 1969). See also : Linda Simon, Genuine Reality, A Life of William James (New York: Harcourt, Brace & Company, 1998).

95 Russell B. Goodman, *American Philosophy And The Romantic Tradition* (Cambridge: Cambridge University Press, 1990). So also Simon, op.cit.

96 " The great Cosmic Intellect terminates and houses itself in mortal men and passing hours.." "Address at The Emerson Centenary in Concord" (1903) in *William James, Memories And Studies* (1911) (New York: Greenwood Press, 1968) at 24.

97 *The Principles of Psychology* (1888) Ch. X. Bellamy did allow for some integration of past with present but he thought of individual identity in terms of stages of personality. see the discussion in Chapter Two, III. above.

98 Ibid. See also Pragmatism A New Name For Some Old Ways Of Thinking Lecture Seven, in *William James, Writings, 1902-1910 Notes & text by Bruce Kuklick, (New York: Library Classics of the United States, 1987) 479-624.*

99 See Israel Schiffler, *Four Pragmatists* (New York: Humanities Press, 1974) that traces the influence of the sociology of George Herbert Mead. Compare the influence of evolutionary thought of John Fiske in Henry Steele Commager, *The Amereican Mind* (New Haven: Yale University Press, 1950) Ch. IV.

100 Louis Menard, *The Metaphysical Club* (New York: Farrar, Straus, Giroux, 2001). See also Simon, op.cit., Ch. 8.

101 *The Collected Papers of Charles Saunders Peirce* Vol. 6. Charles Hartshorne & Paul Weiss, ed., (Cambridge: Harvard University Press, 1934); John E. Smith, *America's Philosophic Vision* (Chicago & London: University of Chicago Press, 1992).

102 William James, " The Dilemma of Determinism" (1884) in *Essays in Pragmatism* Alburey Castell, ed., (New York: Haftner Publishing Co. 1948) See also Smith, op.cit.

103 William James, *Essays in Radical Empiricism* Ch. 2.

104 Smith, *America's Philosophic Vision* Ch. 3.

105 *The Will To Believe And Other Essays in Popular Philosophy (New York: Dover Pub. 1956).*

106 James, " The Moral Philosopher And The Moral Life" (1891) in *Essays In Pragmatism.*

107 Ralph Barton Perry, *The Thought And Character of William James Ch. XXXI; John Patrick Diggins, The Promise of Pragmatism (Chicago & London: The University of Chicago Press, 1994) Ch. 3, 4.*

108 See *The Collected Papers of Charles Saunders Peirce* vol. 5, Bk. II, VI. where Peirce develops the distinction between Pragmaticism and Pragmatism. James acknowledges his indebtedness to Peirce in *Pragmatis*m Lec. Two.

109 According to Peirce, " Pragmatism is the theory that ..a conception, that is the rational purport of a word or other expression, lies exclusively in its conceivable bearing upon the conduct of life." *V Collected Papers* Bk.II, V, sec. 1, 412. Compare James: "..The true, to put it briefly, is only the expedient in the way of our thinking, just as the 'right' is only the

expedient in the way of our behaving...:*Pragmatism*, Lec. Six in William James, Writings 1902-1910 at 583.

110 James chided Henry Adams for not taking sufficient account of time and the possibilities of change that it implies. James strongly objected to Adams' "Letter To American Teachers of History" :"..To tell the truth, it doesn't impress me at all, save by its wit and erudition, and I ask whether an old man soon about to meet his Maker can hope to save himself from the consequences of his life by pointing to the wit and learning he has shown in treating a tragic subject. No sir, you can't do it, can't impress God in that way. ." *The Selected Letters of William James* Elizabeth Hardwick, ed., (New York & London: Anchor Books, 1961) at 266.

111" Materialism means simply the denial that the moral order is eternal and the cutting off of ultimate hopes; spiritualism means the affirmation of an eternal moral order and the letting loose of hope. Surely here is an issue genuine enough for any one who feels it; and as long as men are men it will yield matter for serious philosophic debate.." *Pragmatism* Lecture Three. For a broader discussion of expectations see Josef Pieper, *Hope And History* David Kipp, trans. (San Francisco: Ignatius Press, 1994).

112 William James , *The Varieties of Religious Experience.* A Study of Human Nature. The Gifford Lectures on Natural Religion (1902) Intr. Jaroslav Pelican (New York: Vintage Books, 1990). The lectures are also reprinted in William James , *Writings 1902-1910* pps. 1-477.

113 *The Varieties*, Lec. II.

114 "In a merely human world without a God, the appeal to our moral energy falls short of its maximal stimulating power. Life, to be sure, is even in such a world a genuine ethical symphony; but it is played in the compass of a couple of poor octaves, and the infinite scale of values fails to open up." James, " The Moral Philosopher And The Moral Life" in *Essays In Pragmatism* V. James acknowledges the importance of the transcendentalist tradition of New England, which included a belief that "[N]othing can make that good which is wrong, nor that evil which is right. This is the law of nature- the same in all.." Charles Mayo Ellis " An Essay on Transcendentalism" (1842) in *The American Transcendentalists* Perry Miller, ed. (Garden City: Doubleday, 1957) at 20-35.

115 See the criticism of Emerson in Chapter One II, of the present work. I have discussed Whitman's approach to divinity by an analysis of his poem " Passage to India" in Chapter Two, I.

116 James had to decide upon the proper form of his spirituality. He saw the choice as one between Theism, that kept God and His creation distinct from on another and some form of Pantheism that will allow for an intimacy between God and Man. A Pluralistic Universe (1909) in William James, *Writings 1902-1910*) 625-820. For a discussion of James' religious disposition see A. N. Wilson, *God's Funeral* (New York: W.W. Norton & Company, 1999) and Alfred Kazin, *God And The American Writer* (New York: Random House, 1997) Chapter 8.

117 The character of the designer is harder to discern after the revelation of chance happenings . According to James it is also difficult because of "..the strange mixture of goods and evils that we find in this actual world's particulars." *Pragmatism* Lecture Three. See also, *TheVarieties of Religious Experience* Ch. XX and James' essay " Is Life Worth Living? in *The Will To Believe And Other Essays In Popular Philosophy* (1904) (New York, Dover   Pub.

1959)

118 See the introduction to *The Literary Remains of the Late Henry James Senior* and *A Pluralistic Universe*, Lec. III.

119 " Now the great peculiarity of Mr. James's conception of God is, that it is monistic enough to make God the one and only active principle to satisfy the philosophers, and yet warm and living and dramatic enough to speak to the heart of the common pluralistic man. This double character seems to make of this conception an entirely fresh and original contribution to religious thought. .." *Introduction to The Literary Remains.*

120 See the essay " The importance of individuals" in *The Will To Believe.*

121 ".For pluralistic pragmatism, truth grows up inside of all the finite experiences. They lean on each other, but the whole of them, if such a whole there be, leans on nothing. All 'homes' are in finite experience; finite experience as such is homeless. Nothing outside of the flux secures the issue of it. It can hope for salvation only from its own intrinsic promises and potencies. ." *Pragmatism* Lec. Seven.

122 For James, the religious option is to be preferred, even in the face of doubt. The reason is that "..religion presents the universe to us in a personal form..the universe is no longer a mere It to us, but a Thou if we are religious; and any relation that may be possible from person to person might be possible here..*The Will To Believe* X.

123 " I believe that the only god worthy of the name must be finite" William James, *A Pluralistic Universe* Ch. III.

124 " The Sentiment of Rationality" in *The Will To Believe.* See also ChapterXX of *The Varieties of Religious Experience* and Lecture Eight of *Pragmatism.*

125 " The Importance of Individuals". James insisted that whatever intuition of a higher self we might have must be arrived at ".. in person, in the person of the one who gives his heart to it. " The Sentiment of Rationality" .

126 See the discussion in Chapter One of the present study. On the influence of the will in Calvinism see Sacan Bercovitch, *The Puritan Origins of the American Self* (New Haven & London: Yale University Press, 1975). See further, Henry Adams' view of the weakness of the will in Chapter II.II. above.

127 On the presence of Unitarianism at the Harvard Divinity School see Bruce Kuklick, *The Rise of American Philosophy* Ch. 1.

128 Compare Theodore Parker's externalization of evil with James' observation:"..Not why evil should exist at all, but how we can lessen the actual amount of it, is the sole question in need of consideration.." *A Pluralistic Universe* Lec. III. Parker had been a guest in the James home when William was a child. There are references to Parker in *The Varieties of Religious Experience* Ch. IV.

129 The possibility of the existence of a substantial soul is recognized throughout William James' writing, beginning with the Principles of Psychology. As his experiential orientation developed, James saw the issue as being one of the practical difference the recognition of a substantial principle might make. Otherwise, "..the fact that certain perceptual experiences

seem to belong together is thus all the word substance means.." *Some Problems of Philosophy* Ch. VII. See also the discussion in Lecture III of *Pragmatism*. The issue will be considered again in Chapter Five of this study.

130 *"The Will To Believe"* IX.

131 *As William James Said: Extracts From the Published Writings of William James* selected and edited by Elizabeth Perkins Aldrich, New York: The Vanguard Press, 1942) at 91. On Royce's assessment of James see *William James And Other Essays On The Philosophy of Life* (New York: the MacMillian Company, 1912).

132 Josiah Royce, *The Religious Aspect of Philosophy A Critique of the Bases of Conduct And Faith* (Boston & New York: Houghton Mifflin & Company 1885) Ch. XI, VII.

133 The transition is manifest in the Gifford Lectures that Royce gave at the University of Aberdeen in 1899 and published as *The World And The Individual* in the same year. The development of Royce's thought shall be discussed in the following section of the present chapter.

134 John Clendenning, *The Life And Thought of Josiah Royce*, Rev. ed., (Nashville & London: Vanderbilt University Press, (1999).

135 Josiah Royce, *The Spirit of Modern Philosophy* An Essay In the Form of Lectures (1892) Intr. Ralph Barton Perry (New York: George Braziller, Inc. 1955). The discussion in the text is drawn from Lectures IV to VI.

136 Josiah Royce, " William James And The Philosophy of Life" in *William James And Other Essays*.

137 William James, " The Sentiment of Rationality" in *The Will To Believe And Other Essays*.

138 To James, the God of Isaiah or David was very different from the Absolute of Idealism: ".. That God is an essentially finite being in the Cosmos, not with the cosmos in him, and indeed he had a very local habitation there and very one-sided local and personal attachments. If it should prove probable that the absolute does not exist, it will not follow in the slightest degree that a God like that of David, Isaiah, or Jesus does not exist, or may not be the most important existence in the universe for us to acknowledge.." *A Pluralistic Universe*, Lec. III.

139 "..[T]he absolute things, the last things, the overlapping things, are the truly philosophical concerns; all superior minds feel seriously about them. " *Pragmatism* Lec. III.

140 *Pragmatism* Lec. Eight

141 Josiah Royce, *The World And The Individual* (1899) Second Series, Vol 2, Lec. X (New York: Dover Publications Inc. 1959). The lectures are reprinted in 1 *The Basic Writings of Josiah Royce* edited with an introduction by John McDermott (Chicago & London: The University of Chicago Press, 1969).

142 Josiah Royce, " Immortality" in *William James And Other Essays* This is written in response to James' argument that any reference to an Absolute commits the philosopher to a timeless conception of ultimate reality.

143 " In God you possess your individuality. Your very dependence is the condition of your freedom. .." *The World And the Individual* Vol. 2, X.

144 See Gabriel Marcel, *Royce's Metaphysics* trans. Virginia & Gordon Ringer (Chicago: Henry Regnery Company, 1956).

145 Royce, *The Philosophy of Loyalty* (1908) Intr. John J. McDermott, (Nashville & London: Vanderbilt University Press, 1995) *2 The Basic Writings of Josiah Royce* 855-1013; " Loyalty and Insight" , Essay II in *William James And Other Essays*. Compare Royce's belief that fidelity embraces " loyal steadfastness in obscure service" with a similar recognition by George Eliot at the conclusion of her novel *Middlemarch* : "..that things are not so ill with you and me as they might have been, is half owing to the number who lived faithfully a hidden life and now rest in unvisited tombs." Royce, who was very familiar with English literature, realized the importance of Eliot's insights into human nature. See his "George Eliot as a religious Teacher" in *Fugitive Essays* (1920) (Freeport New York: Books For Libraries Press, Inc. 1968) 261-289. See further, Royce, *The Philosophy of Loyalty* Lec. 3, III.

146 The influence of Hegel is unmistakable. Royce tried to make it clear that his idea of loyalty did not entail devotion to an abstract principle, nor did it require allegiance to any individual or collection of individuals. The purpose of loyalty is to draw individuals together. However, the union in involves something more than their own efforts: " It recognizes that, when apart, individuals fail; but when they try to unite their lives in one common selfhood, to live as if they were the expressions, the instruments, the organs of one ideally beautiful social group, they win the only possible fulfillment of the meaning of human existence. Royce, " Loyalty And Insight" at 56. (emphasis supplied). See also *The Spirit of Modern Philosophy*, Lec. VII. Those whose mentality is formed by sociological tradition tend to reach the same conclusions as those based on Hegelianism; however, a few are more careful to maintain individual distinction. For Example , B. N. Cardozo, the great Supreme Court Justice held that while individual identity is changed by association with others, nevertheless, " .. This does not mean that there is a mystical common will which belongs to the group as a person separate from its members; all that it means is that the wills of individuals, like their habits and desires, are modified by the interaction between mind and mind. The social mind is indeed the sum of the individual minds, but it is the sum of them when associated, and not their sum when dissevered.. *The Paradoxes of Legal Science* (New Haven: Yale University Press, 1928) at 88.

147 *The World And the Individual*, Vol. 2 Second Series, Preface.

148 Ibid., Lec. III.

149 Id., See also Lecture IV.

150 Marcel, op.cit. See also John E. Smith, *Royce's Social Infinite The Community of Interpretation* (New York: The Liberal Arts Press, 1958).

151The Philosophy of Loyalty.

152Josiah Royce, *The Problem of Christianity*, Part II, Ch. IX. Intr. John E. Smith, (Chicago & London: University of Chicago Press : 1968).

153 Ibid. Ch. XI. The significance of the distinction between dyadic and triadic relations to the understanding of human nature is explored by Walker Percy in his *Lost In The Cosmos* under

the title of " A Semiotic Primer of The Self" (New York: Farrar, Straus, & Giroux, 1983). See also Smith, *Royce's Social Infinitive*.

154 *The Problem of Christianity* II, Lec. XII, XIII.

155 Josiah Royce, *The Spirit of Modern Philosophy* (1892) Intr. Ralph Barton Perry, (New York: George Braziller, Inc. 1955) Lecture VIII, Essay V. See also Royce, *Studies In Good And Evil* (1898) (Hamdon, Conn.; Archon Books, 1964) and the chapter entitled " The Religious Mission of Sorrow" in *The Sources of Religious Insight* (1912) (Washington: The Catholic University of America Press, 2001).

156 William James, *Pragmatism* Lecture Eight; Josiah Royce, " Immortality" (1906) in *William James And Other Essays On The Philosophy of Life* Essay V (New York: The MacMillan Company, 1912).

157 Royce, *The Sources of Religious Insight* I.

158 Ibid. Chapter III.

159 " ..For the very essence of the will is that, at every moment of action, it decides absolute issues, because it does irrevocable deeds, and, therefore, if intelligent at all, is guided by opinions that are as absolutely true or false as their intended workings are irrevocable.." *The Sources of Religious Insight*.

160 Bruce Kuklick, *Churchmen And Philosophers From Jonathan Edwards To John Dewey*, (New Haven & London: Yale University Press, 1985) Chapter 16; Josiah Royce, *The Sources of Religious Insight* II, IV.

161 Josiah Royce, *The Philosophy of Loyalty* (1908) John J. McDermott, intro. (Nashville & London: Vanderbilt University Press, 1995) ; *The Sources of Religious Insight*, Chapter V. See also the discussion in Chapter Three, III, of the present work.

162 " ..Our deepest need is to see how the divine will may be done on earth as it is done in heaven. And this is what we have not yet learned to see.." *The Sources of Religious Insight* at 166. Loyalty to Loyalty is defended as a supreme good in *The Philosophy of Loyalty* Lecture 3.

163 This is distinguished from James' speculations about the compounding of consciousness in *A Pluralistic Universe* Lecture V. For a discussion of the interpenetration of self -consciousness and social consciousness see Royce, *Studies of Good and Evil*, Chapter VIII.

164 *The Sources of Religious Insight* V. The good of loyalty brings us a spiritual peace in spite of trials but the serenity does not absolve us from effort. :
" ..The unity of the world is not an ocean in which we are lost but a life which is and which needs all our lives in one. In is no sort of 'moral holiday' that this world life suggests to us . It is precisely as a whole of life of ideal strivings in which we have our place as individual selves and are such selves only in so far as we strive to do our part in the whole.."
The Philosophy of Loyalty 183-184.

165 See the discussion of the exemplary life of the Newport lightkeeper Ida Lewis in *The Sources of Religious Insight* V.v. Royce also has some interesting observations on how personal loyalty helped the development of modern Japan in *Race Questions, Provincialism, And Other*

American Problems, (1908) (Freeport New York: Books For Libraries Press, Inc. 1967) Chapter II; *2 The Basic Writings of Josiah Royce* VIII, c. 33.

166 Josiah Royce, *The Problem of Christianity* (1913) Chapter IV, VIII; Chapter VII, II-III. See also " What is Vital in Christianity" (1909) in *William James And Other Essays On the Philosophy of Life*, Essay Three.

167 Compare William James, P*sychology* Chapter 10 with Josiah Royce, *The Spirit of Modern Philosophy*, Lecture XIII, IV-V.

168 "Our social training thus teaches us to know ourselves through a process which arouses our self-will; and this tendency grows with what it feeds upon. The higher the training and the more cultivated and elaborate is our socially trained conscience, the more highly conscious of our own estimate of our own value becomes, and so, in general, the stronger grows our self-will. Josiah Royce, *The Problem of Christianity* III, VIII. Compare Sigmund Freud, *Civilization And Its Discontents.*

169 " ..But as an ethical personality I have an insatiable need for an opportunity to find, to define, and to accomplish my individual and unique duty. This need of mine is God's need in men and of me. Seen, then, from the eternal point of view, my personal life must be an endless series of deeds." " Immortalilty" Essay V.

170 *The Problem of Christianity* Part II, Chapter IX, IV.

171 Ibid. Chapter V. Divine forgiveness applies to the time before we had a coherent sense of our own life-plans: ".. [T]he past is dead. Grace has saved us. Forgiveness covers the evil deeds that were done . For these deeds, as we now see, were not done by our awakened selves. They were not our own free acts at all. ..the abundance of grace means, henceforth, a new gravity of life.." *The Problem of Christianity* at 157. (emphasis in the original).

172 " In brief, by his own deed of treason, the traitor has consigned himself,- not indeed his whole self, but his self as the doer of this deed,- to what one may call the hell of the irrevocable. Ibid. Chapter V, IX (emphasis in the original)

173 In " What is Vital in Christianity" Royce sketched the elements of positive suffering that , in general, make up for the existence of evil. As an alternative to Stoic resignation Royce develops the image of one who, because extremely loyal, "..is willing to suffer vicariously, freely, devotedly, ills that he might have avoided, but that the cause to which he is loyal, and the errors and sins which he himself did not commit, calls upon him to suffer in order that the world may be brought nearer to its destined union with the divine. *William James And Other Essays On The Philosophy of Life* at 173. In *The Problem of Christianity* a " Suffering Servant" modeled on the Isaiah prophecy, acts on behalf of the community to transfigure the loss caused by a disloyal deed into a positive gain. The improvement draws upon the understanding of the Christian community that the atoning sacrifice of Christ" somehow was so wise and rich and beautiful and divinely fair that, after this work was done, the world was a better world than it would have been had Adam never sinned." Chapter VI, VIII-X. The theme of vicarious suffering appears in Melville's stories, especially *Billy Budd*. See William Ellery Sedgwick, *Herman Melville* Chapter Nine. and Lewis, *The American Adam*, Chapter Seven.

174 "..But however ill comprehended, the 'sign' in which and by which Christianity conquered the world was the sign of an ideal community of all the faithful, which was to become the

community of all mankind, and was to become some day the possession of all the earth, the exponent of true charity, at once the spirit and the ruler of the humanity of the future..Josiah Royce, *The Hope of The Great Community* (1916) (Freeport New York: Books For Libraries Press, Inc., 1967) Chapter Three, pps. 36-7; *2 The Works of Josiah Royce* VIII; at 36.

175 Bruce Kuklick, *Churchmen And Philosophers From Jonathan Edwards to John Dewy* Chapter 16; Louis Menard, *The Metaphysical Club* Chapter Ten.

176 Menard, op.cit.

177 John Dewey, *The Influence of Darwin On Philosophy And Other Essays in Contemporary Thought* (New York: Peter Smith, 1977). See also " From Absolutism to Experimentalism" (1930) in John Dewey, *The Later Works*, 1925-1953 Ed., Jo Ann Boydston (Carbondale & Edwardsville: Southern Illinois University Press, 1984) Vol 5.: 1929-1930, 147-160.

178 John Dewey, *Leibniz's New Essays Concerning The Human Understanding* (1888) (New York: The Hillary House, 1961).

179 Ibid, Chapter X. See also " Kant And Philosophic Method" (1884) in *The Philosophy of John Dewey* John McDermott, ed., (Chicago & London: The University of Chicago Press, 1981). In this essay Dewey begins to connect the idea of an organism with the ultimate truth of social reality.

180 *Leibniz's New Essays* Chapter XII.

181 Josiah Royce, *The Religious Aspect of Philosophy* (1885); *The World And The Individual First Series,* 2 vols. (1899) (New York: Dover Publications: 1959) , See also the discussion in Chapter Three of the present work.

182 John Dewey " A Reply To Professor Royce's Critique of Instrumentalism" in John Dewey *The Middle Works Vol 7 64-*78. See also Dewey's review of The World And The Individual in John Dewey *The Early Works 1882-1898* Vol. 4. These criticism should be compared with Royce's counter -attack in his essay " The Problem of Truth in the Light of Recent Discussion " (1908) in *William James And Other Essays on The Philosophy of Life Essay IV*.

183 Menard, *The Metaphysical Club* Chapter 13. See also William James, "The Meaning of Truth" in *Pragmatism.*

184 James, " Humanism And Truth" in *Pragmatis*m. Dewey's indebtedness to James is acknowledged in several places. See, e.g. " From Absolutism To Experimentalism" 157-159. In writing about Pragmatism, Dewey observes: "..the fundamental idea of an open universe in which uncertainty, choice, hypotheses, novelties and possibilities are natural will remain associated with the name of James; the more he is studied in his historic setting the more original and daring will the idea appear." John Dewey, *Characters And Events* (1929) II, p.440.

185 James *Pragmatism* Lecture Eight.

186 John Patrick Diggins, *The Promise of Pragmatism: Modernism And The Crisis of Knowledge And Authority (Chicago: University of Chicago Press, 1994) Chapter 4.*

187 John Dewey, " The Development of American Pragmatism" (1925) in John Dewey *The Later Works Vol. 2*, pps. 3-21. See also John Dewey, *Logic: The Theory of Inquiry* (New York: Henry Holt & Company, 1938) Chapter XXIV.

188 John Dewey, *Experience And Nature* (New York: W.W. Norton 1929) Chapter Two. Dewey thought it was admissible to treat some determinations as 'quasi-absolutes' but that :" logically absolute truth is an ideal which cannot be realized at least not until all the facts have been registered, or as James says 'logged' and until it is no longer possible to make other observations and other experiences." " The Development of 'American Pragmatism" at 8. For a sound criticism of this aspect of Dewey's philosophy see Jacques Maritain, *Moral Philosophy* (New York: Charles Scribner & Sons 1964) Chapter 14.

189 John Dewey ,*The Quest For Certainty: A Study of The Relation Between Knowledge And Action* (1929) (New York: Capricon Books, 1960), John Dewey, *The Later Works Vol. 4 ; Reconstruction In Philosophy* (1920) (New York: Mentor Books, 1950).

190 John Dewey, *The Public And Its Problems An Inquiry Into Political Theory* (1928) , (Chicago: Gateway Books, 1946).

191 *Experience And Nature* Chapter Six; John Dewey, Individualism Old And New in *The Later Works Vol. 5*, pps. 41-123.

192 See Israel Scheffler, *Four Pragmatists, A Critical Introduction to Peirce, James, Mead And Dewey* (New York: Humanities Press, 1974) Part III. See also George Herbert Mead, " The Philosophies of Royce, James, and Dewey in Their American Setting" *International Journal of Ethics*, Vol. 40, 211-231 (1930).

193 In *Pragmatism* Lecture Three, James adopts Locke's idea of spiritual substance: ".He immediately reduces this notion to its pragmatic value in terms of experience. It means, he says, so much 'consciousness', namely, the fact that at one moment of life we remember other moments, and feel them all as parts of one and the same personal history" *Pragmatism* at 525. James also asserts the same idea when he states that "the fact that certain perceptual experiences do seem to belong together is thus all that the word substance means." *Some Problems of Philosophy A Beginning of An Introduction to Philosophy* (1911) (New York: Greenwood Press, 1968) . Dewey then says that " In spite of the tenderness of James on the topic of the soul he wrote
thought.is itself sufficient proof of the way he whittled down the knowing subject" The Vanishing Subject in the Psychology of James" *Journal of Philosophy*, Vol. 37, 589-99, at 590 (1940).

194 John Dewey, " The Ego as Cause" (1894) *Early Works Vol. 4* 91-98.

195 Dewey, *Experience And Nature* Chapter Six.

196 *Individualism Old And New* Chapter V.

197 As Dewey points out in *Experience and Nature* if the ego is thought of as a transcendental self, the community of selves becomes isolated from natural existence. From a moral point of view, the subjective ego so conceived fails to be an effective instrument for the transformation of society. John Dewey, *Lectures On Ethics Lectures on Social Ethics*, Donald F. Koch ed., (Carbondale & Edwardsville: Southern Illinois University Press, 1991) Three, I.

198 Kuklick, *Churchmen And Philosophers* Chapter 17.

199 Menard, *The Metaphysical Club*, Chapter Twelve.

200 Jane Addams, *Democracy and Social Ethics*, Anne Firor Scott, ed., (Cambridge: Harvard University Press, 1964). See also: Jean Bethke Elshtain, *Jane Addams And The Dream of American Democracy* (New York: Basic Books, 2002).

201 Walt Whitman " Democratic Vistas" (1871) in *The Portable Walt Whitman* that is discussed in Chapter Two , I, of this writing. According to Dewey, " Democracy had its seer in Walt Whitman. It will have its consummation when free social inquiry is indissolubly wedded to the art of full and moving community. " The Search For The great Community "John Dewey, *The Later Works, Vol. 2*, at 528.

202 " The Ethics of Democracy" (1888) in *The Early Works* 1882-1898 Vol. I, 227-249. See also " Christianity And Democracy", The Early Works vol. 4, 3-10. (1971).

203 " The Search For the Great Community".

204 Ibid. See also " Individualism Old And New" Chapter Two.

205 Edward Bellamy, *Looking Backward: 2000-1887* (Boston: Ticknor & Company, 1888). See also the textual discussion in Chapter Two III, and Chapter Five.

206 Herbert Marcuse, *One Dimensional Man Studies In the Ideology of Advanced Industrial Society (Boston : The Beacon Press, 1968)*.

207 See Aldous Huxley, *Brave New World Revisited* (New York: Harper & Row, 1958) that contrasts the government by terror described in George Orwell's *1984* with the non-violent manipulation of the masses in modern society.

208 "Bureaucracy" in Max Weber, *Essays In Sociology* trans. H.H. Gerth & C. Wright Mills, (London: Routledge, 1991) Two, VII. Hanna Arendt describes bureaucracy as the last stage of governance in the nation -state and one that, in some circumstances, can be the cruelest. *The Human Condition* (Chicago: The University of Chicago Press, 1958) II, 6.

209 Marcuse, op.cit. See also Wilfred M. McClay, *The Masterless Self And Society In North America* (Chapel Hill & London: The University of North Carolina Press, 1993).

210 Basic Sources include: John Stuart Mill, *On Liberty* (1859) ed., Gertrude Himmelfarb (New York: Basic Books, 1974); Eugene Samiatin, *We* (1924) trans, Gregory Jilboorg (New York: E.P. Dutton & Company, 1952); Jose Ortega y Gassett, *The Revolt of the Masses* (1929)(New York & London: W.W. Norton & Company, 1932); Karl Jaspers, *Man In The Modern Age* (1933) trans. Eden & Cedar Paul, (London: Routledge, 1959); and Romano Guardini, *The End Of The Modern World* trans. Joseph Theman & Herbert Burke (Chicago: Henry Regnerey & Company, 1956).

211 See Walker Percy, *Lost In The Cosmos: The Last Self-Help Book* (New York: Farrar, Straus & Giroux, 1983).

212 "[Y]ou needn't think you can take me in! This frenzied determination to get things down into their places and make them smaller-typical of this epoch- is a self-tormenting feature of the

mind, an unspeakable enjoyment of the spectacle of how the good can be humiliated, and how wonderfully easily it can be destroyed.." Robert Musil, *The Man Without Qualities* trans. Eithine Wilkins & Ernst Kaiser, (New York: G.P. Putnam's Sons, 1953) Part One, Chapter 72. See also Romano Guardini, *Letters From Lake Como: Explorations in Technology And The Human Race* trans. Geoffrey W. Gromley, (Grand Rapids, Michigan: William Beerdsman Publishing Company, 1994) Letter Seventh.

213 General sources include Josef Pieper, *Abuse of Language, Abuse of Power* trans. Lothar Krauth (San Francisco: Ignatius Press, 1992); Neil Postman, *Technopoly* (New York: Alfred Knopf, 1993) and Pierre Bourdieu, *On Television* trans. Priscilla Parkhurst Ferguson (New York: The New Press, 1998). The observations of the Chairman of the National Endowment of the Arts are also relevant. See Dana Gioia, "Disappearing Ink: Poetry at the End of Print Culture" LVI *The Hudson Review*, Spring, 2003. See generally, Huxley, Brave New World Revisited Chapter V.

214 The Classic study of the partisan tendencies of the modern intelligentsia is Julien Benda, *The Betrayal of the Intellectuals* trans. Richard Aldington, (Boston: The Beacon Press, 1928). Alan Bloom, *The Closing of The American Mind* (New York: Simon & Schuster, 1987) should also be consulted. For the compromises made by scholars to gain access to the mass media, See Bourdieu, op. cit.

215 Under the conditions of modern life the individual "..is merged in the mass, to become something other than he is when he stands alone. On the other hand, in the mass the individual becomes an isolated atom whose individual craving to exist has been sacrificed, since the fiction of a general equality prevails. .." Karl Jaspers, *Man In The Modern Age* Part One, at 42.

216 See the discussion in section I of this chapter.

217 See, e.g. William James, " The Importance of Individuals" in The Will to Belive.

218 Josiah Royce, *Race Questions, Provincialism, And Other American Problems* (1908) in *The Basic Writings of Josiah Royce Vol.* 2, 1089-1110.

219 See David Brooks, " Superiority Complex" in *The Atlantic Monthly* Vol. 290, n. 4, (November, 2002) pps. 32-33.

220 John Dewey, *Liberalism And Social Action* (New York: G.P. Putnam's Sons, 1935) . See also " The Search For The Great Community." in *The Public And Its Problems, Later Works Vol.,* 2, 325-28.

221 In his book *The Rediscovery of America and Chart For Rough Waters* (New York: Duell, Sloan, & Pearce, 1940) Waldo Frank called for a renewal of the spiritual meaning of the individual life as a responsibility that was antecedent to social action. Dewey objected to this proposal to put personal reform ahead of communal obligations . See his *Individualism Old and New* Chapter Four.

222 When there is a proper balance between public and private life " The emotions will be aroused and satisfied in the course of normal living, not in abrupt deviations to secure the fulfillment which is denied them in a situation that is so incomplete that it cannot be admitted into the affections and yet so pervasive that it cannot be escaped. . *Individualism Old And New* , 50. Dewey also defined liberty as " ..that secure release and fulfillment of

personal potentials which takes place only in rich and manifold association with others. ." " The Search For The Great Community" at 295.

223 John Dewey, *The Quest For Certainty.* (1929). See also Dewey, " The Inclusive Philosophical Idea" (1928) in *Later Works Vol. 3*, 41-51.

224 John Patrick Diggins, *The Promise of Pragmatism* Chapter 5. Dewey realized the danger of the experimental method being limited to physical and technical matters, but he continued to insist that only collaborative inquiry operating within an empirical order of existence can elevate human understanding.

225 See Alfred North Whitehead, *The Function of Reason* (Boston: The Beacon Press, 1929) Guardini, *Letters From Lake Como* and Gabriel Marcel, *Man Against Mass Society* (Chicago: Henry Regenery Company, 1952).

226 See John Stuart Mill, *Auguste Comte And Positivism* (Anne Arbor: University of Michigan Press, 1962) Maritain, *Moral Philosophy* Part Two, Chapter 11 and Isaiah Berlin, " Historical Inevitability" in *The Proper Study of Mankind* Henry Hardy & Roger Hausheer, ed., (New York: Farrar, Straus, & Giroux, 1997) 119-190. Dewey expresses his gratitude to Comte in " From Absolutism To Experimentalism" *Later Works Vol. 5* 147-60.

227   Gabriel Marcel , *Man Against Mass Society* .

228 Bruce Kuklick, *Churchmen and Philosophers: From Jonathan Edwards To John Dewey* (New Haven & London: Yale University Press, 1985). Mark A. Noll, *America's God: From Jonathan Edwards to Abraham Lincoln* (Oxford & New York: Oxford University Press, 2002).

229 See " The Religion of Social Solidarity" in Chapter Two of the present work.

230 " The only conception adequate to experience as a whole is organism. What is involved in the notion of organism? Why, precisely the Idea which we had formerly reached of a Reason which is both analytic and synthetic.. Such a Reason..is the ultimate criterion of truth.." " Kant and Philosophic Method" (1884) in *The Philosophy of John Dewey* John J. Mc Dermott, ed., (Chicago & London: University of Chicago Press, 1981) 13-24, 20. See also : " The Inclusive Philosophical Idea" (1928) in *3 The Later Works* , 41-51.

231 John Dewey, " Christianity And Democracy" *4 Early Works 1882-1898* 3-10 (1971).

232 See Dewey's Introduction to Corliss Lamont, *The Illusion of Immortality* (1935). (New York: Continuum Press, 1990) Dewey praises the author for proving that life retains ethical meaning even when there is no hope of personal immortality, and for demonstrating "..the morally and socially injurious consequences of putting practical preoccupation with another world in place of interest in this one..Id. xiii.

233 John Dewey, " What I Believe" (1930), *5 Later Works*, 267-78; *A Common Faith* (New Haven & London: Yale University Press, 1934).

234 " Regarded as an idea, democracy is not an alternative to other principles of associated life. It is the idea of community life itself. It is an ideal in the only intelligible sense of an ideal namely, the tendency and movement of something which exists carried to its final limit, viewed as completed, perfected..." The Search For The Great Community (1927) in *The Public And Its Problems 2 Later Works*..

235 " The Development of American Pragmatism" (1925) *2 Later Works* 3-21.

236 "Well he knew thus dividing good from ill/ Discord should keep the rule of human will." *The Poems of John Dewey* 81 Jo Ann Boydston, ed., (Carbondale & Edwardsville: Southern Illinois University Press, 1977) pps. 59-60. See also John Dewey, *Lectures On Ethics* Donald F. Koch, ed., (Carbondale & Edwardsville: The University of Southern Illinois Press, 1991) Sec. 1.3 and John Dewey *Logic: The Theory of Inquiry* (New York: Henry Holt & Company, 1938) Ch. XXIV .2.

237 *A Common Faith.*

238 Ibid.

239 Dewey preferred the adjective 'religious' to the noun 'religion' because the former implied a disposition that would find spiritual meaning in all the natural conditions and modes of human association that are experienced in modern life, while the latter looks to doctrinal assumptions to interpret such experiences in a way that "..the emotional deposit connected with prior teaching floods the whole situation. *A Common Faith* I, at 13-14. See further, Richard Rorty, " Pragmatism as Romantic Polytheism: in *The Revival of Pragmatism New Essays in Social Thought, Law , and Culture* Morris Dickstein, ed., 21-36 (Durham & London: Duke University Press, 1998).

240 John Dewey, *Liberalism And Social Action* (New York: G. P. Putnam's Sons, 1935).

241 H. Richard Niebuhr, *The Kingdom of God In America* (New York: Harper & Row, 1937).

242 Ibid. See also the authorities cited in note 1, supra.

243 "…The old idea of American Christians as a chosen people who had been called to a special task was turned into the notion of a chosen nation specially favored..The contemplation of their righteousness filled Americans with such lofty and enthusiastic sentiments that they readily identified it with the righteousness of God. .Henceforth, the Kingdom of God was a human possession." Niebuhr, op. cit. at 178-179. See also Noll, op.cit. Part V.

244 On Henry Adams, see " Personal Integrity and General Chaos " in Chapter Two, II, of the present work.

245 See Robert B. Westbrook, *John Dewey And American Democracy* (Ithaca & London: Cornell University Press, 1991).

246 Richard Rorty, *Contingency, Irony And Solidarity* (Cambridge, England: Cambridge University Press, 1981); *The Consequences of Pragmatism* (Essays 1972-1980) (Minneapolis: The University of Minnesota Press, 1982) . There are perceptive evaluations of Rorty in John Diggins, *The Promise of Pragmatism* (Chicago: The University of Chicago Press, 1994) Ch. 10 and James T. Kloppenberg," Pragmatism: An Old Name For Some New Ways of Thinking" in *The Revival of Pragmatism* 83-127.

247 Robert Coles, *The Secular Mind* (Princeton: The Princeton University Press, 1999). Coles argues that Orwell had a deeper insight into the modern psychological problem than did Freud. Recognizing the distortions imposed upon the ego by society, Freud was nonetheless confident that the harassed self could eventually take control of its destiny. Orwell, on the other hand, thought that the acceleration of technological and

organizational forces was making the individual ego " putty in the hands of something larger than any human being. " Op. cit. IV, pps. 155-56.

248 See the evaluation of Rorty in Westbrook, op. cit. Epilogue.

249 " Emerson's master term..is not the 'Mind' but the 'Soul'. The action of the Intellect, though of tremendous importance, was no more than a part of the activity his works celebrate..the action of the conscience, or 'moral sentiment' was at least of equal importance—and underlying both faculties, Emerson believed, was a still more primitive and essential agency, for which he had various names, natural and supernatural.." Jonathan Bishop, *Emerson On The Soul* (Cambridge : Harvard University Press, 1964) at 4.

250 Bruce Kuklick, *Churchmen And Philosophers*, Ch. 2. See also Sacvan Bercovitch, *The Puritan Origins of The American Self* (New York & London: Yale University Press, 1975) and Jeffrey Hammond, *Sinful Self, Saintly Self The Puritan Experience of Poetry* (Athens & London: The University of Georgia Press, 1993). A similar attitude developed within some quarters of Roman Catholicism during the same period. Thus Pascal:"..Self is hateful.. It is unjust in itself since it makes itself the center of everything..*Pensees*, (1656) Ch. VII, 455.

251 R. W. B. Lewis, *The American Adam: Innocence, Tragedy And Tradition In The Nineteenth Century* (Chicago: University of Chicago Press, 1955) Ch. 3.

252 William James, *Some Problems of Philosophy* Ch. VIII; The Will to Believe.

253 Josiah Royce, *The World And The Individual* First Series.

254 John Diggins, *The Promise of Pragmatism*, Ch. 5.

255 Id. See also Charles Taylor, *The Sources of The Self* (Cambridge: Harvard University Press, 1980); Lionel Trilling, *The Opposing Self: Nine Essays In Criticism* (New York, The Viking Press, 1959). Jacques Maritain traces the modern disposition to reject anything beyond interior consciousness to Luther. See, *Three Reformers: Luther, Descartes, Rousseau* (London: Sheed & Ward, 1936).

256 See Charles Mayo Ellis, " An Essay on Transcendentalism" (1842) in *The American Transcendentalists, Their Prose And Poetry* Perry Miller, ed., (Garden City: Doubleday, 1957) 20-35.

257 Henry David Thoreau, *Walden* (1854). See also R. B. Lewis, op.cit., Ch One, III and Vernon L. Parrington, *2 The Main Currents of American Thought* Book III, Part III, III.

258 John Jay Chapman, *Emerson And Other Essays* (1899) (New York: Aims Press, 1965).

259 Compare the analysis in Chapter One, III, of the present work.

260 See Merlin Bowers, *The Long Encounter: Self And Experience In The Writings of Herman Melville (Chicago & London: The University of Chicago Press, 1961).*

261 Jacques Maritain, *The Person and The Common Good John* F. Fitzgerald, trans. (Notre Dame: The University of Notre Dame Press, 1966).

262 See the disintegration of Henry Adams' mentality in Chapter Two of this study.

263 William James, " The Sentiment of Rationality" in *The Will To Believe* See also, *The Varieties of Religious Experience* Ch. XX.

264 Charles Taylor, op. cit.

265 See the criticism of inordinate inwardness in Nicholas Rescher, *Objectivity: The Obligations of Impersonal Reason* (Notre Dame & London: The University of Notre Dame Press, 1997). See also Alan Bloom, *The Closing of The American Mind* (New York: Simon & Schuster,1987).

266 Karol Wojtyla (Pope John Paul II) *The Acting Person* Andre Potovki , trans., (Dodrecht: D. Reidel, Pub. 1979). Basic sources on the natural law tradition are rooted in the writings of Thomas Aquinas *Summa Theologica* II, II, Q. 90-97. Modern expositions include A. P. d'Entreves, *Natural Law* (1951); Jacques Maritain, *Man And The State* (1951) (Washington : The Catholic University of America Press, 1998) Ch. IV.; John Finnis, *Natural Law And Natural Rights* (Oxford: Clarendon Press, 1980). See also my *Modern Legal Philosophy The Tension Between Experiential And Abstract Thought* (Pittsburgh : Duquesne University Press, 1978) Ch. V. There is a good universal defense of objective values in C. S. Lewis, *The Abolition of Man* (New York : MacMillan, 1947).

267 ".. The rightful autonomy of the practical reason means that man possesses in himself his own law, received from the Creator. Nevertheless the autonomy of reason cannot mean that reason itself creates values and moral norms. His Holiness, John Paul II, *The Splendor of Truth* (Veritatis Splendor) Ch. II, sec. 40. (emphasis in original).

268 Actions that realize human nature are primarily expressions of personal existence. Freedom means the power to determine one's own being, but the liberty "..is not from objects of value but freedom for what the self perceives as objective values; values that will perfect him as a person." *The Acting Person Part Two*, Chapter Three, .4-.6.The Second Vatican Council identifies the inner conflict between good and evil in a way that Jonathan Edwards would understand:" For a monumental struggle against the powers of darkness pervades the whole history of man. The battle was joined from the very origin of the world and will continue until the last day, as the Lord has attested. Caught in this conflict, man is obliged to wrestle constantly if he is to cling to what is good , nor can he achieve his own integrity without great efforts and the help of God's grace. *Pastoral Constitution On The Church In The Modern World, III, 37.*

269 " [P] ersonality is an abstraction compared with individuality. All persons have personality in the same sense; there is nothing distinguishingly concrete about it. Individuality, on the other hand, is always differentiated; it is something that specifically characterizes each self. Individuality expresses what one uniquely is.; personality expresses what one has- a property that one may acquire. In this sense, individuality is deeper than personality." John Dewey, " Contributions To Cyclopedia of Education" *7 The Middle Works, 1912-1914*, 295 - 296.

270 The classical Catholic understanding of the human soul is built upon the distinction between matter and form. Matter, as a potency, has what is called " an avidity for being". The metaphysical energy is the form. Together they constitute a substantial unit - that which is both carnal and spiritual:" Soul and matter are the two substantial co-principles of the same being, of one and the same reality called man. Because each soul is intended to animate a particular body, which receives its matter from germinal cells, with all their hereditary content, from which it develops, and because, further, each soul has or is a substantial

relation to a particular body, it has within its very substance the individual characteristics which differentiate it from every other human soul. " Maritain *The Person And The Common Good* III, at 36.

271 Compare Royce's conception of self -awareness , above, Ch. IV, I.

272 Maritain, op.cit.

273 In American thought, this strain begins with the Senior Henry James and continues up to the social philosophy of John Dewey.

274 The text here depends upon two seminal works published by the University of Chicago Press immediately after the Second World War: Hanna Arendt *The Human Condition* (1946) and Michael Polanyi, *Science Faith And Society* (1946).

275 See the critique of Comte in Jacques Maritain, *Moral Philosophy* Part II, Ch. 12 (New York: Charles Scribner & Sons, 1964). See also my *Theories of World Governance* (Washington: The Catholic University of America Press, 1999) Ch. 4 where I dissent from the view, inherited from Comte, that love for one's own society is incompatible with a love for all of humanity.

276 Where citizens are truly free, their civic obligations cannot be imposed by the enforcement of some imagined social contract. In addressing matters of common concern, each must rely upon his or her own conscience. " We must have sovereignty atomized among individuals who are sincerely rooted in a common ground of transcendent obligations. Otherwise, sovereignty cannot fail to be embodied in a social power ruling absolutely over all individuals." Polanyi, op.cit. at 72.

277 Compare the observations of Maritain: " Acting in history, the Christian lawyer or politician must not only consider the truth or falsity of values in themselves and their significance to temporal affairs but also the possibilities of their historical implementation and the consequences.. *Integral Humanism* Ch. VI.

278   There is a good defense of the right of opposition in *The Acting Person* Part Two Ch. 7.

279   See part I of the present chapter. See also Victor Kestenbaum, *The Grace And The Severity of The Ideal John Dewey And The Transcendent.* (Chicago & London: The University of Chicago Press, 2002).

280 For a balanced discussion of the relationship between religious belief and secular citizenship see Wilfred M. McClay, " Two Concepts of Secularism" XXIV *The Wilson Quarterly* no. 3. Summer, 2000, 54-71.

281   The basic work, that we considered in Chapter Two, was *Looking Backward* 2000-1887, published in 1888. Bellamy wrote a sequel that explained the inspiration behind his utopian vision. Edward Bellamy, *Equality* (London: William Heinemann, 1897). It is this later work that is now being considered.

282 *Equality* Ch. XXX-XXXII.

283 According to Pascal, the self , being embarrassed by its faults, becomes hostile to any reproach, especially one that is from religious authority " ..the Catholic religion does not

bind us to confess our sins indiscriminately to everybody; it allows them to remain hidden from all other men save one, to whom she bids us reveal the innermost recesses of our heart, and show ourselves as we are..

Man is so corrupt that he finds even the law of private confession, which shields his faults from public view, too harsh for him to bear.." *Pensees And The Provincial Letters of Blaise Pascal*, (New York: Modern Library, 1941) sec. 100.

284 " But this portion of reason that we possess is a gift of God, and consists in the natural light that has remained in us in the midst of corruption; thus it is in accordance with the whole and it differs from that which is in God , only as a drop of water differs from lthe ocean, or rather as the finite differs from the infinite.." G. W. Leibniz, " On the Conformity of Faith with Reason" in *Theodicy, Essays On The Goodness of God, The Freedom of Man, and The Origins of Evil* (1710) E. M. Huggard, trans., (La Salle, ILL.: Illinois OPen Court, 1885) at 61. Leibniz sincerely believed that he was a Christian philosopher, defending God's cause with a new theory that reflected the advances of his time. However, in the course of this defense, "..the conception of God the Creator gradually changed, until he became the hypostatized quintessence of all fundamental principles; ultimately, God was identified, in Leibniz's mind, with an ideal conception of man.." R. W. Meyer, *Leibniz and the Seventeenth Century Revolution* J. B. Stern, trans. (Cambridge: Bower & Bower, 1952). B, VI.3.

285 Immanuel Kant, *Religion Within the Limits of Reason Alone* (Chicago * London: Open Court Press, 1924) Bk I., i. In the same work Kant affirms :" ..For when the moral law commands that we ought to be better men, it follow inevitably that we must be able to be better men. Ibid., Bk. I, III.

286 Kant does not deny the existence of Divine Grace, but he thought that the general understanding of Grace seemed to remove all inner ground of action other than what a producing external cause had placed there. There was also a conflict between grace and moral freedom because morality implies some good that we must accomplish if we are to be responsible for our actions, while the work of grace seems to imply that the moral good is not our deed but rather the accomplishment of another. *Religion within the Limits of Reason Alone*, Bk I. See also Bk III, Division Two.

287 " The patience of God consists in the fact that he executes his punishment of evil in the criminal only after he has given him the opportunity to improve himself. But, after that, God's Justice is unrelenting. For a judge who pardons is quite unthinkable. .. Immanuel Kant, *Lectures On Philosophical Theology* Allen W. Wood & Gertrude M. Clark, trans. (Ithaca: Cornell University Press, 1978) Second Part, at 126.

288 *Religion Within The Limits of Reason Alone*, Bk.III, Division Two.

289 Brownson was born in Vermont in 1803 and was well acquainted with Emerson, Thoreau, and the Transcendentalist movement. Standard biographies include Theodore Maynard, *Orestes Brownson: Yankee, Radical, Catholic* (New York: MacMillen, 1943) and Arthur M. Schlesinger, Jr. *Orestes Brownson: A Pilgrim's Progress* (Boston : Little Brown, & Co. 1939). See also Leonard Gilhooley, *Contradiction And Dilemma: Orestes Brownson And The American Idea (New York: Fordham University Press, 1972)*

290 See " Decree On Ecumenism" (Nov. 21, 1964) in *The Documents of Vatican II* , Walter M. Abbott, S. J. General Editor (New York: America Press, 1966) 341-366.

291   See the criticisms of James' religious outlook in A. N. Wilson, *God's Funeral* (New York: W.W Norton & Company, 1999) Ch. 14 and Alfred Kazin *God And The American Writer*, (New York: Random House, 1997) Ch. 8.

292   The 'felix culpa' idea of a 'happy sin' that brought us a great Redemption was influential in Protestant theology during the nineteenth century. See R. W. B. Lewis, *The American Adam* Ch. 3.

    At the conclusion of his study of the failures of liberal Protestantism A. N. Wilson observes: ".[I]f this book has established anything, it is that religious experience is not merely individual, but collective.. op.cit. at 338.

293 The whole effect is summarized in Maritain, *True Humanism*

294 Compare the discussion of the Protestant theology of Horace Bushnell in Lewis, Ch. 3 III and Mark Noll, *America's God* Part IV, ch. 15.

Index of Proper Names